Environmental Social Accounting Matrices

T0300501

Policy makers would like to capture all the effects of economic growth resulting from regional economic policies. Those effects can be examined through models that describe the structure of a regional economy. If natural resources are at the base of the economic relationships of a region, then accounting for them as inputs from the ecosystem to the economy system could allow for a more accurate description of this relationship. In addition, doing this could allow for a more complete prediction of the economic flows.

In this book Professors Pablo Martínez de Anguita and John E. Wagner put two disciplines together, regional and ecological economics, presenting a way to understand ecological economic concerns from a regional perspective, and providing a mathematical tool to measure their interrelationships. This book offers different regional economic models that explicitly include the role of natural resources and pollutants in economic regions through the use of social accounting matrices (SAMs) and input–output (I–O) models.

The main objective of this book is to explore I–O and SAM models by expanding the accounts to include natural resources and the environment. The proposed models in this book incorporate the forest and other natural resources and pollutants as a component in a larger model of how the economy and environment of larger areas interact. This book will be of interests to postgraduates, researchers, and scientists in the fields of regional, resource, environmental, or ecological economics.

Pablo Martínez de Anguita is Professor of Sustainable Rural Development and Land Planning at University Rey Juan Carlos, Spain.
John E. Wagner is Associate Professor of Forest Resource Economics at the State University of New York—College of Environmental Science and Forestry, Syracuse, USA.

Environmental Social Accounting Matrices

Theory and applications

Pablo Martínez de Anguita and John E. Wagner

Routledge
Taylor & Francis Group

LONDON AND NEW YORK

First published 2010
by Routledge
2 Park Square, Milton Park, Abingdon, Oxon OX14 4RN

Simultaneously published in the USA and Canada
by Routledge
711 Third Avenue Avenue, New York, NY 10017

Routledge is an imprint of the Taylor & Francis Group, an informa business

Typeset in Times New Roman by
Swales & Willis Ltd, Exeter, Devon

British Library Cataloguing in Publication Data
A catalogue record for this book is available from the British Library

Library of Congress Cataloging-in-Publication Data
Martínez de Anguita, Pablo, 1968–
  Environmental social accounting matrices : theory and applications /
by Pablo Martínez de Anguita and John E. Wagner.
    p. cm.
  Includes bibliographical references and index.
  1. Environmental economics.   2. Social accounting – Environmental
aspects.   3. Natural resources.   4. Sustainable development.
  I. Wagner, John E.   II. Title.
  HD75.6.M3925 2010
  333.701 – dc22   2009040662

ISBN10: 0–415–77630–9 (hbk)
ISBN10: 0–203–85444–6 (ebk)

ISBN13: 978–0–415–77630–1 (hbk)
ISBN13: 978–0–203–85444–0 (ebk)
ISBN13: 978–0–415–53983–8 (pbk)

A la familia de Joana y Alberto Barragan, a todos los que son y a todos los que vendran.

To my wife Janice and my parents Albert and Mirney. And to my professors and students, I have learned from them all.

Contents

Illustrations

Preface

This book tries to offer different regional economic models that explicitly include the role of the natural resources in rural dependent regions through the use of Social Accounting Matrices (SAMs) using forests as the example resource.

Policy makers would like to capture all the effects of economic growth resulting from regional economic policies. Those effects can be examined through regional economic models that describe the structure of a regional economy. If natural resources are at the base of the economic relationships of a region, then accounting for them as inputs from the ecosystem to the economy system could allow for a more accurate description of this relationship. In addition, doing this could allow for a more complete prediction of the economic flows.

The influence of the natural environment on income distribution has increased markedly over time with the greater volume and toxicity of pollutants and higher prices of natural resource commodities (Rose *et al.* 1988). Those factors play an even greater role where impacts stem explicitly from resource development policies. The income distribution that results from changes in the natural resources management regime, and conversely the effects the economic factors have on the resources and their conservation, should be a main component to be studied when designing a regional economic or development policy.

If the region studied is described as rural and resource dependent, economic policies must take into account the role of natural resources in the economic development of this region. If the natural resources are not used in a sustainable manner, the region will not be able to base its economy on those resources for a long time. Unfortunately, regional economic modeling approaches fail to adequately capture the sustainable use of the natural resources. Introducing the concept of sustainability into a regional economic model can be a key to examining the relationship between economic flows and nature flows and stocks. In order to do this, economic flows and natural resources flows must be accounted on a comparable basis.

Regional economic models have tried to incorporate ecological values in order to establish relationships between the environment and the economy. Daly (1968 and 1977), Victor (1972), and Isard (1968) describe input–output (I–O) models considering the flows from the ecosystem to the economic system and vice versa. To fully integrate the flows from the ecosystem into the economic system in I–O models requires accounting not only for the role of the natural resources, but also to establish monetary links between the economic agents and the different kinds of profit that comes from natural resources.

The main objective of this book is to explore SAM models by expanding the accounts considered in a SAM to include the natural resources and the environment. The proposed models in this book incorporate the forest as a component in a larger model of how the economy and environment of larger areas interact. These models are called Environmental Social Accounting Matrices (ESAMs).

Chapters 1 through 4 develop the theory of I–O and SAM models including the estimation of the multiplier effect. Chapter 5 describes how the environment can be introduced in the multiplier theory. Chapter 6 shows how resource and pollutant flows can be incorporated to I–O and SAM mode not only as multipliers but also as endogenous accounts, and introduces the reader to the different I–O and SAM frameworks that have been built to incorporate the environment or the ecology to these models. Finally this chapter also shows how to account for the environment in order to introduce it in different types of ESAM.

Abbreviations

CBS	(Dutch) Central Bureau of Statistics
CBT	commodity-based technology
CGE	computable general equilibrium
CHI	commercial Hicksian income
ECPC	Economic Classification Policy Committee
EF	ecological footprint
ENP	environmental net product
ESA	European system of accounts
ESAM	environmental social accounting matrix
FIA	Forest Inventory and Analysis
FIRE	finance, insurance, and real estate
GRP	gross regional product
IBT	industry-based technology
IEEAF	(European Framework for) Integrated Environmental and Economic Accounting for Forests
I–O	input–output
MEW	measure of economic welfare
MSR	money spent on restoration
NAMEA	national accounting matrix including environmental accounts
NCS	natural commercial stocks
NCSR	non-commercial stock reductions
NDP	net domestic product
NMHI	non-market Hicksian income
NMNC	non-market natural capital
NRP	net regional product
NSC	nature state capitalization
NSCFP	non-sustainable commercial forest profits
NSI	nature state index
NTRP	net timber regional product

REIS	regional economic information system
SAM	social accounting matrix
SAMEA	social accounting matrix and environmental accounts
SEEA	system of environmental and economic accounting
SGRP	sustainable gross regional product
SIC	standard industrial classification
SIOT	symmetric input–output table
SUT	supply use table
TEV	total economic value
THG	total hardwood growth
TSG	totals softwood growth
UN	United Nations
USFS	United States Forest Service

1 Basic concepts in natural resource economics

The economic concept of value and the I–O models

The word "value" has many meanings. Brown (1984) defines it as "an enduring conception of the preferable which influences choice and action." "Preference" is used here to mean the ranking of one thing by an individual below or above another thing because of a notion of betterness. Nevertheless, there are two other nonpreferential related uses of value: a functional or mathematical value of a variable (i.e. if $7n + n^2 = 60$, then the value of $n = 5$), or as Andrews and Waits (1978) describes "functional value relationships." This concept of value refers to a biological or physical relationship of one nonhuman entity to another, for example, the value of nitrogen in corn production. It is the job of applied sciences to determine these functional values. These I–O relationships can exist whether or not humans prefer them or are even aware of them; they are discoverable, but exist no matter what we prefer.

"Value" in the sense of preference can be understood from a philosophical or ethical perspective as "an enduring belief that a specific mode of conduct or end-state of existence is personally or socially preferable to an opposite or converse mode of conduct or end-state of existence" (Rokeach 1973). These are called *held values*.[1] In this case, value is a total concept, as opposed to a marginal concept. Many authors have proposed different ethical approaches based on several notions of value, such as intrinsic value as opposed to utilitarianism, pragmatism, or logical positivism. Examples of intrinsic value have been the idea that the life of nonhuman beings has a value in and of itself (Naess 1984) or the idea of mother earth proposed by James Lovelock (1979) in his work on the "Gaia Hypothesis." We will consider these philosophical values only as held values that may help in understanding the "assigned measures of values."

From an economic perspective, value can be understood as "the relative importance or worth of an object to an individual or group in a given context" (Brown 1984). In this case, value will be a marginal concept. This last economic definition of value has several advantages. It is measured or determined with respect to a person's held values and associated preferences, that is with respect to a person's perception of the object and all other relevant objects. It is also measured with respect to the context in which the measurement takes place; thus, if the context changes, then the economic value changes. This leads to the recognition that economic value depends directly on who is doing the assessing: economic value is a relative or relational concept.

Although "economic measures of value are a small subset of what is encompassed by value every day" (Boulding 1956), they can help in understanding the relative importance or worth of a marginal unit of the good in question to the group entity (Brown 1984). People express their preferences through the choices and tradeoffs that they make, given certain constraints, such as income or available time. These trade-offs must be comparable. This is done quantitatively through prices. Price is defined as a marginal concept. It is not meant to measure the intrinsic value of a good, but only as a means of allocating a scarce good to a specific use. Price therefore can be defined as a measure of relative scarcity.

Any natural resource contains different held values, including intrinsic, economic, cultural, and aesthetic values. These values only translate into economic value in so far as they are scarce and capable of generating human welfare, including spiritual or moral welfare. Thus, if a resource remains unknown; even if it is providing an environmental service, it does not have economic value since it has no relational value with anyone who can give economic value to it: as long as it is not known, it cannot be preferred. Economic theory can measure these preferred and comparable values using theories such as total economic value (TEV) Approach[2] (Pearce 1992).

Value can also refer to a biological or physical relationship of one nonhuman entity to another, and therefore does not depend on any *held values*. These nonpreference meanings of the word "value" applied to natural resources can come from functions such as biological or physical relationships. In this sense, we will address these "values in biophysical terms" as "resource inventory" or simply "inventory."

The object of using the Environmental Social Accounting Matrix (ESAM) framework in this book is to achieve a way to measure sustainability, assess the flow of resources between the economic system and ecosystem, and establish possible limits to the economic system according to the biophysical possibilities of a territory. In this book, two different meanings of the word "value" appear throughout the text and, therefore, a clear distinction is required. We will always refer to biophysical values with the word "inventory" and we will only use the word "value" when indicating a human preference. Finally, we will refer to "economic value" when this preference is assigned through prices. Therefore, economic value will be the result of multiplying the desired good or service by its price; namely, an assigned value indicating its relative scarcity in relation to the specific preference.

There can be many approaches to mix ecosystem goods and services and economic values into a single framework. Using traditional neo-classical utility theory, an ESAM presents a broad framework to combine ecosystem goods and services and economic values allowing for many different interactions between them to be examined. In other words, all values are commensurable and can ultimately be reduced to a single measured unit. Based on this metric, while an ESAM allows accounting for the measures of people's preferences, at the same time, it is also able to expand the accounting system to include "satellite" accounts of other types of values related with ecosystem goods and services included. An ESAM framework uses traditional I–O relationships to describe resource flows between the ecosystem and the economic system; for example, for every dollar of output from the economic system, 0.25 dollars of resource flows into the economic system from the ecosystem are required. Different types of models can be proposed by taking into account different contexts depending on how these concepts are included. The beauty of an ESAM is that it makes it possible to compare different type of models without denying any rule of the theories that underpins both economic models as well as the accounting for ecosystem goods and services.

ESAMs require a large amount of data. As collecting primary data can be very expensive, secondary data are often used. Secondary data sources include various governmental agencies. However, without these data an ESAM would be a very powerful but useless tool.

The concepts of scarcity and sustainability applied to natural renewable resources

According to the dictionary definition, "scarcity" means to be not common or the ability of having an inadequate supply, not sufficient to meet the demand. This definition is too vague and can have several biophysical and economic interpretations. The scarcity of a renewable resource "in physical terms" tends to mean a lack of the resource. But any lack of the resource has to be established according to some reference point. As the objective of this book is to use ESAMs as estimators of regional sustainability, biophysical scarcity will be defined as a distance to a sustainable limit. Thus instead of scarcity, the inventory of a renewable resource is defined with respect to its sustainable limit; decreases or increases in inventory imply moving further or closer to this limit.

The dictionary defines "sustainable" as capable of being sustained or maintained. Biophysical sustainability is defined as the maximum level of use or harvest that can be continually taken from a resource stock for an indefinite period. This is the point that maximizes the growth rate of the natural resource. It also defines the minimum stock of the resource required to maintain this harvest level. When dealing with environmental emission management, we will define the concept of "assimilative capacity" as an upper level above which sustainability declines. This assimilative capacity is the ability of the natural system to accept certain pollutants and to render them benign or inoffensive (Field and Field 2006).

Biophysical sustainability and assimilative capacities are not static concepts. Additionally, there is no single measurement for them. For example, a species, with either a large or small population, can be a sustainable population as long as it breeds and maintains its population. For some resources, such as forests, sustainability can be easier to define because different silvicultural management regimes can provide for a certain percentage of the future losses or increases of populations. In other natural resources, such as fisheries, there are many different levels of sustainability. Defining a sustainable population could be done by relating the studied population not only with its viability (autoecology approach), but also with other populations (sinecology approach) or larger ecosystems (population dynamics approach). Any of these are beyond the scope of this book. If ESAMs are to be used to measure how economies interact with nature and sustainable limits, sustainable limits must be defined and used as an input in the ESAM. Sustainable limits are not an output of an ESAM. The sustainable population, sustainable harvest levels, or assimilative capacity of a natural resource must be measured and defined using a biological science.

Natural resource scarcity can be also defined in economic terms where society does not have sufficient resources to produce enough to fulfil any unlimited subjective wants or needs. Alternatively, scarcity implies that not all of society's goals can be attained at the same time, so that tradeoffs of one good against others are made. In this sense, scarcity is a marginal concept that depends on the allocation of the preferences and the price of the resources.

Assigned values will have a monetary representation and their scarcity will be based only on the relative and economic perception of value. We will refer to this scarcity as their relative "economic scarcity." This economic approach will use price as an economic natural resource scarcity indicator.

The concept of sustainability can be also interpreted in economic terms. From this perspective, "sustainability" means that future production curves are not adversely affected by what we do today. This does not mean that we must maximize environmental quality. It means simply that the environmental impact is reduced enough today to avoid shifting future production possibilities curves back in comparison to today's production possibilities (Field and Field 2006). From this perspective, a resource use rate is called sustainable when the use rate can be maintained over the long run without impairing the fundamental ability of the natural resource base to support future generations (Field and Field 2006). "Sustainability" does not mean that resources must remain untouched; rather, it means that their rates of use must be such that it does not jeopardize future generations. For renewable resources, such as forests, it means establishing use rates that do not exceed the natural productivity. In addition, the assimilative capacity of the ecosystem must also be considered in economic terms.

The difference between biophysical and economic sustainability can be described using the idea of substitution. From a biophysical perspective, if a resource disappears, it is lost forever. From an economic point of view, finding a substitute for the lost resource eliminates the problem. Thus sustainability will be defined as biophysical and scarcity will be defined in terms of prices.

Using the idea of "scarcity" only in an economic sense can be dangerous. Policy decisions are most frequently determined on economic criteria, and as Spash (2000) explains, if this monetary value fails to represent the values individuals associate with the environment, the interpreted responses as trade processes will result in misrepresentation of the motives lying behind the economic valuation. In such circumstances people may find the use made of their statements unacceptable (Burgess *et al.* 1995). On the other hand, using the same word for two different concepts can be misguiding. This is the reason we will also include the ideas of inventory increases and reductions.

ESAM is a framework where price can be used as well as other relative scarcity or value indicators. Using money is only one way to measure how important ecosystem services are to people. ESAM as a framework can provide the opportunity to use other indicators. Whatever the indicator used, the products or results obtained through an ESAM analysis will be always subject to the limitations of the nature of data provided.

The TEV of natural renewable resources

Measuring resources in economic terms, with the limitations mentioned above, allows for estimating the value that ecosystem services provide by using different tools. The first one is market: fish or lumber, for example, are bought and sold in markets and their trading prices can be registered. But the most important services from "nature," like a day of wildlife viewing or a view of the ocean, are not traded in markets. Thus, people do not pay directly for many ecosystem services. This economic value can be estimated by accounting for the number of people who are willing and able to pay to preserve or enhance the services. Thus, it is not necessary for ecosystem services to be bought and sold in markets in order to measure their value in dollars. What is required is a measure of how much purchasing power (in dollars) people are willing and able to give up to get the service of the ecosystem, or how much people would need to be paid in order to give it up, if they were asked to make a choice similar to one they would make in a market. This is the base of the TEV Approach (Pearce 1992) that will be used to account for natural resources in economic terms in the ESAM framework: total economic value can be defined by the sum of a number of components when adding all of this "purchasing power" (Pearce 1993; Randall and Stoll 1983).

This approach is not free of controversy. Ecological function and existence values are difficult to analyze and estimate scientifically and economically. Also, asking for a willingness to pay or using any other estimating method has difficulties: people are not familiar with purchasing such goods, and their willingness to pay may not be clearly defined. However, even considering these limitations, TEV is the widest possible method that allows estimating economic values for the services of ecosystems in dollar terms (Costanza *et al.* 1997a).

TEV is defined as the area under the demand curve bounded by a set quantity minus the variable production costs (the opportunity cost of the inputs),[3] and it encompasses the following types of use and non-use values:

1 Use values

   a   *Direct use values*: the value in use (e.g. crops and recreation).

   b   *Ecological functional or indirect use values*: referred to as an indirect use value of an environmental service (e.g. flood control and waste assimilation).

2 Non-use values

   a   *Option values*: they capture the resources a consumer would be willing and able to give up in order to retain the opportunity to consume a resource. That is, the preservation of the stock is valuable merely to keep consumers' options open.

   b   *Existence values*: existence values are not associated with actual use, or even with the option to use the thing (Turner *et al.* 1993). People may even be willing and able to pay to simply preserve the existence of some environmental amenity. Also, the desire to leave an unspoiled planet for one's descendants (*a bequest value*) will also endow species or ecosystems with existence value.

Within the rather theoretical concept of the TEV, the entire range of natural resources outputs can be more practically seen as market, potential market, and non-market values. In addition, the classic distinction made by public economics between private and public goods, with all the intermediate categories of local and club goods, can be recalled (Figure 1.1).

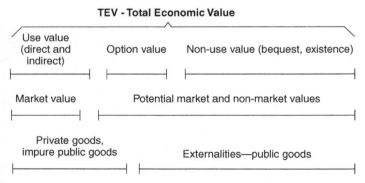

Figure 1.1 Classification of the TEV according to Merlo and Jöbstl.
Source: Merlo and Jöbstl (1999).

The TEV of forests

The objective of the final part of this book is to provide an accounting framework for sustainability of renewable resources. While only forests are used in this final part of this book, conceptually, any renewable resource or pollutant could be introduced in an ESAM framework. This gives an idea of the relational complexity that an ESAM can capture by expanding its accounts to include the economic or even non-economic value of a natural resource, and relating it to the circular flow of the economy in a region.

The reason for using forests to illustrate the examples and applications comes from the simplicity of its measurement: Forest inventory can be easily accounted for given the state of development of the dendrometry. Therefore measuring the sustainability of its management can be done more freely of controversy than in any other resource. This can be done by defining sustainability in terms of silvicultural possibility defined normally as the mean annual increment given an established forest management regime. In opposition to the easy way of measuring timber production, measuring the economic value for biodiversity as such can be much more difficult. The same can be said about the quality of the water, the amount of fisheries in the oceans, or the level of pollutants in the atmosphere which can change from one day to the next. Measuring the sustainability of these natural resources is more technically difficult than measuring forest growth and removals.

Also, TEV as defined in Table 1.1 including use value (including direct and indirect) plus non-use value (including bequest and existence) and option value can be applied more easily to forests than to other resources. In a forest, direct use values include revenues from timber and values of non-timber forest products. By contrast, indirect use values or "functional" values relate to the ecological functions performed by forests, such as global biogeochemical cycling, the protection of soils, and the regulation of watersheds. Option value or quasi-option value (Arrow and Fisher 1974; Henry 1974) can be understood as the expected value of the information on the benefits of an asset, conditional on its preservation and enabling an increase in the stock of knowledge relevant to the utilization of the asset. A frequently evoked example of quasi-option value is associated with genetic resources, for example, future pharmaceuticals developed from plant materials.

Existence value relates to the value of environmental assets, irrespective of current or optional uses. Empirical measures of existence values based on donations to conservation organizations or on the contingent valuation method suggest these can be a significant element in TEV, especially in contexts where the asset has unique characteristics or cultural significance.

Table 1.1 shows the possible components of the TEV of a forest according to Merlo *et al.* (1999).

Table 1.1 TEV in a forest including positive externalities

---

1 Use values
1.1 Direct use values
1.1.1 Timber, firewood, cork, resin, sparto grass, decorative plants, mushrooms, medicine plants, berries, truffles, etc.
1.1.2 Grazing, honey, etc.
1.1.3 Hunting, mushrooms, recreation, etc.

1.2 Indirect use values
1.2.1 Watershed management: soil conservation, avalanche prevention, flood prevention, etc.
1.2.2 Micro-climate regulation
1.2.3 Water quality and purification (including capture of nutrients and pollutants)
1.2.4 Carbon storage
1.2.5 Landscape

2 Option values
2.1.1 Personal future recreation and environmental interests
2.1.2 Potential source of energy and raw materials
2.1.3 Potential unknown source of bio-diversity, medicine plants, etc.
2.1.4 Potential use of unused landscape resources

3 Non-use values
3.1 Bequest values
3.1.1 Landscape, recreation, energy and raw material availability, biodiversity, environmental conditions, e.g. related to carbon storage, affecting future generations

3.2 Existence values
3.2.1 Bio-diversity, environmental conditions, e.g. related to carbon storage, affecting other species, respect for the right or welfare of non-human beings including the forest

OTHER EXTERNALITIES THAT NEGATIVELY AFFECT THE TEV
(if previously not considered)
• erosion, floods, and avalanches due to poor management;
• loss of landscape value due to excessive expansion of forest land use;
• risk of damage by forest fires;
• loss of biodiversity or landscape value due to plantation forestry;
• loss of recreation opportunities due to intensive plantation forestry and poor management;
• pollen and other allergic factors.

Source: Adapted from Merlo and Briales (2000).

The concept of sustainability applied to rural resource-dependent regions

Any economic system exists within the natural world, and the laws of nature govern many of the processes and changes that have to be considered in an economy, such as the production function. The natural world provides raw materials and energy inputs without which production and consumption would be impossible (Hall *et al.* 1986). Production and consumption activities also produce waste products called residuals, and sooner or later they find their way back into the natural ecosystem. Economies make direct use of natural assets of all types. The dependence on natural resources, especially on forests, becomes more evident in rural areas and needs to be accounted for. Indicators of this dependence should be incorporated in regional economic models.

Sustainability is a key concept in a rural resource-dependent region. Regional economic models are often built on the assumption that the relationships among the elements of the model will remain constant in the future. However, depletion or degradation of natural resources can change the relationship among the actors of an economic model. If a model does not consider the possibility of depletion or degradation of the natural resources in the future, it could easily give erroneous predictions simply by considering the rate at which resources are used is going to remain constant. Accurate predictions are especially important in a forest economy-based region that depends on the continuous flow of timber. Any change in the availability of the raw material would mean a change that models, without constantly reviewed parameters, would not take into consideration. Thus, the concept of sustainability must be included in any regional economic model that tries to accurately estimate future economic predictions.

Natural resources accounting systems

Different approaches to account for natural resources

There is substantial current interest in expanding national accounting systems to include services appropriated from the ecological systems. Forests are among the resources receiving the most interest. In this regard, a recent review by Vincent and Hartwick (1997) revised more than 100 such applications. Efforts by international organizations have underlined the importance attached to expanding natural resources accounts.

It is clear that conventional economic accounting systems can shed light only on a subset of the many ways in which the forest contributes to human welfare. This is due to the fact that conventional accounting systems are essentially restricted to goods and services that pass through markets. Although there are aspects of forests that contribute to human welfare, such as certain recreation activities, they nevertheless do not pass through conventional markets. In addition, there are religious and cultural uses of natural resources that serve to enhance human welfare, although the value of such services are not (and perhaps should not) be registered in any economic account. For example, forest soil and species are part of the biogeochemical cycles. They fulfil several ecological functions, such as promoting biodiversity and fostering other ecosystems and even if they are not accounted for, they are intrinsically important to many economic sectors. Conventional economic accounts indirectly include some of these services, but certainly not all.

The origins of integrated environmental and economic accounting can be traced to the early 1970s. Nordhaus and Tobin (1973) provided a calculation of an adjusted national product, called Measure of Economic Welfare (MEW). Official attempts were subsequently undertaken in Norway and the Netherlands. Also, international initiatives, such as the Brundtland Commission on Sustainable Development and the Rio Conference 1992, were important in shaping the United Nations (UN) draft handbook on the System of Environmental and Economic Accounting (SEEA), which is the most comprehensive current proposal on expanded green accounting. The draft manual of the SEEA, the UN's system, contains detailed examples of how forest accounts should be compiled. In fact, some terms of the manual have served as the base for some definition concepts in the ESAM framework: the biophysical value of depletion in forestry is defined as "that part of the value of removals or losses of non-cultivated standing timber (and other of the forest's non-cultivated biological assets) due to logging, harvesting, hunting and clearance of forests, which exceeds the sustainable use." Meanwhile, the economic value of depletion can be defined as "the value of decrease in the market value of land due to degradation resulting from forestry, logging or other forest-related activities and deforestation (clearance of forest land)."

Three other ideas from the SEEA are adapted and included in the ESAM accounting framework. The first idea is to focus the ESAM accounting system of forestry or any other renewable resource on sustainability in order to be able to build sustainability indexes based on signals that allow the prediction of whether a particular development path is sustainable or not. The second one is to base the system on modular structures, in which more complex measurements can be added on progressively. The third one, also applied to forestry, is to allow both market and non-markets registers. Many authors discuss whether or not one should try to value non-marketed services in a monetary metric, or to limit the system to accounting in physical terms. The ESAM allows both. An objective of a forest accounting system can be to trace the stocks and the relevant flows throughout the economy over time and space. In this sense, physical accounts, the ingoing and outgoing stock over the accounting period, must be recorded. In addition, economic flows must be traced throughout the economy. Physical information, useful for many purposes, finds difficulties when trying to put monetary values on non-marketed goods. The ESAM tries to overcome these difficulties by providing different formats of real and "virtual" flows.

Difficulties when introducing natural resources in accounting systems

Field and Field (2006) defines "the economy" as the collection of technological, legal, and social arrangements through which individuals in society seek to increase their material and spiritual well-being. The two elementary economic functions are production and consumption. Two observations concerning the production and the consumption of natural resources can be made in order to characterize the economy of a rural resource-dependent region. First, nature is an important provider of goods and services as well as the basic building block of an economy. Second, it is important to establish links between who pays and who profits from the different aspects of the renewable resources.

Forests also produce public goods. Public goods are associated with market failures. Market failures are not currently included in national accounting systems. When interpreting the flows of public goods between forestry and other sectors, we must note that monetary equivalents may be derived from market simulations, which means that in order to deal with externalities we need to simulate markets to obtain monetary values that will be included in some of our models.

As a consequence, it is necessary to extend the definition of "production" to include flows of public goods between institutional sectors as well as to have an extended definition of the term "real estates" including natural assets.

In addition to private goods, forestry provides numerous public goods that are consumed or used as intermediate goods in other sectors.

A complete depiction of macroeconomic activities of forestry within national accounting, therefore, demands a consideration and quantification of these flows. Only information about the complete extent of all relations to other sectors may facilitate decisions on the allocation of scarce resources. Thus, recently an increasing demand for information exists referring to dimensions and structures of non-market goods in an economy (Klaus 1994). A provision of different economic methods to measure monetary values of external effects and public goods requires a critical discussion of their positions within circular-flow analysis.

The contribution of forest resources to regional development is complex, especially the manner in which income is generated and distributed to regional households. In forested regions, forest management provides important market and non-market inputs into regional value-added activities. Some non-market forest inputs provide benefits for sectors that neither own nor manage the forest resources, such as the tourism sector. Many of the recent analyses conducted by regional economists have tended to ignore the non-market, or public good aspect, of natural resources, and this aspect is particularly important when considering the increasing relevance of recreation-based industries in these remote natural resource-dependent regions (Marcouiller and Deller 1997). A concise framework including relationships between stakeholders and market as well as flows of non-market goods from natural resources into the economic system should also be incorporated into regional economic models[4] of rural resource-dependent regions.

2 Regional I–O economic models

The basic I–O table

I–O analysis is the name given to a systematic framework for analyzing the interdependence of industries in an economy (Miller and Blair 1985). I–O models are a branch of economic statistics. This analysis dates from the development by Wassily Leontief (1936) of a general production theory based on the economic interdependence of producing industries within an economy. I–O analysis is widely used for measuring impacts of forest-related activities on output, employment, income taxes, exports, and imports in different sectors. This framework is useful for explaining how important a segment of forest industry is to a region's economy or for gauging the effects of changes in forest management (Klemperer 1996).

A regional economy may be characterized by the participants involved in economic activities. In an I–O setting, industries are the principal actors in a region's economy. Industries are characterized by two related activities: (1) they sell the output they produce; and (2) they buy the inputs they need to produce their output. The output is sold to other local industries as inputs into their production process; to final consumption by households, governments, private investment, or to exports. Equation (2.1) describes the ith industry's total output in terms of sales or receipts:

$$x_1 = z_{11} + z_{12} + \cdots + z_{1j} + \cdots + z_{1n} + y_1 + e_1$$
$$\vdots$$
$$x_i = z_{i1} + z_{i2} + \cdots + z_{ij} + \cdots + z_{in} + y_i + e_j$$
$$\vdots$$
$$x_n = z_{n1} + z_{n2} + \cdots + z_{nj} + \cdots + z_{nn} + y_n + e_n \tag{2.1}$$

where
x_i denotes the ith industry's total output in monetary terms, namely, sales or receipts;
z_{ij} denotes the amount of the ith industry's total output sold to the jth industry as an input;
y_i denotes the amount of the ith industry's total output sold to final demand consumption, namely, households (H), governments (G), and private investment (In); and
e_i denotes the amount of the ith industry's total output sold as exports.

To produce their output, an industry must purchase locally produced inputs (often called intermediate factors of production), pay labor and capital (often called primary factors of production), and buy imported intermediate or primary factors of production. Equation (2.2) describes the jth industry's total outlay in terms of purchases or expenditures:

$$x_1 = z_{11} + z_{21} + \cdots + z_{i1} + \cdots + z_{n1} + w_1 + m_1$$
$$\vdots$$
$$x_j = z_{1j} + z_{2j} + \cdots + z_{ij} + \cdots + z_{nj} + w_j + m_j$$
$$\vdots$$
$$x_n = z_{1n} + z_{2n} + \cdots + z_{in} + \cdots + z_{nn} + w_n + m_n \qquad (2.2)$$

where
x_j denotes the jth industry's total outlay in monetary terms, namely, purchases or expenditures;
z_{ij} denotes the amount of the jth industry's total outlay used to purchase inputs from the ith industry;
w_j denotes the amount of the jth industry's total outlay used to pay for labor (L) and capital (K); and
m_j denotes the amount of the jth industry's total outlay used to pay for imports.

Comparing equations (2.1) and (2.2) reveals five factors. First, output is not defined in physical terms: It is defined in monetary terms. This allows the comparison of output among very different industries, for example, the automobile industry with the wood products industry. Second, output (receipts) and outlay (expenditures) are defined in monetary terms; accounting rules dictate that for any industry receipts must equal expenditures. Therefore, the left-hand side of equation (2.1) must equal the left-hand side of equation (2.2). Third, as there are "n" industries in a region, there are "n" equations that define expenditures and "n" equations defining receipts. Fourth, common to the expenditures, equation (2.1), and the receipts, equation (2.2), are the *interindustry* flows, z_{ij}s. Finally, the structures of equations (2.1) and (2.2) allow the development of an I–O table showing how these two equations are related.

To develop the I–O table, we will start with equation (2.1) showing industry receipts. Table 2.1a represents equation (2.1).

The final demand column in Table 2.1a shows the components of household, government, and private investment consumption explicitly. Summing across the rows of Table 2.1a gives equation (2.1). In a similar manner, Table 2.1b represents equation (2.2). The value-added column in Table 2.1b shows the components of labor and capital explicitly. Summing down the columns of Table 2.1b gives equation (2.2). Table 2.1c combines Tables 2.1a and 2.1b show each industry's expenditures and receipts. Table 2.1c illustrates what equations (2.1) and (2.2) define mathematically, that a fundamental building block of an I–O table is the z_{ij}s or the interindustry flows.

Table 2.1a Industry receipts

Receipts		Industry 1 ... n		Final demand			Exports	Total output
Industry	1	z_{11}	$\cdots$ z_{1n}	y_{1H}	y_{1G}	y_{1In}	e_1	x_1
	$\vdots$	$\vdots$	$\ddots$ $\vdots$	$\vdots$	$\vdots$	$\vdots$	$\vdots$	$\vdots$
	n	z_{n1}	$\cdots$ z_{nn}	y_{nH}	y_{nG}	y_{nIn}	e_n	x_n

Table 2.1b Industry expenditures

		Expenditures Industry 1 ... n	
Industry	1	z_{11}	$\cdots$ z_{1n}
	$\vdots$	$\vdots$	$\ddots$ $\vdots$
	n	z_{n1}	$\cdots$ z_{nn}
Value added		w_{L1}	$\cdots$ w_{Ln}
		w_{K1}	$\cdots$ w_{Kn}
Imports		m_1	$\cdots$ m_n
Total outlay		x_1	$\cdots$ x_n

Table 2.1c Industry expenditures versus receipts

Receipts		Expenditures				
		Industry 1 ... n	Final demand			Exports	Total output

Receipts		Industry 1 ... n	Final demand			Exports	Total output
Industry	1	z_{11} ... z_{1n}	y_{1H}	y_{1G}	y_{1In}	e_1	x_1
	:	: ⋱ :	:	:	:	:	:
	n	z_{n1} ... z_{nn}	y_{nH}	y_{nG}	y_{nIn}	e_n	x_n
Value added		w_{L1} ... w_{Ln} w_{K1} ... w_{Kn}					
Imports		m_1 ... m_n					
Total outlay		x_1 ... x_n					

Table 2.1d I–O table

Receipts		Industry 1 ... n	Final demand			Exports	Total output
Industry	1	z_{11} ... z_{1n}	y_{1H}	y_{1G}	y_{1In}	e_1	x_1
	:	: ⋱ :	:	:	:	:	:
	n	z_{n1} ... z_{nn}	y_{nH}	y_{nG}	y_{nIn}	e_n	x_n
Value added		w_{L1} ... w_{Ln} w_{K1} ... w_{Kn}	w_{LH} w_{LG} w_{LIn} w_{KH} w_{KG} w_{KIn}			w_{Le} w_{Ke}	L K
Imports		m_1 ... m_n	m_H	m_G	m_{In}	m_e	M
Total outlay		x_1 ... x_n	H	G	In	E	

The next step in the development of the I–O table requires filling the bottom right portion of Table 2.1c and interpreting the economic information, if any, contained in each column. Table 2.1d shows the I–O table. We will interpret the economic information in the bottom right portion starting with the intersection of the value-added row and the final demand column components:

w_{LH} denotes the purchase of labor by households, for example domestic help;

w_{KH} denotes the interest payments by households for the use of private capital, for example, a loan;

w_{LG} denotes the purchase of labor by governments; and

w_{KG} denotes interest payments by governments for the use of private capital;

w_{LIn} denotes the purchase of labor by private investment (this is often zero filled); and
w_{KIn} denotes interest payments by private investment for the use of capital (this is often zero filled).

The intersection of the value-added row and exports component is as follows:

w_{Le} denotes payments to foreign labor; and
w_{Ke} denotes interest payments for the use of foreign capital.

The intersection of the imports and final demand components is as follows:

m_{C} denotes the purchase of imported good and services by households;
m_{K} denotes the purchase of imported good and services by governments; and
m_{In} denotes the purchase of imported good for private investment.

The intersection of the imports and exports components, m_{e}, denotes the transshipment of goods, or those good that were imported and then exported. As with total output and total outlay by industries, the sum of the value-added row elements and the sum of the final demand column elements can determine the total output (receipts) and the total outlay (expenditures) for each, respectively:

Total output (receipts)
L denotes the total receipts for labor; and
K denotes the total receipts for capital.

Total outlay (expenditures)
H denotes total household expenditures;
G denotes total government expenditures; and
In denotes total private investment expenditures.

Finally, the row sum for imports, M, defines the total receipts allocated to imports which accrue to foreign suppliers and column sum for exports, E, defines the total expenditures allocated to exports which accrue to local suppliers.

The I–O table is also related to the system of national and regional accounts. A region's total expenditures is given by equation (2.3):

$$\text{Total expenditures} = x_1 + \cdots + x_n + \text{H} + \text{G} + \text{In} + \text{E} \tag{2.3}$$

Likewise, a region's total income is given by equation (2.4):

$$\text{Total income} = x_1 + \cdots + x_n + \text{L} + \text{K} + \text{M} \tag{2.4}$$

As a nation's or region's expenditures must equal its income, equation (2.3) must equal equation (2.4). This is shown in equation (2.5a):

$$x_1 + \cdots + x_n + \text{H} + \text{G} + \text{In} + \text{E} = x_1 + \cdots + x_n + \text{L} + \text{K} + \text{M} \tag{2.5a}$$

$$\text{H} + \text{G} + \text{In} + (\text{E} - \text{M}) = \text{L} + \text{K} \tag{2.5b}$$

Equation (2.5b) defines gross national or regional product. The left-hand side and right-hand side of equation (2.5b) define the expenditure and income approach to estimate gross national or regional product, respectively.

Table 2.2 illustrates a hypothetical I–O table as given in Table 2.1d.

Table 2.2 I–O table

Receipts	Expenditures						Exports	Total output
	Ind 1	Ind 2	Ind 3	HH	Govt	Invest		
Intermediate factors								
Ind 1	100	90	85	90	60	50	60	535
Ind 2	95	75	70	60	45	25	40	410
Ind 3	90	80	65	75	40	20	50	420
Value added								
Labor	85	60	90	10	25	0	45	315
Capital	80	50	55	20	30	0	55	290
Imports	85	55	55	30	50	55	30	360
Total outlay	535	410	420	285	250	150	280	

Notes: The following notation is used: Ind 1 denotes industry 1; Ind 2 denotes industry 2; Ind 3 denotes industry 3; HH denotes household final demand expenditures; Govt denotes government final demand expenditures; and Invest denotes private investment expenditures.

Table 2.2 shows that the total outlays (expenditures) equal the total output (receipts) for each industry. In addition, the sum of the final demand components (households + governments + private investment

+ exports) equals total payments (value added + imports). The region's total expenditures is:

$$
\begin{aligned}
\text{Total expenditures} &= x_1 + x_2 + x_3 + H + G + \text{In} + E \\
&= 553 + 410 + 420 + 285 + 250 + 150 + 280 \\
&= 2{,}330
\end{aligned}
\tag{2.6}
$$

The region's total income is:

$$
\begin{aligned}
\text{Total income} &= x_1 + x_2 + x_3 + L + K + M \\
&= 553 + 410 + 420 + 315 + 290 + 360 \\
&= 2{,}330
\end{aligned}
\tag{2.7}
$$

The gross regional product is:

$$
\begin{aligned}
H + G + \text{In} + (E - M) &= L + K \\
285 + 250 + 150 + (280 - 360) &= 315 + 290 \\
605 &= 605
\end{aligned}
\tag{2.8}
$$

The basic I–O model: demand-driven

The basic I–O model is both descriptive and predictive. The descriptive model is shown in Table 2.1d. The demand approach predictive model will be developed in this section. The question to be answered by the demand approach predictive model is "What is the impact on a region's industrial output if final demand changes?" The logic of answering this question is as follows: if the final demand changes for one or more of the regionally produced outputs, this will cause a change in the amount of output produced locally to satisfy this change in final demand. However, in order for these industries to satisfy this change in output, they must change the amount of input they use. Thus, all industries backward linked to the initial industries will have to change the amount of output they produce, as will all the industries linked to these industries etc. The demand approach predictive model must then develop a direct relationship between final demand and these production relationships.

To develop these relationships we will start with our focus on Table 2.1a and equation (2.1). Table 2.3 is a simplified version of Table 2.1a.

Table 2.3 I–O model: demand approach

Receipts		Industry 1 ... n	Final demand	Total output
Industry	1 : n	Z	y	x

The interindustry transactions are defined by the $n \times n$ matrix Z, the $n \times 1$ column vector of final demands (y) are calculated using equation (2.9):

$$\begin{bmatrix} y_{1H} & y_{1G} & y_{1In} & e_1 \\ \vdots & \vdots & \vdots & \vdots \\ y_{nH} & y_{nG} & y_{nIn} & e_n \end{bmatrix} \cdot \begin{bmatrix} 1 \\ \vdots \\ 1 \end{bmatrix} = y \tag{2.9}$$

and the total output by industry is defined as the $n \times 1$ column vector x. As can be seen by equation (2.9), the final demand vector will include exports. Table 2.3 and equation (2.1) can be written in matrix notation as:

$$Z \cdot \begin{bmatrix} 1 \\ \vdots \\ 1 \end{bmatrix} + y = \begin{bmatrix} x_1 \\ \vdots \\ x_n \end{bmatrix} = x \tag{2.10}$$

The problem with equation (2.10) is that it is descriptive but not predictive. To convert equation (2.10) into a predictive model, we must tie changes in final demand to changes in production. Leontief (1936) accomplished this by using the transactions matrix, Z, whose column elements z_{ij} show the flow from industry i to industry j and assuming constant returns to scale. That is if the amount of output that an industry produces doubles, x_j, they must use twice the amount of inputs, z_{ij} for $i = 1,2, \ldots ,n$. This allows the amount of input use to be tied directly to the amount of output produced. Mathematically, constant returns to scale imply a ratio of input to output or z_{ij}/x_j. This ratio is called a technical coefficient and is denoted as a_{ij}:

$$a_{ij} = \frac{z_{ij}}{x_j} \tag{2.11a}$$

Or in matrix notation as:

$$A = Z\hat{X}^{-1} \tag{2.11b}$$

where $\hat{X}$ denotes a diagonal matrix whose diagonal elements are defined as the total output of each industry, x_j. The jth column of the technical coefficients matrix, A, defines the jth industry's production function. The assumptions of constant return to scales imply that production technology is held constant and no changes in the relative prices. Table 2.4 illustrates the calculation of the technical coefficients matrix, A, using the hypothetical I–O table given in Table 2.2.

Table 2.4 The technical coefficient or direct requirements matrix

	Z			$\hat{X}^{-1}$		
	Ind 1	Ind 2	Ind 3	Ind 1	Ind 2	Ind 3
Ind 1	100	90	85	0.001869	0	0
Ind 2	95	75	70	0	0.002439	0
Ind 3	90	80	65	0	0	0.002381

	A		
	Ind 1	Ind 2	I nd 3
Ind 1	0.186916	0.219512	0.202381
Ind 2	0.17757	0.182927	0.166667
Ind 3	0.168224	0.195122	0.154762

Notes: The technical coefficients matrix $A = Z\hat{X}^{-1}$. Ind 1 denotes Industry 1. Ind 2 denotes Industry 2. Ind 3 denotes Industry 3.

Given equation (2.11b), it can be shown that:

$$Ax = Z \cdot \begin{bmatrix} 1 \\ \vdots \\ 1 \end{bmatrix}$$

and

$$Ax + y = x \tag{2.12}$$

Solving equation (2.12) for x gives the demand approach predictive model:

$$Ax + y = x$$
$$y = x - Ax$$
$$y = (I - A)x$$
$$x = (I - A)^{-1} y$$
$$\Delta x = (I - A)^{-1} \Delta y \qquad (2.13)$$

where I denotes the identity matrix and Δ denotes a change. Equation (2.13) can be used to predict the change in output, Δx, given a change in final demand, Δy. The $(I - A)^{-1}$ term is called the Leontief inverse. Table 2.5 illustrates the calculation of the Leontief inverse matrix, $(I - A)^{-1}$, using the hypothetical I–O table given in Table 2.2.

Table 2.5 The Leontief inverse

	A			$(I - A)$		
	Ind 1	Ind 2	Ind 3	Ind 1	Ind 2	Ind 3
Ind 1	0.18692	0.21951	0.20238	0.81308	− 0.21951	− 0.20238
Ind 2	0.17757	0.18293	0.16667	− 0.17757	0.81707	− 0.16667
Ind 3	0.16822	0.19512	0.15476	− 0.16822	− 0.19512	0.84524

	$(I - A)^{-1}$		
	Ind 1	Ind 2	Ind 3
Ind 1	1.42705	0.48796	0.43791
Ind 2	0.38626	1.41643	0.37178
Ind 3	0.37319	0.42410	1.35608

Notes: The Leontief inverse is given by $(I - A)^{-1}$. Ind 1 denotes industry 1. Ind 2 denotes industry 2. Ind 3 denotes industry 3.

Finally, Table 2.6 shows an application of the demand approach predictive model, equation (2.13), using the hypothetical I–O table given in Table 2.2. Assume that the final demand for the output of Industry 2 increases by 50 dollars. Using equation (2.13), we can see that this change in final demand will cause the output of industry 1 to increase by 24.40 dollars, the output of industry 2 to increase by 70.82 dollars (the initial 50 plus another 20 more), and the output for industry 3 to increase by 21.20 dollars. This gives an overall change in region's total output of 116.42 dollars.

Table 2.6 The demand-driven predictive model

	Δx		(I − A)⁻¹			Δy
Ind 1	24.40		1.42705	0.48796	0.43791	0
Ind 2	70.82	=	0.38626	1.41643	0.37178	• 50
Ind 3	21.20		0.37319	0.42410	1.35608	0
Total	116.42					

Notes: The demand-driven predictive model is given by $\Delta x = (I - A)^{-1}\,\Delta y$. Ind 1 denotes industry 1. Ind 2 denotes industry 2. Ind 3 denotes industry 3.

Assumptions of the basic I–O model: demand driven

Using equation (2.13) to predict the impact on a region's economy, as measured by output, relies on a number of assumptions:

1   Only an exogenous change in final demand will cause a change in regional economic activity. The region's economy as described by the I–O table (e.g. Tables 2.1d or 2.2) is in equilibrium.
2   Production functions exhibit constant returns to scale. In other words, the production functions are linear homogeneous, technology is known and fixed, and changes in relative prices will not affect the proportion of an input used.
3   There are no spatial characteristics associated with the predicted economic impacts. A regional economy is also defined by geographic boundaries. One cannot state that the economic impacts will occur only in the southwest corner.
4   There is nothing in the predictive model, equation (2.13), that defines how long it will take the economic impacts to occur.
5   Increases or decreases in the final demand for industry "*j*" will always have the same impact, but of opposite sign, on the economy.
6   The economy is on the frontier of its production possibility curve, but there exists excess resources (at a constant price) to draw from when there is an increase in final demand.
7   The larger the leakages from a regional economy due to imports, for example, the smaller the economic impacts.

The basic I–O model: supply-driven

In the basic demand approach I–O model, the Leontief inverse highlights the backward linkages among industries. For example, the first column in the hypothetical I–O table, Table 2.2, shows that industry 1 buys from itself and industries 2 and 3. Thus if industry 1's output increases its output due to an exogenous change in final demand it must increase its purchases from industries 1, 2, and 3. This will cause an increase in the output that industry 2 produces. In order for industry 2 to increase its output, it must increase its purchases from industries 1, 2, and 3. Ghosh (1958) and Augusztinovics (1970) proposed an alternative interpretation of the basic I–O table that highlights the forward linkages; namely, the primary inputs (i.e. the value-added components plus imports) to industrial output.

The development of the supply-side I–O model, as with the demand approach, will begin with the transactions matrix, Z. While the demand approach focused on the columns of the transactions matrix (i.e. expenditures), the supply-side model will focus on the rows of the transactions matrix (i.e. receipts). While the predictive demand model focused on changes in final demand (i.e. equations (2.9) and (2.13)), the predictive supply model will focus on changes in payments made to the value-added components and imports. To develop these relationships we will start with our focus on Table 2.1b and equation (2.2). Table 2.7 is a simplified version of Table 2.1b.

Table 2.7 I–O model: supply approach

		Expenditures
		Industry
		1 ... n
Industry	1 ⋮ n	Z
Payments		w^{T}
Total outlay		x^{T}

The interindustry transactions are defined by the n × n matrix Z, the 1 × n row vector of payments (w^{T}) are calculated using equation (2.14):[1]

$$\begin{bmatrix} 1 & 1 & 1 \end{bmatrix} \cdot \begin{bmatrix} w_{L1} & \cdots & w_{Ln} \\ w_{K1} & \cdots & w_{K1} \\ m_1 & \cdots & m_n \end{bmatrix} = w^{\mathrm{T}} \tag{2.14}$$

and the total outlay by industries is defined as the 1 × n row vector x^{T}. As can be seen by equation (2.14), the payments vector will include the value-added components and imports. Table 2.7 and equation (2.2) can be written in matrix notation as:

$$x^T = \begin{bmatrix} 1 & \cdots & 1 \end{bmatrix} \cdot Z + w^T \qquad (2.15)$$

The problem with equation (2.15) is that it is descriptive but not predictive. To convert equation (2.15) into a predictive model, we must tie changes in payments to changes in output. This is accomplished by using the transactions matrix, Z, whose row elements z_{ij} show the flow or sales of industry i's output as an input into industry j's production process as described by equation (2.2). If the sale from industry i to industry j is stable, then doubling the output from industry i doubles the sales of that output as an input to industry j. Thus, each industry's sales can be a constant proportion of their output or z_{ij}/x_i. These fixed output coefficients are:

$$\theta_{ij} = \frac{z_{ij}}{x_i} \qquad (2.16a)$$

Or in matrix notation:

$$\theta = \hat{X}^{-1}Z \qquad (2.16b)$$

where $\hat{X}$ is defined as a diagonal matrix whose diagonal elements are total outlay. Given equation (2.16b), it can be shown that:

$$x^T\theta = \begin{bmatrix} 1 & \cdots & 1 \end{bmatrix} \cdot Z \qquad (2.17)$$

and:

$$x^T = x^T\theta + w^T$$
$$x^T - x^T\theta = w^T$$
$$x^T(I - \theta) = w^T$$
$$x^T = w^T(I - \theta)^{-1}$$
$$\Delta x^T = \Delta w^T(I - \theta)^{-1} \qquad (2.18)$$

where I denotes the identity matrix and Δ denotes a change. Equation (2.18) can be used to predict how changes in payments, Δw^T, will change total output, Δx^T. Table 2.8 illustrates the calculation of the fixed output coefficients matrix, θ. Table 2.9 illustrates calculating $(I - \theta)^{-1}$, using the hypothetical I–O table given in Table 2.2.

Finally, Table 2.10 shows an application of the supply-driven predictive model, equation (2.18), using the hypothetical I–O table given in Table 2.2. Assume that the payments of industry 2 increase by 50 dollars. Using equation (2.18), we can see that this change in payments

Table 2.8 The fixed output coefficient matrix

$\hat{X}^{-1}$		
0.001869	0	0
0	0.002439	0
0	0	0.002381

Z		
100	90	85
95	75	70
90	80	65

θ		
0.186916	0.168224	0.158879
0.231707	0.182927	0.170732
0.214286	0.190476	0.154762

Notes: The technical coefficients matrix $\theta = \hat{X}^{-1}Z$. Ind 1 denotes industry 1. Ind 2 denotes industry 2. Ind 3 denotes industry 3.

Table 2.9 The output inverse

	θ		
	Ind 1	Ind 2	Ind 3
Ind 1	0.18692	0.16822	0.15888
Ind 2	0.23171	0.18293	0.17073
Ind 3	0.21429	0.19048	0.15476

	$(I - \theta)$		
	Ind 1	Ind 2	Ind 3
	0.81308	−0.16822	−0.15888
	−0.23171	0.81707	−0.17073
	−0.21429	−0.19048	0.84524

	$(I - \theta)^{-1}$		
	Ind 1	Ind 2	Ind 3
	1.42705	0.37395	0.34378
	0.50402	1.41643	0.38085
	0.47537	0.41400	1.35608

Notes: The output inverse is given by $(I - \theta)^{-1}$. Ind 1 denotes industry 1. Ind 2 denotes industry 2. Ind 3 denotes industry 3.

Table 2.10 The supply-driven predictive model

Δx^{T}		
Ind 1	Ind 2	Ind 3
25.20	70.82	19.04
	Total	115.07

$$=$$

Δw^{T}		
Ind 1	Ind 2	Ind 3
0	50	0

$\cdot$

	$(I - \theta)^{-1}$		
	Ind 1	Ind 2	Ind 3
	1.42705	0.37395	0.34378
	0.50402	1.41643	0.38085
	0.47537	0.41400	1.35608

Notes: The supply driven model is given by $\Delta x^{\mathrm{T}} = \Delta w^{\mathrm{T}}(I - \theta)^{-1}$. Ind 1 denotes industry 1. Ind 2 denotes industry 2. Ind 3 denotes industry 3.

will cause the output of industry 1 to increase by 25.20 dollars, the output of industry 2 to increase by 70.82 dollars (the initial 50 plus another 20.82 more), and the output for industry 3 to increase by 19.04 dollars. This gives an overall change in region's total output of 115.07 dollars.

Assumptions of the basic I–O model: supply-driven

Using equation (2.13) to predict the impact on a region's economy, as measured by output, relies on a number of assumptions:

1   Producers face a monopoly situation. It is not easy for them to find substitutes in the short run.
2   There is sufficient scarcity of other resources and factors of production such that the economic behaviors of producers will not change in the short run.
3   There is not sufficient time for producers to find substitutes for the scarcity.
4   The smaller the region, the smaller the probability of producers finding alternatives to the scarcity in the short run.

Park (2007) provides a review of the literature associated with supply-driven I–O models. Historically, the main criticism of supply I–O models was described as their implausibility; namely, given the final demands, y in equation (2.9), if consumption reacts perfectly to any changes in supply. For example, an increase in lumber could be supplied to the construction industry to produce housing without an increase in the corresponding supply of nails. Park (2007) review focuses on the work of Ghosh (1958), Oosterhaven (1989), and Dietzenbacher (1997) primarily. The basic concept of value added can be illustrated by wage × labor or price × quantity. Value added can be changed in two ways: (1) holding quantity constant (i.e. labor) and changing price (i.e. wage); and (2) allowing both quantity and price to change. The main components of value added are labor and capital.

The relationship between demand- and supply-driven I–O models

A mathematical relationship can be established between the demand- and supply-driven models based on the definitions of A, equation (2.11b), and θ, equation (2.16b):

$$A = \hat{X}\theta\hat{X}^{-1} \tag{2.19}$$

$$\theta = \hat{X}^{-1}A\hat{X} \tag{2.20}$$

Based on these equations, the technical coefficients and the fixed output coefficients matrices, A and θ respectively, are defined as similar matrices. Thus, the traces of these matrices are equal: That is the sum of the principle diagonal of A and θ are equal, $\Sigma_i a_{ii} = \Sigma_i \theta_{ii}$ for $i = 1,2,\ldots,n$. In fact, based on the definition of $\hat{X}$, $a_{ii} = \theta_{ii}$ for $i = 1,2,\ldots,n$; namely, the elements of the principle diagonal for the technical coefficients and the fixed output coefficients matrices are equal. The economic interpretation of this is that the purchases and sales as a proportion of output an industry makes to itself must be equal.

Likewise, a mathematical relationship can be established between $(I - A)$ and $(I - \theta)$:

$$(I - A) = I - \hat{X}\theta\hat{X}^{-1} = \hat{X}(I - \theta)\hat{X}^{-1} \tag{2.21a}$$

$$(I - \theta) = I - \hat{X}^{-1}A\hat{X} = \hat{X}^{-1}(I - A)\hat{X} \tag{2.21b}$$

and $(I - A)^{-1}$ and $(I - \theta)^{-1}$:

$$(I - A)^{-1} = \hat{X}(I - \theta)^{-1}\hat{X}^{-1} \tag{2.22a}$$

$$(I - \theta)^{-1} = \hat{X}^{-1}(I - A)^{-1}\hat{X} \tag{2.22b}$$

By definition $(I - A)$ and $(I - \theta)$, and $(I - A)^{-1}$ and $(I - \theta)^{-1}$ are similar matrices and their traces are equal. In fact, based on the definition of $\hat{X}$, $(I - A)^{-1}_{ii} = (I - \theta)^{-1}_{ii}$ for $i = 1,2,\ldots,n$; namely, the elements on the principle diagonal are equal. In addition, if Δw^T and Δy are zero filled with $(\Delta w^T)_i = (\Delta y)_i \neq 0$, or if the ith element of either the payments or final demand vector of equations (2.18) and (2.13) respectively are equal, then $(\Delta x^T)_i = (\Delta x)_i$ as shown in Tables 2.6 and 2.10.

I–O models for multi-product industries

In the traditional I–O tables there was a one-to-one correspondence between industries and commodities (Miller and Blair 1985). That is an industry (sometimes called a sector or activity) produced a commodity or product that was reflective of the industry's classification. For example the agricultural industry produced agricultural commodities that it sold to other industries, final demand, and exports. However, many industries produce more than one output. To modify the I–O tables to allow for an industry producing a primary product and one or more secondary products requires creating two separate accounts: industry accounts and commodity accounts.

Industry accounts

To develop these accounts, industries are grouped together based on the similarity of their production technology. This is termed a "production-oriented," "supply-based," or "supply-side" framework. The Economic Classification Policy Committee (ECPC) defined a production-oriented industry as one in which "the production technology of the industry— described by the production process itself, the materials used, type of labor employed, or some combination of these—uniquely defines the industry" (ECPC Report 1 Economic Concepts Incorporated in the Standard Industrial Classification of Industries in the United States, August 1994; http://www.census.gov/epcd/naics/ecpcrpt1, accessed on October 28, 2008). An example of this type of industrial classification system is the 2007 North American Industry Classification System (NAICS) (http://www.census.gov/eos/www/naics/, accessed on October 23, 2008). In the production-oriented framework, if an enterprise produces more than one output, the enterprise is assigned to an industry based on the output or the primary product that generates the most revenue (NAICS 2007; Miller and Blair 1985). The assumption is that the primary product uses the most resources and is the most indicative of the production process (NAICS 2007).

Commodity accounts

Those same product descriptions used in the industry accounts can be used to define commodities. The commodity accounts provide two important functions. First, they allow an industry to purchase commodities as part of its production process: it does not matter if this commodity is a primary product or a secondary product of some other industry. Second, they allow an industry to account for all of the commodities that it may produce. These will be classified as a primary product or secondary products.

The industry and commodity accounts allow the traditional I–O tables to be expanded to (1) identify the commodities used in an industry's production process, and (2) identify the commodities the industry produces as a primary product or secondary products. This expansion takes the form of two new matrices: the make or supply matrix and the use matrix.

The make or supply matrix

The make matrix, V, represents the amount of commodity "c" produced by industry "i."

Table 2.11a The make or supply matrix

		Commodity 1 ... c		Total output (industry)
Industry	1 ⋮ n	v_{11} ... v_{nc} ⋮ ⋱ ⋮ v_{n1} ... v_{nc}		x_1 ⋮ x_n
Total production (commodity)		q_1 ... q_c		

Table 2.11b The make or supply matrix, matrix notation

		Commodity 1 ... c	Total output (industry)
Industry	1 ⋮ n	V	x_n
Total production (commodity)		q_c^{T}	

As shown by Tables 2.11a and 2.11b, the make matrix is defined as an industry-by-commodity (I × C) matrix. By definition the number of commodities, c, can be greater than or equal to the number of industries, n; thus c ≥ n and the make matrix is not necessarily square. The principle diagonal elements of the make matrix denote the primary products while the off-diagonal elements denote any secondary products. The column sum of the make matrix denotes the total amount of the cth commodity produced or supplied within the region. This is given by equation 2.23:

$$q_c^T = \begin{bmatrix} q_1 & \cdots & q_c \end{bmatrix} = \begin{bmatrix} 1 & \cdots & 1 \end{bmatrix} \cdot V \qquad (2.23)$$

Market shares matrix

The relationship given in equation (2.23) allows the development of a matrix that shows the fraction of the cth commodity produced by the ith industry. This matrix is the market shares matrix, *D*, and is given by equation (2.24):

$$D = V\left(\hat{Q}\right)^{-1} \qquad (2.24)$$

where $\hat{Q}$ is a diagonal matrix whose diagonal elements are the vector q_c from equation (2.23). D is an $I \times C$ matrix of commodity output proportions or the market shares matrix, because the columns show the percent of the cth commodity produced by the ith industry; $0 \le d_{ic} \le 1$ and $\Sigma_i d_{ic} = 1$.

By-products matrix

The row sums of the make matrix denote the total amount of output produced by the ith industry. This is given by equation (2.25):

$$x_n = V \cdot \begin{bmatrix} 1 \\ \vdots \\ 1 \end{bmatrix}$$

(2.25)

The relationship given in equation (2.25) allows the development of a matrix that shows the fraction of the ith industry's total production that is made up of the primary product versus all secondary products. This matrix is the by-products matrix, G, and is given by equation (2.26):

$$G = V^{\mathrm{T}} \left(\hat{X} \right)^{-1}$$

(2.26)

G is $C \times I$ matrix of industry output proportions or the by-products matrix, because the columns of the G matrix show the percent of the cth commodity produced by the ith industry; $0 \le g_{ci} \le 1$ and $\Sigma_c g_{ci} = 1$.

The use matrix

The use matrix, U, represents the amount of commodity "c" used by industry "i" in its production process.

As shown by Tables 2.12a and 2.12b, the use matrix is defined as a commodity-by-industry ($C \times I$) matrix. As with the make matrix, $c \ge n$ and the use matrix is not necessarily square.

The column sums of the use matrix including the payments vector define the ith industry's total outlay or expenditures. This is given by equation (2.27):

$$x_n^T = \begin{bmatrix} x_1 & \cdots & x_n \end{bmatrix} = \begin{bmatrix} 1 & \cdots & 1 \end{bmatrix} \cdot U + \begin{bmatrix} w_1 & \cdots & w_n \end{bmatrix}$$
$$= \begin{bmatrix} 1 & \cdots & 1 \end{bmatrix} \cdot U + w_n^T$$

(2.27)

Table 2.12a The use matrix

		Industry 1 ... n	Final demand	Exports	Total output (commodity)
Commodity	1 : c	u_{11} ... u_{1n} : u_{c1} ... u_{cn}	f_{1H} f_{1G} f_{1In} : f_{nH} f_{nG} f_{nIn}	e_1 : e_c	q_1 : q_c
Value added		w_{L1} ... w_{Ln} w_{K1} ... w_{Kn}			
Imports		m_1 ... m_n			
Total outlay (industry)		x_1 ... x_n			

Table 2.12b The use matrix, matrix notation

		Industry 1 ... n	Final demand	Total output (commodity)
Commodity	1 : c	U	f_c	q_c
Payments		w^T		
Total outlay (industry)		x_n^T		

where w_n^T is defined in equation (2.14). The rows of the use matrix show the uses of locally produced commodities in terms of inputs into various production process and final demand. The row sums of the use matrix including final demand define the total amount of the cth commodity produced. This is given by equation (2.28):

$$q_c = \begin{bmatrix} q_1 \\ \vdots \\ q_c \end{bmatrix} = U \cdot \begin{bmatrix} 1 \\ \vdots \\ 1 \end{bmatrix} + \begin{bmatrix} f_{1H} & f_{1G} & f_{1In} & e_1 \\ \vdots & \vdots & \vdots & \vdots \\ f_{cH} & f_{cG} & f_{cIn} & e_c \end{bmatrix} \cdot \begin{bmatrix} 1 \\ \vdots \\ 1 \end{bmatrix}$$

$$= U \cdot \begin{bmatrix} 1 \\ \vdots \\ 1 \end{bmatrix} + \begin{bmatrix} f_1 \\ \vdots \\ f_c \end{bmatrix} = U \cdot \begin{bmatrix} 1 \\ \vdots \\ 1 \end{bmatrix} + f_c$$

(2.28)

where f_c is a column vector defining final demand for commodities.

The absorption matrix

The use matrix serves a function similar to the interindustry trans-actions matrix, Z, in the traditional I–O model. The ith column of the interindustry transactions matrix defined the ith industry's production function in terms of purchasing intermediate inputs from other regional industries. The technical coefficients or direct requirements matrix, $A = Z\hat{X}^{-1}$, provides the flows on a per dollar of industry output basis. The ith column of the use matrix may also be interpreted as the ith industry's production function. However, instead of defining the flows in terms of purchases for local industries, the flows are defined in terms of local commodities. Just as a technical coefficients or direct require-ments matrix is calculated from the interindustry transactions matrix, an analogous direct requirements matrix can be calculated from the use matrix. This matrix is called the absorption matrix, B:

$$B = U\hat{X}^{-1} \tag{2.29}$$

where $\hat{X}$ is a diagonal matrix whose diagonal elements are the vector x_n^{T} from equation (2.27). The absorption matrix, B, is a commodity-by-industry, $C \times I$, matrix with b_{ci} denoting the dollars' worth of commodity "c" required to produce one dollar's worth of industry i's output.

Expanded I–O tables

Including the distinction between industries and commodities in the I–O table results in an expanded I–O table shown in Tables 2.13a and 2.13b.

Table 2.13a Expanded I–O table

	Commodity 1 ... c	Industry 1 ... n	Final demand	Total output
Commodity 1 ⋮ c		u_{11} ... u_{1n} ⋮ ⋱ ⋮ u_{c1} ... u_{cn}	f_{1H} f_{1G} f_{1In} e_1 ⋮ ⋮ ⋮ ⋮ f_{cH} f_{cG} f_{cIn} e_c	q_1 ⋮ q_c
Industry 1 ⋮ n	v_{11} ... v_{nc} ⋮ ⋱ ⋮ v_{n1} ... v_{nc}			x_1 ⋮ x_n
Payments		w_{L1} ... w_{Ln} w_{K1} ... w_{Kn} m_1 ... m_n	w_{LH} w_{LG} w_{LIn} e_L w_{KH} w_{KG} w_{KIn} e_K m_H m_G m_{In} m_e	L K M
Total input	q_1 ... q_c	x_1 ... x_n	H G In E	

Table 2.13b Expanded I–O table, matrix notation

	Commodity 1 ... c	Industry 1 ... n	Final demand	Total output
Commodity 1 ⋮ c		U	f_c	q_c
Industry 1 ⋮ n	V			x_n
Payments		w^T	α	β
Total input	q_c^T	x_n^T	β	

As can be seen Table 2.13a (or Table 2.13b in matrix notation), this is an expanded version of Table 2.1d. The intersection of the payment and the final demand accounts in Table 2.13a is interpreted in the same manner as in Table 2.1d. In the matrix notation, the intersection of payments and final demand accounts is a scalar found by equation (2.30):

$$\alpha = \begin{bmatrix} 1 & 1 & 1 \end{bmatrix} \cdot \begin{bmatrix} w_{LH} & w_{LG} & w_{LIn} & e_L \\ w_{KH} & w_{KG} & w_{KIn} & e_K \\ m_H & m_G & m_{In} & m_e \end{bmatrix} \cdot \begin{bmatrix} 1 \\ 1 \\ 1 \\ 1 \end{bmatrix} \tag{2.30}$$

The column sum of the final demand account is a scalar found by equation (2.31):

$$\beta = \begin{bmatrix} 1 & \cdots & 1 \end{bmatrix} \cdot \begin{bmatrix} f_1 \\ \vdots \\ f_c \end{bmatrix} + \alpha \tag{2.31}$$

The row sum of the payments account is a scalar and found by equation (2.32):

$$\beta = \begin{bmatrix} w_1 & \cdots & w_n \end{bmatrix} \cdot \begin{bmatrix} 1 \\ \vdots \\ 1 \end{bmatrix} + \alpha \tag{2.32}$$

The fact that equations (2.31) and (2.32) are equal is no coincidence: β is by definition the gross national or regional product. This is the same as given by equation (2.5b).

The expanded I–O table, Table 2.13a, is the same as that used by the European System of Accounts (ESA) entitled "a simplified combined supply and use table" (ESA, 1995, Chapter 9—Input-Output Framework; http://circa.europa.eu/irc/dsis/nfaccount/info/data/ESA95/en/een00438.htm, accessed on October 29, 2008).

Symmetric versus non-symmetric I–O tables

A predictive I–O model requires calculating a total requirements matrix. For example, in the demand-driven I–O model it is the Leontief inverse, $(I - A)^{-1}$, given in equation (2.13). The foundation of the Leontief inverse is the technical coefficients matrix, A (see equation (2.11b)). This is an industry-by-industry matrix and square or symmetric and $(I - A)$ is invertible. In the supply-driven I–O model it is the output inverse, $(I - \theta)^{-1}$, given in equation (2.18). The foundation of the output inverse is the direct-output coefficients matrix, θ (see equation (2.16b)). This is an industry-by-industry matrix and square or symmetric and $(I - \theta)$ is invertible.

The previous paragraph leads to two observations. First, a necessary condition for a predictive I–O model is a square or symmetric co-efficients matrix. Second, the traditional I–O table, as illustrated in Table 2.1d, is by definition a symmetric input–output table (SIOT). However, it is limited as it only uses industry accounts.

As is shown by Tables 2.13a and 2.13b, the use and make (supply) matrices employ both industry and commodity accounts. However, these matrices are potentially non-symmetric as the number of commodities may be greater than or equal to the number of industries, $c \geq n$. Thus, Tables 2.13a and 2.13b can be described as non-symmetric I–O tables. The advantage of non-symmetric I–O table (often called a supply use table (SUT)) is the added flexibility that combining industry and commodity accounts allows in describing a regional economy. The potential disadvantage is creating a predictive I–O model given the non-symmetric use and make matrices; namely deriving a total requirements matrix from non-symmetric use and make matrices.

Given the dimensions of the use and make matrices, $C \times I$ and $I \times C$, respectively, two possible symmetric matrices are guaranteed; namely, a commodity-by-commodity, $C \times C$, or an industry-by-industry, $I \times I$, total requirements matrix. Developing the $I \times I$ or $C \times C$ total require-ments matrix from the use and make matrices depends on nature of the secondary products and the assumption used to account for secondary products. Secondary production can be categorized as:

1   Subsidiary products—a secondary product whose production process is technically unrelated to the primary product (Braibant 2002; Miller and Blair 1985). Miller and Blair (1985) use the example of an automobile manufacturer producing a small number of military tanks in a plant unrelated to the production of automobiles, the primary product.
2   By-products—a secondary product whose production process is technically related to the primary product (Braibant 2002; Miller and Blair (1985)). Miller and Blair (1985) use the example of an automobile manufacturer producing automobile parts as well as fully assembled automobiles. Producing automobile parts is the by-product.
3   Joint products—secondary products that are produced simultaneously with another product (Braibant 2002; Miller and Blair 1985). The classic example of the joint products are beef and hides.

The two assumptions of accounting for secondary products are termed industry-based technology (IBT) and commodity-based technology (CBT). The IBT assumption states that each industry has the same input structure regardless of its mix of commodity outputs (Braibant 2002) or all commodities produced by an industry are produced with the same input structure (Miller and Blair 1985). The CBT assumption states that each commodity has its own input structure regardless of the producing industry (Braibant 2002; Miller and Blair 1985). Braibant (2002) and Miller and Blair (1985) state the nature of subsidiary products lend themselves better to a total requirements matrix built based on the CBT assumption and the nature of by-products lend themselves better to a total requirements matrix built based on the IBT assumption. Joint products can lend themselves to either a total requirements matrix built on either the CBT or IBT assumptions. Joint products generally imply that the number of commodities is greater than the number of industries.

    Braibant (2002) and Miller and Blair (1985) describe different approaches to modify the use matrix based on information contained in the make or supply matrix and employing either the IBT or CBT assumption. However, transforming a SUT into an SIOT may have many complications and limitations. For example, surveys of industries usually provide general information about the type of commodities used and produced. This is the information contained in the SUT.

However, information in terms of the intermediate and primary factors of production for each specific commodity produced is not collected. Thus, general information arranged from a SUT is a starting point for constructing an SIOT. The non-symmetric make or supply and use matrices can be converted into a C × C or I × I matrix by adding extra statistical information on the input structures (intermediate and primary factors of production) or by assuming constant input structures by commodity or by industry (ESA, 1995, Chapter 9—Input-Output Framework; http://circa.europa.eu/irc/dsis/nfaccount/info/data/ESA95/en/een00438.htm, accessed on October 29, 2008).

Total requirements matrices

As stated previously, a predictive I–O model requires calculating a total requirements matrix. The traditional predictive I–O model was given by equation (2.13). This model can be described as industry-by-industry approach as the I–O table (Table 2.1d) only referenced industries. However, the flexibility of distinguishing between commodities and industries (Tables 2.13a and 2.13b) allows for developing approaches that include both commodities and industries. Equation (2.33) follows from Tables 2.13a and 2.13b and defines the accounting relationship equating total commodity output with that used in production and final demand commodity consumption:

$$
q_c = U \begin{bmatrix} 1 \\ \vdots \\ 1 \end{bmatrix} + f_c
$$

$$(2.33)$$

The definition of the absorption matrix, B equation (2.29), allows the relationship given in equation (2.33) to be defined in terms of commodity and industries (equation (2.34)):

$$
q_c = Bx + f_c
$$
$$(2.34)$$

Unfortunately, a predictive model cannot be developed directly from equation (2.34). However, assuming IBT or CBT and using the definitions of the market shares matrix, D equation (2.24), and the by-products matrix, G equation (2.26), we can develop predictive models that take advantage of the flexibility shown in Tables 2.13a and 2.13b. A standard approach to develop these predictive models is to assume that the number of commodities equals the number of industries. While Miller and Blair (1985, 2009) provide very detailed discussions on developing these models, we will only summarize their discussion in what follows.

The first three predictive models are developed by examining the market shares matrix:

$$D = V\hat{Q}^{-1}$$

$$D\hat{Q} = V$$

$$D\hat{Q} \begin{bmatrix} 1 \\ \vdots \\ 1 \end{bmatrix} = V \begin{bmatrix} 1 \\ \vdots \\ 1 \end{bmatrix}$$

The last equation can be rewritten as equation (2.35):

$$Dq_c = x \tag{2.35}$$

Substituting equation (2.35) into (2.34) gives equation (2.36):

$$q_c = BDq_c + f_c \tag{2.36}$$

This substitution allows developing the first predictive model given in equation (2.37):

$$q_c = (I - BD)^{-1} f_c \tag{2.37}$$

Examining equation (2.37) reveals four observations. First, it defines a commodity-driven model in that the external final demand change is defined by commodity purchases, f_c. Second, the total requirement matrix, $(I - BD)^{-1}$, is a $C \times C$ matrix. Third, the BD matrix defines the commodity inputs per dollar of commodity output and describes IBT (Miller and Blair 1985, 2009). Finally, using the definitions of the absorption matrix, B, and the market shares matrix, D, the BD matrix can be defined in terms of the use and make matrices (equation (2.38)):

$$BD = \left[U\hat{X}^{-1} \right] \cdot \left[V\hat{Q}^{-1} \right] \tag{2.38}$$

Thus, the first model is formally defined as a commodity-driven commodity-by-commodity model given IBT.

The second predictive model can be developed by rewriting equation (2.35) as:

$$q_c = D^{-1}x \tag{2.39}$$

assuming D is symmetric and nonsingular. Equation (2.39) and equation (2.37) can be combined giving:

$$x = D(I - BD)^{-1}f_c \tag{2.40}$$

Examining equation (2.40) reveals three observations. First, it defines a commodity-driven model in that the external change in final demand is defined by commodity purchases, f_c; however, the impact is defined in terms of industry output x. Second, the total requirement matrix, $D(I - BD)^{-1}$, is an I × C matrix. Finally, as with equation (2.37), the total requirements matrix describes IBT (Miller and Blair 1985, 2009). The second model is a commodity-driven industry-by-commodity given IBT.

The third predictive model (equation (2.41)) is developed by substituting equation (2.39) into equation (2.34):

$$D^{-1}x = Bx + f_c$$
$$x = DBx + Df_c \tag{2.41}$$

The term Df_c requires some interpretation. This will be done by re-examining equation (2.35), $Dq_c = x$. The relationship states that pre-multiplying the total commodity output vector, q_c, by the market shares matrix, D, converts it into a total industry output vector, x, using IBT. The f_c vector denotes the final demand in terms of commodities. Thus pre-multiplying f_c by the market shares matrix would convert it into final demand in terms of industries, or $Df_c = y$, again in terms of IBT. The y vector is defined by equation (2.9). Equation (2.41) then reduces to (equation 2.41a):

$$x = DBx + y \tag{2.41a}$$

The predictive model is given by equation (2.42):

$$x = (I - DB)^{-1}y \tag{2.42}$$

Examining equation (2.42) reveals four observations. First, it defines an industry-driven model in that the external final demand change is defined by industry purchases, *y*. Second, the total requirement matrix, $(I - DB)^{-1}$, is an I × I matrix. Third, the *DB* matrix defines the industry inputs per dollar of industry output and describes IBT (Miller and Blair 1985, 2009). Finally, using the definitions of the absorption matrix, *B*, and the market shares matrix, *D*, the *DB* matrix can be defined in terms of the use and make matrices (equation (2.43)):

$$DB = \left[V\hat{Q}^{-1} \right] \cdot \left[U\hat{X}^{-1} \right]$$
(2.43)

Thus, the third model is formally defined as an industry-driven industry-by-industry model given IBT.

The predictive model given in equation (2.42) is analogous to the traditional demand-driven I–O model given in equation (2.13). However, $(I - DB)^{-1} \neq (I - A)^{-1}$ almost assuredly. If the make matrix is diagonal, $\hat{V}$, (namely, that is there is a one-to-one relationship between industries and commodities) then $\hat{V}$ becomes essentially an I × I rather than an I × C matrix. If $\hat{V}$ is diagonal, then $\hat{V} = \hat{V}^T$ and if $\hat{X} = \hat{V}$ then:

$$A = Z\left(\hat{X}\right)^{-1} = U\left(\hat{V}\right)^{-1}$$
(2.44)

Equation (2.44) gives an I × I direct requirements matrix defined using either IBT or CBT because $\hat{V}$ is diagonal and there are no secondary, joint, or by-products. In addition equation (2.44) implies that $Z = U$. Consequently:

$$(I - A)^{-1} = \left(I - U\left(\hat{V}\right)^{-1} \right)^{-1}$$
(2.45)

This relationship (equation (2.45)), while appearing unique, may occur in less developed economies (e.g. Thomas and Bautista 1999).

The next three predictive models are developed by examining the by-products matrix:

$$G = V^T \hat{X}^{-1}$$

$$G\hat{X} = V^T$$

$$G\hat{X} \begin{bmatrix} 1 \\ \vdots \\ 1 \end{bmatrix} = V^T \begin{bmatrix} 1 \\ \vdots \\ 1 \end{bmatrix}$$

The last equation can be rewritten as equation (2.46):

$$Gx = q_c \qquad (2.46)$$

and equation (2.47):

$$x = G^{-1}q_c \qquad (2.47)$$

Equation 2.47 requires that G^{-1} be symmetric and nonsingular. Equation (2.47) can be substituted into equation (2.34) giving:

$$q_c = BG^{-1}q_c + f_c \qquad (2.48)$$

Equation (2.48) is used to develop the fourth predictive model:

$$q_c = \left(I - BG^{-1}\right)f_c \qquad (2.49)$$

Examining equation (2.49) reveals four observations. First, it defines a commodity-driven model in that the external change is defined by commodity purchases, f_c. Second, the total requirement matrix, $(I - BG^{-1})^{-1}$, is a C × C matrix. Third, the BG^{-1} matrix defines that a commodity has the same input structure regardless of the industry that produces it and describes CBT (Miller and Blair 1985, 2009). Finally, using the definitions of the absorption matrix, B, and the market shares matrix, D, the BG^{-1} matrix can be defined in terms of the use and make matrices:

$$BG^{-1} = U\left(V^T\right)^{-1} \qquad (2.50)$$

Thus, the fourth model is formally defined as a commodity-driven commodity-by-commodity model given CBT. Masui (2005) uses the relationship given in equation (2.50) to posits that if (1) $A = BG^{-1}$ and is defined as C × C matrix; (2) V is defined as I × C; and (3) both matrices are given as part of a region's data base, then the use matrix maybe estimated using $U = AV^T$.

The fifth predictive model can be found by combining equation (2.46) with equation (2.49):

$$Gx = \left(I - BG^{-1}\right)f_c$$
$$x = \left[G^{-1}\left(I - BG^{-1}\right)^{-1}\right]f_c \qquad (2.51)$$

Examining equation (2.51) reveals three observations. First, it defines a commodity-driven model in that the external change in final demand is defined by commodity purchases, f_c; however, the impact is defined in terms of industry output x. Second, the total requirement matrix, $G^{-1}(I - BG^{-1})^{-1}$, is an I × C matrix. Finally, as with equation (2.49), the total requirements matrix describes CBT (Miller and Blair 1985, 2009). The fourth model is a commodity-driven industry-by-commodity given CBT.

The final predictive model we will develop will start by combining equation (2.34) and (2.46):

$$Gx = Bx + f_c$$

$$x = G^{-1}Bx + G^{-1}f_c \tag{2.52}$$

The term $G^{-1}f_c$ requires some interpretation. This will be done by re-examining equation (2.47), $G^{-1}q_c = x$. The relationship states that pre-multiplying the total commodity output vector, q_c, by the inverse of the by-products matrix, G^{-1}, converts it into a total industry output vector, x, but using CBT. The f_c vector denotes the final demand in terms of commodities. Thus pre-multiplying f_c by the inverse of the by-products matrix would convert it into final demand in terms of industries, or $G^{-1}f_c = y$, again using CBT. Equation (2.52) then reduces to (equation (2.52a)):

$$x = G^{-1}Bx + y \tag{2.52a}$$

The last predictive model is given by equation (2.53):

$$x = \left(I - G^{-1}B\right)^{-1} y \tag{2.53}$$

Examining equation (2.53) reveals four observations. First, it defines an industry-driven model in that the external final demand change is defined by industry purchases, y. Second, the total requirement matrix, $(I - G^{-1}B)^{-1}$, is an I × I matrix. Third, the $G^{-1}B$ matrix describes CBT (Miller and Blair 1985, 2009). Finally, using the definitions of the absorption matrix, B, and the by-product matrix, G, the $G^{-1}B$ matrix can be defined in terms of the use and make matrices (equation (2.54)):

$$G^{-1}B = \left[\hat{X}\left(V^{T}\right)^{-1}\right] \cdot \left[U\hat{X}^{-1}\right] \tag{2.54}$$

Thus, the final model is formally defined as an industry-driven industry-by-industry model given CBT.

Summary of predictive models

Tables 2.14b and 2.14c provide a summary of the predictive models developed using traditional I–O models and make (supply) and use tables, respectively.

Table 2.14a Total requirements matrices

	Industry-based technology	Commodity-based technology
Commodity-by-commodity	$(I - BD)^{-1}$	$(I - BG^{-1})^{-1}$
Industry-by-industry	$(I - DB)^{-1}$	$(I - G^{-1}B)^{-1}$

Source: Miller and Blair (1985).

Notes: The number of commodities may be greater than or equal to the number of industries (IBT). The number of commodities must equal the number of industries (CBT).

Table 2.14b Summary of predictive models for traditional I–O

	Demand-side traditional I–O	Supply-side traditional I–O
Industry-by-industry	$\Delta x = (I - A)^{-1}\Delta y$	$\Delta x^{\mathrm{T}} = \Delta w^{\mathrm{T}}(I - \theta)^{-1}$

Table 2.14c Summary of predictive models derived from make and use matrices

	Industry-based technology	Commodity-based technology
Commodity-driven commodity-by-commodity	$\Delta q_c = (I - BD)^{-1}\Delta f_c$	$\Delta q_c = (I - BG^{-1})^{-1}\Delta f_c$
Commodity-driven industry-by-commodity	$\Delta x = [D(I - DB)^{-1}]\Delta f_c$	$\Delta x = [G^{-1}(I - BG^{-1})^{-1}]\Delta f_c$
Industry-driven industry-by-industry	$\Delta x = (I - DB)^{-1}\Delta y$	$\Delta x = (I - G^{-1}B)^{-1}\Delta y$

Source: Miller and Blair (1985 and 2009).

Note: IBT: The number of commodities may be greater than or equal to the number of industries. CBT: The number of commodities must equal the number of industries.

Examining Table 2.14c shows that we did not develop any industry-driven commodity-by-industry models using either IBT or CBT. Miller and Blair (2009) do develop the total requirements matrices and models for those predictive models. However, the most common approaches are the ones we have summarized. Second, the direct requirements matrices from the commodity-by-commodity (equations (2.38) and (2.50)) or industry-by-industry (equations (2.43) and (2.54)) models are functions of the use and make matrices. In equation (2.44), we defined the relationship $A = U\hat{V}^{-1}$ given the industry-driven industry-by-industry model given IBT and assuming the make matrix was defined as a diagonal implying a one-to-one relationship between industries and commodities. However, if the make matrix is diagonal, then the direct requirements matrices given by equations (2.38), (2.50), (2.43), and (2.54) all reduce to $A = U\hat{V}^{-1}$. Finally, the CBT predictive models all require that the by-products matrix be symmetric and nonsingular. Millar and Blair (2009) develop alternative forms for the total requirements matrices given CBT that do not require an inverse of the by-products matrix.

Braidant (2002) describes alternative approaches for deriving I × I and C × C SIOTs from a SUT that are not always shown easily using matrix algebra. For example, Braidant (2002) develops a C × C SIOT from an SUT assuming that "each product [commodity] is produced in its own specific way, irrespective of the industry where it is produced." The implication of this CBT assumption is that only one technique exists for producing each commodity and the number of commodities must equal the number of industries. This requires that the secondary commodities are transferred from the industries where they are produced to the industries of which they are the primary commodity. The result is a C × C SIOT. In this case the resulting total requirements matrix is the same as $(I - BG^{-1})^{-1}$ described by Miller and Blair (1985, 2009) and given in Table 2.14c. However, a C × C SIOT developed using the assumption that "each industry has its own specific way of production, irrespective of its product mix" or an IBT assumption is not the same as $(I - BD)^{-1}$ described by Miller and Blair (1985, 2009) and given in Table 2.14c. The implication of this IBT assumption is that the number of commodities may be greater than or equal to the number of industries.

The ESA uses a C × C SIOT developed from a SUT given the number of commodities may be greater than the number of industries. This requires allocating secondary commodities in the make or supply table to the industries where they are the principal commodity. ESA defines two approaches one based on a CBT and the second based on IBT assumptions as described by Braidant (2002). However, the choice of which assumption to apply is not an easy one. It depends on the structure of national industries, e.g. the degree of specialization, and on the homogeneity of the national technologies used to produce commodities within the same commodity group. For example, boots may be made from leather and from plastic. Assuming the same product technology for all boots (or, when a higher level of aggregation is used, e.g. footwear) can thus be problematic; assuming industry technology may then be a better alternative (http://circa.europa.eu/irc/dsis/nfaccount/info/data/esa95/en/een00441.htm, accessed on December 31, 2008).

Bohlin and Widell (2006) analyze how SIOTs and the SUT differ from each other when calculated from different technology assumptions. They conclude that the IBT and CBT are only two extreme solutions to all the infinitely many SIOTs that are consistent with the use and make matrices. This is shown by the differences between direct requirements and total requirements matrices determined by Miller and Blair (1985) and Braidant (2002). Thus care should be taken when calculating SIOTs.

3 Social accounting matrices

SAM models: general background

From a regional perspective, the structure of a regional economy can be described by its production, income distribution, consumption of goods and services, savings and investments, and trade. A SAM gives a comprehensive picture of the flow of income among households, primary factors of production (land, labor, and capital), and economic institutions. A SAM has two principal objectives. The first is concerned with the organization of information, usually information about the economic and social structure of a country or region in a particular year, though the spatial and temporal dimensions can change. Once the data in a particular country has been organized in the form of a SAM, they present a static image that can reveal much about the country's economic structure. The second objective of a SAM is to provide the statistical basis for the creation of a plausible model (King 1985).

The principle of a SAM is the same as that of an I–O model. It is really nothing more than double-entry bookkeeping. A SAM is a series of accounts where what is "incoming" into one account must be "outgoing" from another account. In this respect, a SAM resembles traditional accounts and embodies the information normally included in national or regional accounts and more. In a SAM, the double entries are achieved by only a single entry in a matrix that resembles an oversized chessboard (King 1985). Each account consists of one row across the board and one column down it, both identically numbered. How large the matrix is depends on the limitations of the available data and the motivation in which it was constructed. In principle there is no limit to the level of detail, but in practice, both the data and the effort available for constructing the SAM impose limitations. While the traditional I–O model focus on flows among actors involved in production (see Tables 2.1d and 2.13a and Tables 2.15a and 2.15b), a

SAM is better described as a socioeconomic model as it includes not only flows among the actors involved in production but also the inter-dependence of production with the rest of society (Thorbecke 1998).

Table 2.13a illustrates an expanded I–O model developed using make (supply) and use matrices. Table 3.1 disaggregates the payments and final demand accounts in Table 2.13a to better show the inter-dependence of production with the rest of the economy and describes the potential detail of a SAM.

Table 3.2 illustrates a SAM for Zimbabwe developed using make (supply) and use matrices as shown in Table 3.1.

There are two unique features of the Zimbabwe SAM that are not shown in Table 3.1. First, the transaction costs row and column do not appear in Table 3.1. On closer inspection, the transaction costs can be aggregated into a diagonal marketing margins matrix. Second, house-holds according to Table 3.1 purchase commodities not industries. However, in an economy such as Zimbabwe, households do purchase directly from industries in the form of subsistence or direct home consumption of the agricultural commodities they produce.

This type of SAM can be very useful for regions where agricultural production can have an important weight and its data can be intro-duced mostly on a per-hectare basis as well as per head per year for milk cows, ewes, does, and breeding males through the use matrix. This allows consideration of different intensity levels in terms of yield and corresponding combinations of inputs (new seed, fertilizer, better management, etc.).

For small regions, even villages, a make (or supply) and use matrices can be useful as the product sales (the make matrix) can account for the total amount of the products that are sold in the domestic or village market (domestic product markets) while the intermediate factors of production (the use matrix) account for the necessary purchases of intermediate inputs for the production and total amount of production for the commodities. Dixon *et al.* (2004) also include two additional cells for this case in order to account both the transaction costs, between inputs and commodities, and the household consumption of inputs, both recorded as a loss of commodities.

To demonstrate this circular flow, Table 3.2 shows that urban and rural households purchase the four commodities (commodity rows and household columns). These commodities are produces by the local industries (the make matrix; industry rows, and commodity columns). In order for the local industries to produce these commodities, they must purchase intermediate factors of production (the use matrix, commodity rows, and industry columns) and value added (factors rows and industry columns). Finally, the payments to labor from the factor rows are distributed to urban and rural households. The circle is complete: consumption = > commodity production = > labor income = > income distribution = > consumption. While the circular flows are more complicated than this if each individual row and column is analyzed, this demonstrates that what is "outgoing" from one account must be "incoming" into another account and that column totals must equal row totals.

Basic SAM accounts

Highlighting these interdependent flows and ultimately developing a predictive model can get lost in the detail provided in Table 3.1 and Table 3.2. Thus Table 3.1 will be aggregated into a symmetric industry-by-industry SAM shown in Table 3.3.

We will use four main accounts (or row/column headings) to define the SAM shown in Table 3.3:

Industry accounts: The industry accounts are used to describe the production activity within the area and all expenditures and receipts associated with production processes.

Factor accounts: The factor accounts denote the primary factors of production such as (1) wages, salaries, and benefits paid to labor, and (2) proprietary income and other property income, and rent.

Institutions accounts: The institutional accounts denote households, governments, enterprises, and capital investment.

Import/export or rest of the world accounts: The import/export accounts, also called the rest of the world accounts, describe the trade flows into and out of the region. Imports are represented by rows and exports by columns.

Description of SAMs

Interindustry transaction matrix (S_{11}): This matrix represents the interindustry transaction matrix. Table 3.1 uses both industry and commodity accounts in the form of use and make matrices to depict production. Chapter 2 discusses the creation of a symmetric industry-by-industry from use and make matrices. If marketing margins exist they will be included in the use matrix using matrix summation. The relationship between an I–O transactions matrix, Z, and S_{11} developed using the use and make matrices is also discussed in Chapter 2.

Table 3.1 Detailed SAM layout

Receipts	Ind (1)	Com (2)	Factor (3)	Expenditures Ent (4)
Ind (1)		Make		
Com (2)	Use	Marketing margins		
Factor (3)	Value added			
Ent (4)			Capital income	
HH (5)			Labor income	Retained earning
Govt (6)	Indirect business taxes	Import tariff	Factor taxes	Corp taxes
Capital (7)				Corp savings
Imports (8)		Imports	Payments to foreign labor	Payments to foreign ent
Totals (9)	Total prod cost	Total com supply	Total value added	Total ent exp

Source: Based on the SAM described by Dixon *et al.* (2004), Taniguchi (2004), and Thomas an
Bautista (1999).

Notes:
Ind (1)—Industry; Com (2)—Commodity; Factor (4)—Primary factors of production such as
(a) wages, salaries, and benefits paid to labor, and (b) proprietary income, other propert
income, and rent; Ent (5)—Enterprises; HH (6)—Households; Capital (7)—Capital; Gov
(8)—Governments; Import/Export (9)—Imports and exports; Use (2,1)—Use matrix; Value
added (3,1)—Sum of the primary factors of production; Indirect business taxes (6,1)—Indirec
business taxes include excise, property, and sales taxes, and licenses and fees.; Total prod cos
(9,1)—Total production costs, this is a sum of the elements in column (1); Make (1,2)—Mak
matrix; Marketing margins or transaction costs (2,2)—Difference among domestic, export
and import products to reflect deficiencies in trade and transport infrastructure; Import tariff
(6,2)—A duty or tax in certain imported commodities; Imports (8,2)—Imported commodities
Total com supply (9,2)—Total commodity supply, this is a sum of the elements in column (2
Capital income (4,3)—Distribution of value added to capital; Labor income (5,3)—Distri
bution of wages and salaries to households; Factor taxes (6,3)—Payments to governments b
primary factors of production.; Payments to foreign labor (8,3)—Distribution of (a) wages
salaries, and benefits paid to labor, and (b) proprietary income, other property income, and ren
to foreign households and enterprises; Total value added (9,3)—This is a sum of the element
in column (3)

Expenditures				
HH (5)	Govt (6)	Capital (7)	Exports (8)	Totals (9)
HH direct consump				Total ind prod
HH market consump	Govt consump	Investment exp	Com exports	Total com demand
				Total factor income
	Transfers to ent			Total ent income
InterHH transfers	Transfers to HH		Foreign payments HH	Total HH income
Income tax			Foreign grants	Total govt income
HH savings	Govt savings		Foreign savings	Total savings
HH imports	Govt imports		Transship	Total imports
Total HH exp	Total govt exp	Total investment	Total exports	

Investment exp (2,7)—Investment expenditures on commodities; Total investment (9,7)—This is a sum of the elements in column (7); Com exports (2,8)—Commodity exports; Foreign payments HH (5,8)—Foreign payments to households; Foreign grants (6,8)—Payments in the form of grants to local governments from foreign governments; Foreign savings (7,8)—Payments from foreign enterprises, household, and governments in the form of savings; Transship (8,8)—Transshipments or commodities imported then exported.; Total exports (9,8)—This a sum of the elements in column (8); Total ind prod (1,9)—Total industry production, this is a sum of the elements in row (1); Total com demand (2,9)—Total commodity demand, this is a sum of the elements in row (2); Total factor income (3,9)—This is a sum of the elements in row (3); Total ent income (4,9)—Total enterprise income is a sum of the elements in row (4); Total HH income (5,9)—Total household income is a sum of the elements in row (5); Total govt income (6,9)—Total government income is a sum of the elements in row (6); Total saving (7,9)—This is a sum of the elements in row (7); Total imports (8,9)—This is a sum of the elements in row (8)

Table 3.2 Example of a supply and use SAM

Category	Industries					Commodities				Transaction costs			Factors			Households		Other institutions								Total
	1	2	3	4	5	6	7	8	9	10	11	12	13	14	15	16	17	18	19	20	21	22	23	24	25	
Industries																										
1 Agriculture large scale	0	0	0	0	0	5250	0	0	0	0	0	0	0	0	0	0	0	0	0	0	0	0	0	0	0	5250
2 Agriculture small-scale	0	0	0	0	0	670	0	0	0	0	0	0	0	0	0	685	0	0	0	0	0	0	0	0	0	1355
3 Industry	0	0	0	0	0	0	17859	0	0	0	0	0	0	0	0	0	0	0	0	0	0	0	0	0	0	17859
4 Transportation	0	0	0	0	0	0	0	8263	0	0	0	0	0	0	0	0	0	0	0	0	0	0	0	0	0	8263
5 Other services	0	0	0	0	0	0	0	0	15781	0	0	0	0	0	0	0	0	0	0	0	0	0	0	0	0	15781
Commodities																										
6 Agriculture	244	7	2697	0	97	0	0	0	0	0	0	0	0	0	0	617	629	0	0	0	0	0	2963	0	−30	7224
7 Industry	1145	165	5859	3075	3619	0	0	0	0	0	0	0	0	0	0	5236	7255	0	310	0	0	0	2515	3399	−495	32083
8 Transportation	38	29	176	183	282	0	0	0	0	3445	1689	986	0	0	0	604	662	0	169	0	0	0	0	0	0	8263
9 Other services	715	30	281	421	1685	0	0	0	0	0	0	0	0	0	0	1913	2561	0	4295	0	0	0	1598	2784	0	16283
Transaction costs																										
10 Domestic sales	0	0	0	0	0	657	2788	0	0	0	0	0	0	0	0	0	0	0	0	0	0	0	0	0	0	3445
11 Imports	0	0	0	0	0	9	1680	0	0	0	0	0	0	0	0	0	0	0	0	0	0	0	0	0	0	1689
12 Exports	0	0	0	0	0	580	406	0	0	0	0	0	0	0	0	0	0	0	0	0	0	0	0	0	0	986

	1	2	3	4	5	6	7	8	9	10	11	12	13	14	15	16	17	18	19	20	21	22	23	24	25	Total
Factors																										
13 Labor	755	684	2936	2446	6028	0	0	0	0	0	0	0	0	0	0	0	0	0	0	0	0	0	0	0	0	12849
14 Capital	1719	260	5386	1950	3524	0	0	0	0	0	0	0	0	0	0	0	0	0	0	0	0	0	0	0	0	12839
15 Land	458	137	0	0	0	0	0	0	0	0	0	0	0	0	0	0	0	0	0	0	0	0	0	0	0	595
Households																										
16 Rural	0	0	0	0	0	0	0	0	0	0	0	0	1605	1979	595	0	259	5526	1113	0	0	0	102	0	0	11179
17 Urban	0	0	0	0	0	0	0	0	0	0	0	0	11218	127	0	0	0	3306	346	0	0	0	0	0	0	14997
Other institutions																										
18 Enterprise	0	0	0	0	0	0	0	0	0	0	0	0	0	10733	0	0	0	0	1209	0	0	0	0	0	0	11942
19 Government	0	0	0	0	0	0	0	0	0	0	0	0	0	0	0	0	0	0	0	3727	1477	1861	291	0	0	7356
20 Direct taxes	0	0	0	0	0	0	0	0	0	0	0	0	0	0	0	709	1351	1667	0	0	0	0	0	0	0	3727
21 Indirect taxes	176	43	524	188	546	0	0	0	0	0	0	0	0	0	0	0	0	0	0	0	0	0	0	0	0	1477
22 Import tariffs	0	0	0	0	0	10	1800	0	51	0	0	0	0	0	0	0	0	0	0	0	0	0	0	0	0	1861
23 Rest of the world	0	0	0	0	0	48	7550	0	451	0	0	0	26	0	0	0	0	535	418	0	0	0	0	0	0	9028
24 Saving investments	0	0	0	0	0	0	0	0	0	0	0	0	0	0	0	1415	2280	908	-504	0	0	0	1559	0	0	5658
25 Stock exchange	0	0	0	0	0	0	0	0	0	0	0	0	0	0	0	0	0	0	0	0	0	0	0	-525	0	-525
Total	5250	1355	17859	8263	15781	7224	32083	8263	16283	3445	1689	986	12849	12839	595	11179	14997	11942	7356	3727	1477	1861	9028	5658	-525	

Source: Standard SAM for Zimbabwe, 1991. Thomas and Bautista (1999).

Note: Data are presented in million Zambian dollars.

Table 3.3 Traditional SAM layout

Receipts	Expenditures				Total
	Industry (1)	Factor (2)	Institutions (3)	Exports (4)	
Industry (1)	S_{11}	0	S_{13}	S_{14}	x^d_1
Factor (2)	S_{21}	0	0	S_{24}	x^d_2
Institutions (3)	S_{31}	S_{32}	S_{33}	S_{34}	x^d_3
Imports (4)	S_{41}	S_{42}	S_{43}	S_{44}	x^d_4
Total	$x^{s\,T}_1$	$x^{s\,T}_2$	$x^{s\,T}_3$	$x^{s\,T}_4$	

Notes:
Matrices
S_{11}—Interindustry transactions matrix; S_{21}—Value-added matrix; S_{31}—Sales and taxes matrix; S_{41}—Imports
S_{32}—Distribution matrix; S_{42}—Factor imports
S_{13}—Final demand matrix; S_{33}—Transfers matrix; S_{43}—Institutional import matrix
S_{14}—Industry export matrix; S_{24}—Factor export matrix; S_{34}—Institutional export matrix; S_{44}—Transshipment matrix

Row totals
x^d_1—Column vector of the sum of the row elements of the Industry Accounts (1). Total Industry Output
x^d_2—Column vector of the sum of the row elements of the factor accounts (2). Total factor income
x^d_3—Column vector of the sum of the row elements of the institutional accounts (3). Total institutional income
x^d_4—Column vector of the sum of the row elements of the import accounts (4). Total imports

Column totals
x^{sT}_1—Row vector of the sum of the column elements in the industry accounts (1). Total industry expenditures or outlay
x^{sT}_2—Row vector of the sum of the column elements of the factor accounts (2). Total factor expenditures
x^{sT}_3—Row vector of the sum of the column elements of the institution accounts (3). Total institution expenditures
x^{sT}_4—Row vector of the sum of the column elements of the export accounts (4). Total exports

Value-added matrix (S_{21}): This matrix defines payments to the primary factors of production, by the different industries. These include: (a) wages, salaries, and benefits paid to labor, and (b) proprietary income, other property income, and rent. The sum of value added from each production account define gross regional product, an index of overall economic activity.

Sales and taxes matrix (S_{31}): This matrix defines payments by industries to the various institutions. Expenditures by industries to households would be payments for inputs (other than labor) used in the production process. Expenditures by industries to governments are (a) indirect business taxes (e.g. excise, property, and sales taxes, and licenses and fees) and (b) import tariffs.

Import matrix (S_{41}): This matrix defines the import of intermediate inputs used by each industry in producing its output.

Distribution matrix (S_{32}): This matrix defines the distribution of factor income to institutions. A row defines the amount of a household's income comprising of salaries and interest payments. A column defines the distribution of salaries between households and governments (e.g. taxes paid on salary income).

Factor import (S_{42}): This matrix defines payments for (a) wages, salaries, and benefits paid to labor and (b) proprietary income, other property income, and rent to foreign households and enterprises.

Final demand matrix (S_{13}): This matrix describes the purchases of goods and services by households and other institutions for final consumption. These purchases are final demand because the items purchased are not used in any further production process.

Transfer matrix (S_{33}): This matrix defines the movement of funds between institutions; for example, the transfer from federal government to households or to local government.

Institutional import matrix (S_{43}): This matrix defines the expenditures on imported good and services used in final consumption by institutions.

Industry export matrix (S_{14}): This matrix describes industry exports to the rest of the world. That is goods and services produced within the region and exported to the rest of the world. Domestic and foreign trade may be aggregated into one sector.

Factor export matrix (S_{24}): This matrix defines payments to local capital or labor from foreign institutions. This matrix can be used also to capture moneys sent back to households.

Institutional export matrix (S_{34}): This matrix defines the export of institutional goods and services; for example, households providing labor to foreign enterprises or the sale of governmental goods and services.

Transshipments matrix (S_{44}): This submatrix defines the cross hauling of goods (e.g. goods imported to meet export demand).

SAM row totals

Total industry output (x_1^d): This column vector denotes the row sum of industry receipts and defines total industry output. The ith element of this vector is:

$$\left(x_1^d\right)_i = \sum_{g=1}^{4}\sum_j \left(S_{1g}\right)_{ij} \tag{3.1}$$

The elements of this vector are determined by adding the row elements of the interindustry transaction matrix, the final demand matrix, and the activity export matrix.

Total factor income (x_2^d): This column vector denotes the row sum of factor receipts or total factor income. The ith element of this vector is:

$$\left(x_2^d\right)_i = \sum_{g=1}^{4}\sum_j \left(S_{2g}\right)_{ij} \tag{3.2}$$

The elements of this vector are determined by adding the row element of the value-added matrix and the factor export matrix.

Total institutional income (x_3^d): This column vector denotes the row sum of institutions receipts or institutional income. The ith element of this vector is:

$$\left(x_3^d\right)_i = \sum_{g=1}^{4}\sum_j \left(S_{3g}\right)_{ij} \tag{3.3}$$

The elements of this vector are determined by adding the row element of the sales and taxes matrix, distribution matrix, transfer matrix, and institutional export matrix.

Total imports (x_4^d): This column vector denotes the row sum of total import expenditures or gross payments to the rest of the world. The ith element of this vector is:

$$\left(x_4^d\right)_i = \sum_{g=1}^{4}\sum_j \left(S_{4g}\right)_{ij} \tag{3.4}$$

The elements of this vector are determined by adding the row element of the activity import matrix, the factor import matrix, the institutional import matrix, and the transshipment matrix.

SAM column totals

Total industry outlays (x_1^{sT}): This row vector denotes the column sum of industry expenditures. The jth element of this vector is:

$$\left(x_1^{s^T}\right)_j = \sum_{k=1}^{4}\sum_i (S_{k1})_{ij} \tag{3.5}$$

The elements of this vector are determined by adding the column elements of the interindustry transaction matrix, the value-added matrix, the sales and taxes matrix, and the activity import matrix.

Total factor outlay or expenditures (x_2^{sT}): This row vector denotes the column sum of factor expenditures. The jth element of this vector is:

$$\left(x_2^{s^T}\right)_j = \sum_{k=1}^{4}\sum_i (S_{k2})_{ij} \tag{3.6}$$

The elements of this vector are determined by adding the column elements of the distribution matrix plus the factor import matrix.

Total institutional expenditures (x_3^{sT}): This row vector denotes the column sum of institution expenditures. The jth element of this vector is:

$$\left(x_3^{s^T}\right)_j = \sum_{k=1}^{4}\sum_i (S_{k3})_{ij} \tag{3.7}$$

The elements of this vector are determined by adding the column elements of the final demand matrix, the transfer matrix, and the institutional import matrix.

Total exports (x_4^{sT}): This row vector denotes the column sum of exports or total trade receipts from the rest of the world. The jth element of this vector is:

$$\left(x_4^{s^T}\right)_j = \sum_{k=1}^{4}\sum_i (S_{k4})_{ij} \tag{3.8}$$

The elements of this vector are determined by adding the column elements of the activity export matrix, the factor export matrix, the institutional export matrix, and the transshipment matrix.

By definition:

$$x_k^d = x_k^{s^T} ; \forall k \tag{3.9}$$

Table 3.4 illustrates a symmetric industry-by-industry SAM shown in Figure 3.3.

Table 3.4 Industry-by-industry SAM for Onondoga County, New York

		(1)	(2)	(3)	(4)	(5)	(6)	(7)	(8)	(9)	(10)	(11)
Ag	(1)	2.11	0.00	0.49	16.73	0.03	1.03	1.66	0.54	0.05	0.00	0.00
Mining	(2)	0.01	0.07	0.21	4.55	1.06	0.04	0.01	0.07	0.20	0.00	0.00
Const	(3)	1.88	2.33	1.04	53.25	38.88	20.26	175.00	53.33	53.35	0.00	0.00
Manuf	(4)	15.25	0.97	234.21	1,515.52	81.07	143.30	25.90	265.16	24.33	0.00	0.00
TCPU	(5)	4.18	0.52	27.86	255.57	216.77	87.70	57.92	141.42	22.93	0.00	0.00
Trade	(6)	7.63	0.33	100.03	459.21	34.05	85.07	12.21	94.77	3.86	0.00	0.00
FIRE	(7)	6.65	0.87	17.79	107.51	41.59	123.35	402.60	251.86	9.81	0.00	0.00
Serv	(8)	2.64	0.43	107.32	397.37	167.55	310.15	217.93	735.11	20.07	0.00	0.00
Govt	(9)	0.34	0.03	3.31	31.49	15.32	23.85	31.47	57.15	4.66	0.00	0.00
Other	(10)	0.00	0.00	0.00	1.77	1.43	0.41	0.18	0.33	0.17	0.00	0.00
EC	(11)	21.36	6.79	485.46	1,877.66	596.06	1,502.17	917.68	2,258.05	1,658.89	11.57	0.00
PI	(12)	2.50	1.89	92.51	90.54	128.39	104.74	111.83	626.62	0.00	0.00	0.00
OPI	(13)	13.83	11.26	30.94	833.43	891.98	482.64	1,721.95	277.84	116.69	6.69	0.00
IBT	(14)	2.01	1.40	8.05	160.56	221.18	534.57	383.79	65.80	0.00	0.00	0.00
HH	(15)	0.00	0.01	0.00	4.55	3.69	1.05	0.46	0.85	0.43	0.00	6,402.70
Fed govt	(16)	0.03	0.00	0.26	2.06	0.28	0.21	0.06	0.33	0.05	0.00	1,143.50
S/L govt	(17)	0.25	0.03	7.73	29.69	11.58	21.07	14.50	49.16	1.38	0.00	158.80
Ent	(18)	0.00	0.00	0.00	0.00	0.00	0.00	0.00	0.00	0.00	0.00	7.50
Capital	(19)	0.01	0.01	0.00	7.80	6.33	1.81	0.80	1.46	0.74	0.00	0.00
Inv red	(20)	0.02	0.00	0.26	1.70	0.09	0.16	0.03	0.29	0.03	0.00	0.00
FIm	(21)	2.43	1.31	26.79	230.75	25.58	14.86	3.20	26.41	5.68	0.00	0.00
DIm	(22)	42.01	4.89	186.61	1,541.95	246.63	243.53	276.60	451.19	42.87	0.00	1,623.10
Total		125.13	33.16	1,330.89	7,623.67	2,729.55	3,701.94	4,355.79	5,357.73	1,966.19	18.26	9,335.60

Source: Data provided by the Minnesota Implan Group, 1725 Tower Drive West, Suite 140, Stillwater, MN (http://www.implan.com/)

Notes:
Ag—Agriculture; Const—Construction; Manuf—Manufacturing; TCPU—Transportation, communications, public utilities; Trade—Wholesale and retail trade; FIRE—Finance, insurance, and real estate; Serv—Services; Govt—Government goods and services;

SAM models versus I–O models

An I–O model as described in Chapter 2 is a worthwhile system of accounting because it can be used to derive a powerful predictive model using a set of simple assumptions. However, as stated earlier a traditional I–O model focuses on flows among actors involved in production and a SAM includes not only flows among the actors involved in production but also the interdependence of production with the rest of society (Bulmer-Thomas 1982; Rose *et al.* 1988; Thorbecke 1998). While an I–O model is able to do similar analysis as a SAM, the latter is a more thorough methodology. In fact, an I–O model is a subset of a SAM (Wagner 1997).

(12)	(13)	(14)	(15)	(16)	(17)	(18)	(19)	(20)	(21)	(22)	Total
0.00	0.00	0.00	4.33	0.01	0.72	0.00	0.04	0.12	6.01	91.26	125.13
0.00	0.00	0.00	0.31	0.04	0.05	0.00	0.16	0.01	1.73	24.64	33.16
0.00	0.00	0.00	0.00	36.10	341.76	0.00	511.28	0.00	0.24	42.20	1,330.89
0.00	0.00	0.00	1,149.35	125.15	134.41	0.00	570.71	32.73	1,288.14	2,017.48	7,623.67
0.00	0.00	0.00	544.91	9.08	86.31	0.00	27.50	4.53	126.55	1,115.79	2,729.55
0.00	0.00	0.00	1,746.73	3.03	41.62	0.00	236.19	42.88	169.04	665.29	3,701.94
0.00	0.00	0.00	1,493.86	1.48	50.58	0.00	57.51	0.00	103.64	1,686.69	4,355.79
0.00	0.00	0.00	2,001.27	31.35	112.92	0.00	16.28	0.02	33.67	1,203.65	5,357.73
0.00	0.00	0.00	100.82	210.89	1,339.41	0.00	2.37	0.35	7.68	137.03	1,966.19
0.00	0.00	0.00	4.77	0.52	0.22	0.00	0.00	0.59	7.86	0.00	18.25
0.00	0.00	0.00	0.00	0.00	0.00	0.00	0.00	0.00	0.00	0.00	9,335.69
0.00	0.00	0.00	0.00	0.00	0.00	0.00	0.00	0.00	0.00	0.00	1,159.01
0.00	0.00	0.00	0.00	0.00	0.00	0.00	0.00	0.00	0.00	0.00	4,387.26
0.00	0.00	0.00	0.00	0.00	0.00	0.00	0.00	0.00	0.00	0.00	1,377.35
1,096.80	982.10	0.00	268.10	1,818.30	787.10	413.70	775.40	1.50	20.20	0.00	12,576.96
52.20	1.10	240.90	1,386.00	406.70	0.70	410.90	4.40	0.10	2.40	3.40	3,665.58
0.00	22.20	1,136.40	808.90	386.60	1,441.50	185.60	195.90	0.30	3.60	86.50	4,561.70
0.00	1,534.80	0.00	0.00	63.50	0.80	0.00	0.00	0.00	0.00	0.00	1,606.60
0.00	1,596.50	0.00	844.60	451.90	1.00	596.40	0.00	2.60	34.70	605.40	4,152.06
0.00	0.00	0.00	1.30	0.10	0.10	0.00	117.10	0.00	1.40	2.40	124.99
0.00	15.70	0.00	151.00	22.40	14.50	0.00	1,262.90	3.50	0.00	0.00	1,807.01
0.00	234.90	0.00	2,070.90	98.20	208.20	0.00	374.10	35.90	0.00	0.00	7,681.58
1,159.00	4,387.30	1,377.30	12,577.15	3,665.37	4,561.89	1,606.60	4,151.85	125.13	1,806.84	7,681.73	

Other—Nonclassified industries; EC—Employee compensation; PI—Proprietary income; OPI—Other property income; IBT—Indirect business taxes; HH—Households; Fed govt—Federal government; S/L govt—State and local government; Ent—Enterprises; Inv red—Inventory reductions (row), Inventory additions (column); FIm—Foreign imports (row), Foreign exports (column; DIm—Domestic imports (row), Domestic exports (column)

There are two basic accounting differences between an I–O model and a SAM:

1   In an I–O model, the expenditures of the intermediate factors of production and the receipts of the industries are accounted for only once. The SAM uses a double accounting framework. Value added, institution demands, and import-exports (rest of the world) are accounted for both as columns and rows.
2   The lower right quadrant of the expanded I–O table should show the flow between primary inputs and final demand. SAM provides a framework to develop this flow as well as all other possible flows among all economic agents.

Descriptive and predictive SAM models

Thorbecke (1985) states the interindustry transaction submatrix, S_{11}, should be closed to contain all the necessary behavioral and technical relationships of the economic system in a consistent way. For notational ease we will let Table 3.5 describes the industry-by-industry SAM given in Table 3.3 based on an aggregation depicted by Thorbecke (1998).

Expenditures and receipts are divided into endogenous and exogenous accounts. The endogenous account, S, is composed of the industry, S_{11}, and factor, S_{21}, accounts plus the household and enterprise components of the institution accounts. The final demand column vector, f, which defines the exogenous account is composed of the government and capital investment components of the institution accounts plus exports. The row vector, m^T, which defines the exogenous account is composed of the government and capital investment components of the institution accounts plus imports receipts. Finally the intersection of the column and row vector exogenous accounts gives a scalar, m_4, denoting transshipments. Given Table 3.5, a procedure analogous to that used in Chapter 2 to develop the demand-side I–O model can be used develop the SAM model given in equation (3.10):

$$x^d = \left(I - S\hat{X}^{-1}\right)^{-1} f \tag{3.10}$$

where $\hat{X}$ is a diagonal matrix whose diagonal elements are the vector x^d or x^s. The predictive SAM model can be described as:

$$\Delta x^d = \left(I - S\hat{X}^{-1}\right)^{-1} \Delta f \tag{3.11}$$

Table 3.5 Aggregated industry-by-industry SAM layout

		Expenditures				
		Endogenous accounts			Exogenous accounts	
Receipts		Industry	Factors	HH, Ent	Govt, Cap, Ex	Total
Endogenous accounts	Industry Factors HH Ent		S		f	x^{d}
Exogenous accounts	Govt, Cap, Im		m^{T}		m_4	x_4^{d}
	Totals		x^{sT}		x_4^{sT}	

Notes:

Endogenous accounts
Industry
Factors
Households (HH)
Enterprises (Ent)

Exogenous accounts
Governments (Govt)
Capital investment (Cap)
Export/Imports (Ex, Im)

Using equation (3.11) to predict the impact on a region's economy, as measured by output, relies on the same seven assumptions given in Chapter 2 for the demand-side I–O model.

Data limitations of I–O models and SAMs

Limitations of national non-survey methods affect any I–O or SAM analysis (Bergstrom *et al.* 1990). These commonly recognized limitations are therefore implicitly associated with databases and analyses available with programs such as IMPLAN (http://www.implan.com/, accessed on March 16, 2009). The most important concern deals with the ability of non-survey methods to generate an accurate picture of the economy. Secondary data sources used to derive county-level estimates of final demand, final payments, gross output, and employment can be incomplete, inconsistent, and inaccurate (Alward *et al.* 1993). In addition, an analysis tool such as IMPLAN assumes that the industries within a regional economy remain stable over time. Thus, care should be taken if there are any potential changes in the structure of the regional economy since the database's creation. For example, industries may both enter and leave the region over time and in a rural economy, the subtraction or addition of only one industry may cause a "shock" to the economy. It is therefore important to periodically evaluate and update the structure of county-level industries contained in any database.

Another limitation resulting from non-survey based framework is the application of national technical coefficient (or production functions) to every region. This procedure ignores geographical differences in production processes and production variations between firms and industries (Alward *et al.* 1993). On the other hand, if the user has better information of production processes for an industry in a region, analysis tools such as IMPLAN generally provide the capability for the user to adjust regional technical coefficients.

Despite their limitations, analysis tools such as IMPLAN are both applied widely and are accepted professionally. Although caution must be exercised when applying analysis tools such as IMPLAN, they are a useful and powerful approach for economic impact analysis.

SAMs and CGE models

The literature on Computable General Equilibrium (CGE) models is as rich as that associated with SAMs. It is not our intention to also develop CGE models in this book, but to introduce the relationships between a SAM and CGE models briefly. Once the linkage is made, it is up to the reader to pursue it further with respect to including the flow of environmental resources into the economy and the flow pollution from the economy in an ESAM, then using this ESAM as the basis for a CGE model.

CGE models can be defined as a class of economic model that may be used to estimate how an economy might react to changes in policy, technology or other external factors. CGE models are also referred to as a specific type of Applied General Equilibrium (AGE) model. They build upon the data, accounting, and equilibrium structure defined in an I–O or SAM model. Simply put, CGE models build upon the circular flow depicted in a SAM shown in Table 3.1; that is, expenditures must equal receipts (conservation of value) and supply must equal demand (conservation of product).

A CGE model generally starts with an assumption that households maximize their utility subject to their income and the prices of goods and producers maximize their profits subject to production technology. A household's utility is a function of consumption and savings. A producer's profit is total revenue minus the cost of intermediate and primary factors production. This constrained maximization can be solved for households' demand for commodities and producers' demand for intermediate and primary factors of production. For the economy to be in equilibrium given the assumption of utility maximization by households and profit maximization by producers expenditures must equal receipts (conservation of value) and supply must equal demand (conservation of product). What ties these households' and producers' demand functions together are the accounting and equilibrium structure defined in a SAM. The problem is to solve for the producer output levels given commodity prices and primary factor of production prices that leaves the economy in equilibrium. Given the possible nonlinearity and complexity of the households' and producers' demand functions the only solution techniques are numerical; thus the term "computable" general equilibrium model.

4 Regional economic multipliers

Multiplier analysis: general background

One of the major uses of I–O and SAM models is to assess the effects on an economy when there are changes in elements that are exogenous to the model of that economy (Miller and Blair 1985). For example, when tourists visit natural areas, they spend money at various local business activities. These expenditures create additional economic activity as the monies flow within the region economy. Regional economic multipliers are measures of economic changes that summarize these responding effects.

Multiplier analysis: traditional demand-driven I–O models: general background

Open versus closed models

The I–O model developed in Chapter 2 is given in equation (4.1) and the predictive model is given in equation (4.2):

$$x = (I - A)^{-1}y \tag{4.1}$$

$$\Delta x = (I - A)^{-1}\Delta y \tag{4.2}$$

where x denotes a column vector of total industry output, I denotes the identity matrix, A denotes the technical coefficients matrix, and y denotes a column vector of final demands. The $(I - A)^{-1}$ term is the total requirements matrix or the Leontief inverse. The I–O model described in equation (4.1) is called an "open model" because it only includes the interindustry transactions as defined by the technical coefficients matrix, A (see equations (2.11a) and (2.11b) and Table 2.1d in Chapter 2).

As described by Miller (1998) and Miller and Blair (1985), the open model given in equation (4.1) is criticized as underestimating the regional economic impacts because it does not include households. Having households exogenous to the model omits the impact of households' spending of wage and salary income as a result of the change in final demand for an industry's output. Table 4.1 illustrates "closing" the I–O model with respect to households.

Table 4.1 The "closed" I–O table

Receipts	Industry 1 ... n	H	Final demand		Exports	Total output
Industry 1 : n	z_{11} ... z_{1n} : ∴ : z_{n1} ... z_{nn}	y_{1H} : y_{nH}	y_{1G} y_{1In} : : y_{nG} y_{nIn}		e_1 : e_n	x_1 : x_n
Labor	w_{L1} ... w_{Ln}	w_{LH}	w_{LG} w_{LIn}		w_{Le}	L
Value added	w_{K1} ... w_{Kn}	w_{KH}	w_{KG} w_{KIn}		w_{Ke}	K
Imports	m_1 ... m_n	m_H	m_G m_{In}		m_e	M
Total outlay	x_1 ... x_n	H	G In		E	

Notes: L denotes labor; K denotes capital; H denotes households; G denotes governments; In denotes private investment.

Let $\bar{Z}$ denote the interindustry transactions matrix closed with respect to households:

$$\bar{Z} = \begin{bmatrix} z_{11} & \cdots & z_{1n} & y_{1H} \\ \vdots & \ddots & \vdots & \vdots \\ z_{n1} & \cdots & z_{nn} & y_{nH} \\ w_{L1} & \cdots & w_{Ln} & w_{LH} \end{bmatrix} \tag{4.3}$$

Let $\bar{A}$ denote the technical coefficients matrix closed with respect to households:

$$\bar{A} = \bar{Z}\left(\hat{X}\right)^{-1} \tag{4.4}$$

where

$$\hat{X} = \begin{bmatrix} x_1 & 0 & 0 & 0 \\ 0 & \ddots & 0 & 0 \\ 0 & 0 & x_n & 0 \\ 0 & 0 & 0 & H \end{bmatrix}$$

$$(4.5)$$

The "closed model" is given by equation (4.6) and the predictive closed model is given by equation (4.7):

$$\bar{x} = \left(I - \bar{A}\right)^{-1} \bar{y} \tag{4.6}$$

$$\Delta\bar{x} = \left(I - \bar{A}\right)^{-1} \Delta\bar{y} \tag{4.7}$$

where $\bar{y}$ is an n × 1 column vector given by equation (4.8):

$$\bar{y} = \begin{bmatrix} y_{1G} & y_{1In} \\ \vdots & \vdots \\ y_{nG} & y_{nIn} \\ w_{LG} & w_{LIn} \end{bmatrix} \cdot \begin{bmatrix} 1 \\ 1 \end{bmatrix}$$

$$(4.8)$$

The regional economic impacts can be measured in terms of direct and indirect given the open model from equation (4.1) and direct, indirect, and induced effects given the closed model from equation (4.6). Direct effects are production changes associated with the immediate effects of final demand changes. For example, a change in the demand for wood furniture would cause the manufacturer to produce more output. Indirect effects are production changes in backward-linked industries caused by the changing input needs of directly affected industries. For example, the wood furniture manufacturer would demand more lumber, glue, and furniture hardware, etc. causing an increase in production from all industries that supply these inputs. Induced effects are the changes in regional household spending patterns caused by changes in regional employment generated from the direct and indirect effects. The change in final demand would cause income and employment to increase, stimulating spending in the economy in general. For example, the induced effect would include the purchases generated by new personnel employed (Alward *et al.* 1993).

There are three general regional economic impacts that are of most concern: (1) output; (2) employment; and (3) income. I–O multipliers can be used to summarize these regional economic impacts. Multipliers are basically a ratio of total impacts to initial impacts. If total impacts are defined as direct plus indirect effects, then the multiplier is identified as a Type I multiplier. All Type I multipliers are derived from the Leotief inverse, $(I - A)^{-1}$. If the total impacts are defined as direct plus indirect plus induced, then the multiplier is identified as a Type II multiplier. All Type II multipliers are derived from the closed Leotief inverse, $(I - \overline{A})^{-1}$. Unfortunately, consistency within the literature at identifying multipliers ends with these definitions (Miller 1998). Table 4.2 defines the classification system we will use.

Table 4.2 I–O multiplier classifications

Multiplier	Notation	Total effect	Direct effect
Open model			
Type I—output/output	T1-O/O	Output	Output
Type I—income/output	T1-I/O	Income	Output
Type I—employment/output	T1-E/O	Employment	Output
Type I—income/income	T1-I/I	Income	Income
Type I—employment/ employment	T1-Emp/Emp	Employment	Employment
Closed model			
Type II—output/output	T2-O/O	Output	Output
Type II—income/output	T2-I/O	Income	Output
Type II—employment/output	T2-E/O	Employment	Output
Type II—income/income	T2-I/I	Income	Income
Type II—employment/ employment	T2-Emp/Emp	Employment	Employment

Notes: In a Type I multiplier the total effect is defined as the direct plus indirect effects. In a Type II multiplier the total effect is defined as the direct plus indirect plus induced effects.

Type I—output/output

The most basic multiplier is the Type I output/output multiplier often called the output multiplier. The output multiplier for the jth industry is defined as the total value of production in all sectors of the economy that is necessary in order to satisfy a dollar's worth of final demand for industry j's output (Miller and Blair 1985). Thus, the direct effect is defined as $1.00. Let α_{ij} denote an element of the Leontief inverse given in equation (4.9):

$$\begin{bmatrix} \alpha_{11} & \cdots & \alpha_{1n} \\ \vdots & \ddots & \vdots \\ \alpha_{n1} & \cdots & \alpha_{nn} \end{bmatrix} = \left(I - A\right)^{-1}$$

(4.9)

The jth output multiplier (O_j) is found by summing jth column of the Leontief inverse matrix as given in equation (4.10):

$$O_j^{(\text{T1-O/O})} = \sum_{i=1}^{n} \alpha_{ij}; j = 1,2,3,\ldots,n$$

(4.10)

Type I—income/output

The Type I—income/output multiplier is often called the income multiplier and relates the change in final demand for the jth industry's output in terms of the wage income it generates. As with the Type I—output/output multiplier the direct effect is defined as \$1.00. Let ω^T denote a 1xn row vector given by equation (4.11):

$$\omega^T = \begin{bmatrix} \dfrac{w_{L1}}{x_1} & \cdots & \dfrac{w_{Ln}}{x_n} \end{bmatrix}$$

(4.11)

where w_{Lj} denotes the wage payments by the jth industry (see Table 2.1d). The jth income multiplier $(\mathcal{H}_j^{(\text{T1-I/O})})$ is found by equation (4.12):

$$\mathcal{H}_j^{(\text{T1-I/O})} = \sum_{i=1}^{n} \omega_i a_{ij}; j = 1, \ldots,n$$

(4.12)

where a_{ij} denotes an element of the Leontief inverse given in equation (4.9).

Type I—employment/output

The Type I—employment/output multiplier is often called the employment multiplier and relates the change in final demand for the jth industry's output in terms of the employment it generates. As with the Type I—output/output multiplier the direct effect is defined as \$1.00. Let ε^T denote a $1 \times n$ row vector given by equation (4.13):

$$\varepsilon^T = \begin{bmatrix} \dfrac{emp_1}{x_1} & \cdots & \dfrac{emp_n}{x_n} \end{bmatrix}$$

(4.13)

where emp_j denotes the employment in the jth industry and $\dfrac{emp_j}{x_j}$ denotes the employment per \$1.00 worth of output of the jth industry. The jth employment multiplier ($Emp_j^{(T1\text{-}Emp/O)}$) is found by equation (4.14):

$$Emp_j^{(T1\text{-}Emp/O)} = \sum_{i=1}^{n} \varepsilon_i \alpha_{i,j}; \, j = 1,\ldots,n \qquad (4.14)$$

where α_{ij} denotes an element of the Leontief inverse given in equation (4.9).

The previous multipliers defined the direct effect as change in the final demand for the jth industry's output. The next two Type I multipliers define the direct effect in terms of income and employment respectively.

Type I—income/income

If the initial or direct effect is not described in terms of output, but with respect to income, then the Type I income/income multiplier is more appropriate. For example, a new industry is moving into the region and regional economic planners would like to estimate the total income effect due to the increased wage income; or an existing industry is moving out of the region and regional economic planners would like to estimate the total income effect due to the decreased wage income. The direct effect is an increase or decrease in the wage payments of the jth industry. The total effect is an increase or decrease in regional income as measured by wage payments:

$$\mathcal{H}_j^{(T1\text{-}I/I)} = \dfrac{\left(\sum_{i=2}^{n} \omega_i \alpha_{i,j}\right)}{\omega_j} = \dfrac{\mathcal{H}_j^{(T1\text{-}I/O)}}{\omega_j}; \, j = 1,\ldots,n \qquad (4.15)$$

where ω_j denotes the wage payments per output by the jth industry given in equation (4.11) and α_{ij} denotes an element of the Leontief inverse given in equation (4.9).

Type I—employment/employment

If the initial or direct effect is not described in terms of output, but with respect to employment, then the Type I employment/employment multiplier is more appropriate. For example, a new industry is moving into the region and regional economic planners would like to estimate the total employment effect due to the increased employment from the new industry; or an existing industry is moving out of the region and regional economic planners would like to estimate the total employment effect due to the loss in employment. The direct effect is an increase or decrease in employment of the jth industry. The total effect is the increase or decrease in regional employment:

$$Emp_j^{(T1\text{-}Emp/Emp)} = \frac{\sum_{i=1}^{n} \varepsilon_i \alpha_{i,j}}{\varepsilon_j} = \frac{Emp_j^{(T1\text{-}Emp/O)}}{\varepsilon_j} \; ; j = 1,\ldots,n \tag{4.16}$$

where ε_j denotes the employment per output by the jth industry given in equation (4.13) and α_{ij} denotes an element of the Leontief inverse given in equation (4.9).

Each Type I multiplier has its corollary using a closed model. As was discussed earlier, a Type I multiplier may be criticized as underestimating the regional economic impacts due to not including households impact on the economy (Miller 1998; Miller and Blair 1985). Type II multipliers address this issue.

As with the Type I multipliers, the fundamental component of calculating the Type II multipliers is the total requirements matrix or the closed Leontief inverse $(I - \bar{A})^{-1}$. Let $\bar{\alpha}_{ij}$ denote an element of the closed Leontief inverse given in equation (4.17):

$$\left(I - \bar{A}\right)^{-1} = \left(I - \bar{Z}\hat{X}^{-1}\right)^{-1} = \begin{bmatrix} \bar{\alpha}_{11} & \cdots & \bar{\alpha}_{1n} & \bar{\alpha}_{1,n+1} \\ \vdots & \ddots & \vdots & \vdots \\ \bar{\alpha}_{n1} & \cdots & \bar{\alpha}_{nn} & \bar{\alpha}_{n,n+1} \\ \bar{\alpha}_{n+1,1} & \cdots & \bar{\alpha}_{n+1,n} & \bar{\alpha}_{n+1,n+1} \end{bmatrix} \tag{4.17}$$

Type II—output/output

As with the Type I—output/output multiplier the Type II—output/output multiplier is the column sum of the closed Leontief inverse given in equation (4.18):

$$O_j^{(T2\text{-}O/O)} = \sum_{i=1}^{n+1} \bar{\alpha}_{ij} \; ; j = 1,2,3,\ldots,n \tag{4.18}$$

where $\bar{a}_{ij}$ denotes the an element of the closed Leontief inverse given in equation (4.17). This multiplier for the jth industry is defined as the total value (direct plus indirect plus induced effect) of production from all the region's industries that is necessary in order to satisfy a dollar's worth of final demand for industry j's output. The direct effect, as before, is defined as $1.00.

Type II—income/output

The Type II—income/output multiplier for the jth industry is defined as the total value (direct plus indirect plus induced effect) of wage income generated from all the region's industries that is necessary in order to satisfy a dollar's worth of final demand for industry j's output. The direct effect, as before, is defined as $1.00. This multiplier is given in equation (4.19):

$$\mathcal{H}_j^{(\text{T2-I/O})} = \sum_{i=1}^{n} \omega_i \bar{a}_{i,j} = \sum_{i=1}^{n} \bar{a}_{n+1,i} \bar{a}_{i,j}; \, j = 1, \ldots, n \qquad (4.19)$$

where ω_i denotes the wage payments per output by the ith industry given in equation (4.11) and $\bar{a}_{ij}$ denotes the an element of the closed Leontief inverse given in equation (4.17).

Type II—employment/output

The Type II—employment/output multiplier for the jth industry is defined as the total value (direct plus indirect plus induced effect) of employment generated from all the region's industries that is necessary in order to satisfy a dollar's worth of final demand for industry j's output. The direct effect, as before, is defined as $1.00. This multiplier is given in equation (4.20):

$$Emp_j^{(\text{T2-Emp/O})} = \sum_{i=1}^{n} \varepsilon_i \bar{\alpha}_{ij}; \, j = 1, \ldots, n \qquad (4.20)$$

where ε_i denotes the employment per output by the ith industry given in equation (4.13) and $\bar{a}_{ij}$ denotes the an element of the closed Leontief inverse given in equation (4.17).

Type II—income/income

A Type II—income/income multiplier is a ratio of (direct plus indirect plus induced effects) to (direct effect). The direct effect is in terms of wages that a producer would have to pay to produce \$1.00 worth of output. The direct effect or the wage income required to produce \$1.00 worth of output is defined by equation (4.11). For example if you produce \$200 worth of output and pay \$75 to labor, the direct effect would be 0.375 (= 75/200). Thus for every \$1.00 of output you produce, \$0.375 is used to pay for labor. The jth industry's Type II—income/income is given by equation (4.21):

$$\mathcal{H}_j^{(\text{T2-I/I})} = \cfrac{\cfrac{\left(\sum_{i=1}^{n}\omega_i\bar{a}_{i,j}\right)}{\omega_j} = \cfrac{\mathcal{H}_j^{(\text{T2-I/O})}}{\omega_j}}{\cfrac{\left(\sum_{i=1}^{n}\bar{a}_{n+1,i}\bar{a}_{i,j}\right)}{\bar{a}_{n+1,j}} = \cfrac{\mathcal{H}_j^{(\text{T2-I/O})}}{\bar{a}_{n+1,j}}} \qquad ; j = 1, \ldots, n \qquad (4.21)$$

where $\omega_i = \bar{a}_{n+1,i}$ denotes the wage payments per output by the ith industry given in equation (4.11) and $\bar{a}_{ij}$ denotes the an element of the closed Leontief inverse given in equation (4.17).

Type II—employment/employment

The Type II—employment/employment multiplier calculates the total employment effect (direct plus indirect plus induce effects) if the initial or direct effect is in terms of the employment required to produce \$1.00 worth of output. The jth industry's Type II—employment/employment is given by equation (4.22):

$$Emp_j^{(\text{T2-Emp/Emp})} = \cfrac{\sum_{i=1}^{n}\varepsilon_i\bar{\alpha}_{ij}}{\varepsilon_j} = \cfrac{Emp_j^{(\text{T2-Emp/O})}}{\varepsilon_j} ; j = 1, \ldots, n \qquad (4.22)$$

where ε_i denotes the employment per output by the ith industry given in equation (4.13) and $\bar{a}_{ij}$ denotes an element of the closed Leontief inverse given in equation (4.17).

Using the multipliers listed in Table 4.2 and described above to predict the impacts on a region's economy relies on the seven assumptions given in Chapter 2 for the demand-side I–O model.

Table 4.3 Aggregated industry-by-industry SAM layout

Receipts		Expenditures				
		Endogenous accounts			Exogenous accounts	
		Industry	Factors	HH, Ent	Govt, Cap, Ex	Total
Endogenous accounts	Industry					
	Factors		S		f	x^d
	HH, Ent					
Exogenous accounts	Govt, Cap, Im		m^T		m_4	x_4^d
	Totals		x^{sT}		x_4^{sT}	

Notes:

Endogenous accounts
Industry
Factors
Households (HH)
Enterprises (Ent)

Exogenous accounts
Governments (Govt)
Capital investment (Cap)
Export/Imports (Ex, Im)

Multiplier analysis: SAM

The SAM model, developed in Chapter 3 and illustrated in Table 4.3, is given in equation (4.23) and the predictive model is given in equation (4.24):

$$x^d = \left(I - S\hat{X}^{-1}\right)^{-1} f \tag{4.23}$$

$$\Delta x^d = \left(I - S\hat{X}^{-1}\right)^{-1} \Delta f \tag{4.24}$$

where $\hat{X}$ is a diagonal matrix whose diagonal elements are the vector x^d of x^s. Expenditures and receipts are divided into endogenous and exogenous accounts. The endogenous account, S, is composed of the industry, S_{11} in Table 3.3, and factor, S_{21} in Table 3.3, accounts plus the household and enterprise components of the institution accounts. The final demand column vector, f, which defines the exogenous account is composed of the government and capital investment components of the institution accounts plus exports. The row vector, m^T, which defines the exogenous account is composed of the government and capital investment components of the institution accounts plus

Table 4.4 Endogenous accounts of an aggregated industry-by-industry SAM—the transactions matrix

| | | Expenditures | | |
		Industry	Factors	HH, Ent
Receipts	Industry	S_{11}	0	S_{13}
	Factors	S_{21}	0	0
	HH, Ent	S_{31}	S_{32}	S_{33}

Notes:
S_{11}—Interindustry transactions matrix
S_{21}—Value-added matrix
S_{31}—Sales and taxes matrix
S_{32}—Distribution matrix
S_{33}—Transfers matrix

imports receipts. Finally the intersection of the column and row vector exogenous accounts gives a scalar, m_4, denoting transshipments.

As a practical matter, the choice between multiplier effects depends on the nature of the exogenous change whose impact is being studied. Thorbecke (1985) states the interindustry transaction submatrix should be closed to contain all the necessary behavioral and technical relationships of the economic system in a consistent way. Pyatt and Round (1985) also state that multipliers should reflect the circular flow of income that characterizes the process of demand, production, and income distribution. For example, Stone (1985) and Bulmer-Thomas (1982) define a SAM output multiplier by closing the interindustry transaction submatrix (S_{11}; Table 3.3) with respect to wage and capital payments to households and household consumption.

For the purposes of this discussion, we will continue the closure described by Thorbecke (1998) given in Table 4.3 and detailed explicitly in Table 4.4. The technical coefficients matrix, $S\hat{X}^{-1}$ in equations (4.23) and (4.24), is given by equation (4.25):

$$A_n = S\hat{X}^{-1} = \begin{bmatrix} A_{11} & 0 & A_{13} \\ A_{21} & 0 & 0 \\ A_{31} & A_{32} & A_{33} \end{bmatrix} \tag{4.25}$$

Equation (4.23) can be re-written using equation (4.25) as:

$$x^d = \left(I - A_n\right)^{-1} f = R_a \cdot f \tag{4.26a}$$

Table 4.5 SAM multiplier classifications

Multiplier	Notation	Total effect	Direct effect
Accounting multiplier			
SAM—Accounting	AC		
Industry account multipliers			
SAM—output/output	O/O	Output	Output
SAM—income/output	I/O	Income	Output
SAM—value added/output	VA/O	Value added	Output
SAM—employment/output	Emp/O	Employment	Output
SAM—income/income	I/I	Income	Income
SAM—value added/value added	VA/VA	Value added	Value Added
SAM—employment/ employment	Emp/Emp	Employment	Employment

Notes:
The total effect is defined as the direct plus indirect plus induced. However, the total effect as defined by a SAM would include at the minimum three endogenous accounts not a simple closing of the industrial technical coefficients matrix with respect to household as with a Type II multiplier.
The SAM accounting multiplier is summed across all three of the endogenous accounts as shown in Figure 4.3.
The SAM industry account multipliers are summed across the region's endogenous industries.

where $R_a = (I - A_n)^{-1}$ denotes the SAM's total requirements matrix or the multiplier matrix. More specifically R_a is defined as the *accounting multiplier matrix* as it explains the results obtained from the SAM and not the process by which the SAM was generated (Thorbecke 1998; Pyatt and Round 1985).

The same mechanics that were used to derive the Type I and Type II I–O multipliers may also be used to derive SAM multipliers. As with the I–O multipliers, Table 4.5 defines the classification system we will use for SAM multipliers.

SAM accounting multiplier

The jth sector's SAM accounting multiplier, $SAM_j^{(AM)}$, is calculated by summing the columns of the accounting multiplier matrix, R_{ai}:

$$SAM_j^{(AM)} = \sum_i (R_a)_{ij}; \text{ for all j} \tag{4.27}$$

where $(R_a)_{ij}$ denotes an element of the SAM's accounting multiplier matrix. Thus a SAM accounting multiplier is calculated for each industrial activity, primary factor of production, household, and enterprise.

Caution should be used when using and interpreting this multiplier as it implies that average expenditures as described by A_n in equation (4.25) hold for all of the endogenous accounts. While this may be tenable for changes in final demand in the industry accounts, A_{11}, this is not tenable for injections into the household accounts specifically, A_{13} (Thorbecke 1998; Thorbecke and Jung 1996; Pyatt and Round 1985). A standard approach to deal with this issue is to develop a fixed price multiplier matrix, R_c. In equation (4.25), let $(C_{13})_{ij} = \eta_{ij}(A_{13})_{ij}$ where η_{ij} is the income elasticity of the jth institution and ith output (Thorbeck 1998; Thorbecke and Jung 1996; Pyatt and Round 1985; Pyatt and Round 1979). Thus equation (4.25) can be re-written as:

$$A_c = \begin{bmatrix} A_{11} & 0 & C_{13} \\ A_{21} & 0 & 0 \\ A_{31} & A_{32} & A_{33} \end{bmatrix}$$

(4.25a)

and equation (4.26) can be re-written as:

$$x^d = (I - A_n)^{-1} f = R_a \cdot f \qquad (4.26a)$$

where R_c is denoted as the *fixed price multiplier matrix*. The jth sector's SAM fixed price multiplier, $SAM_j^{(FP)}$, is calculated by summing the columns of the accounting multiplier matrix, R_c:

$$SAM_j^{(FP)} = \sum_i (R_c)_{ij}; \text{ for all j} \qquad (4.27a)$$

However, as Thorbecke (1998) pointed out that while the fixed price multipliers are superior to the accounting multipliers, multipliers derived from the accounting multiplier matrix are often used in applied work as they are easily derived from limited data. Thus, we will develop the following multipliers using the accounting multiplier matrix.

SAM industry account multipliers

The next sets of SAM multipliers are derived from the endogenous industries of the accounting multiplier matrix, R_a. They are similar to the truncated multipliers Miller and Blair (1985) developed using the closed Leontief inverse.

SAM output/output multiplier

A SAM output/output multiplier, $SAM_j^{(O/O)}$, for the jth industry is given by equation (4.28):

$$SAM_j^{(O/O)} = \sum_{i=1}^{n} (R_a)_{ij} \; ; j = 1,\ldots,n \tag{4.28}$$

where $i,j = 1, \ldots ,n$ denote the "n" regional industries and $(R_a)_{ij}$ denotes an element of the SAM's accounting multiplier matrix. This multiplier defines the total value (direct plus indirect plus induced effect) of production from all the region's industries that is necessary in order to satisfy a dollar's worth of final demand for industry j's output. The direct effect, as before, is defined as \$1.00.

SAM income/output multiplier

A SAM income/output multiplier, $SAM_j^{(I/O)}$, for the jth industry is given by equation (4.29):

$$SAM_j^{(I/O)} = \sum_{i=1}^{n} \omega_i (R_a)_{ij} \; ; j = 1,\ldots,n \tag{4.29}$$

where $i,j = 1, \ldots ,n$ denote the "n" regional industries, ω_i denotes the ith element of the ω^T $1 \times n$ row vector given by equation (4.11), and $(R_a)_{ij}$ denotes an element of the SAM's accounting multiplier matrix. This multiplier defines the total value (direct plus indirect plus induced effect) of wage income generated from all the region's industries that is necessary in order to satisfy a dollar's worth of final demand for industry j's output. The direct effect, as before, is defined as \$1.00.

SAM value-added/output multiplier

A SAM value-added/output multiplier, $SAM_j^{(VA/O)}$, for the jth industry is given by equation (4.30):

$$SAM_j^{(VA/O)} = \sum_{i=1}^{n} v_i (R_a)_{ij} \; ; j = 1,\ldots,n \tag{4.30}$$

where $i,j = 1, \ldots ,n$ denote the "n" regional industries, v_i denotes the ith element of the v^T $1 \times n$ row vector given by equations (4.31a) and (4.31b):

$$[s_{21}]^T = [1 \quad \cdots \quad 1] \cdot S_{21} \tag{4.31a}$$

$$v^T = \left[\frac{(s_{21})_1}{x_1^d} \quad \frac{(s_{21})_2}{x_2^d} \quad \cdots \quad \frac{(s_{21})_n}{x_n^d} \right] \tag{4.31b}$$

and $(R_a)_{ij}$ denotes an element of the SAM's accounting multiplier matrix. This multiplier defines the total value added generated (direct plus indirect plus induced effect) from all the region's industries that is necessary in order to satisfy a dollar's worth of final demand for industry j's output. The direct effect, as before, is defined as \$1.00.

SAM employment/output multiplier

A SAM employment/output multiplier, $SAM_j^{(Emp/O)}$, for the jth industry is given by equation (4.32):

$$SAM_j^{(I/O)} = \sum_{i=1}^{n} \varepsilon_i (R_a)_{ij} \, ; \, j = 1,\ldots,n \tag{4.32}$$

where $i,j = 1, \ldots ,n$ denote the "*n*" regional industries, ε_i denotes the ith element of the ε^T $1 \times n$ row vector given by equation (4.13), and $(R_a)_{ij}$ denotes an element of the SAM's accounting multiplier matrix. This multiplier defines the total value (direct plus indirect plus induced effect) of employment generated from all the region's industries that is necessary in order to satisfy a dollar's worth of final demand for industry j's output. The direct effect, as before, is defined as \$1.00.

SAM income/income multiplier

A SAM income/income multiplier, $SAM_j^{(I/I)}$, for the jth industry is given by equation (4.33):

$$SAM_j^{(I/I)} = \frac{\sum_{i=1}^{n} \omega_i (R_a)_{ij}}{\omega_j} \, ; \, j = 1,\ldots,n \tag{4.33}$$

where $i,j = 1, \ldots ,n$ denote the "*n*" regional industries, ω_i denotes the ith element of the ω^T $1 \times n$ row vector given by equation (4.11), and $(R_a)_{ij}$ denotes an element of the SAM's accounting multiplier matrix. This multiplier defines the total income effect (direct plus indirect plus induce effects) if the initial or direct effect is in terms of the wage income required to produce \$1.00 worth of output.

SAM value-added/value-added multiplier

A SAM value-added/value-added multiplier, $SAM_j^{(VA/VA)}$, for the jth industry is given by equation (4.34):

$$SAM_j^{(VA/VA)} = \frac{\sum_{i=1}^{n} v_i (R_a)_{ij}}{v_j}; \, j = 1,\dots,n$$

(4.34)

where i,j = 1, . . . ,n denote the "*n*" regional industries, v_i denotes the ith element of the v^T 1 × n row vector given by equation (4.30b), and $(R_a)_{ij}$ denotes an element of the SAM's accounting multiplier matrix. This multiplier defines the total value-added effect (direct plus indirect plus induce effects) if the initial or direct effect is in terms of the value-added required to produce $1.00 worth of output.

SAM employment/employment multiplier

A SAM employment/employment multiplier, $SAM_j^{(Emp/Emp)}$, for the jth industry is given by equation (4.35):

$$SAM_j^{(Emp/Emp)} = \frac{\sum_{i=1}^{n} \varepsilon_i (R_a)_{ij}}{\varepsilon_j}; \, j = 1,\dots,n$$

(4.35)

where i,j = 1, . . . ,n denote the "*n*" regional industries, ε_i denotes the ith element of the ε^T 1 × n row vector given by equation (4.13), and $(R_a)_{ij}$ denotes an element of the SAM's accounting multiplier matrix. This multiplier defines the total employment effect (direct plus indirect plus induce effects) if the initial or direct effect is in terms of the employment required to produce $1.00 worth of output.

Using the SAM industry account multipliers listed in Table 4.5 and described above to predict the impacts on a region's economy relies on the seven assumptions given in Chapter 2 for the demand-side I–O model.

The SAM accounting multiplier matrix decomposition

The SAM accounting multiplier matrix can be decomposed into three multiplicative components: intragroup effects, intergroup effects, and extragroup effects (Thorbecke 1998; Subramanian 1988; Pyatt and Round 1979, 1985; Stone 1985; Bulmer-Thomas 1982). The intragroup effects estimate impacts within the account where the change is first introduced. For example, the intragroup effect of a tourist purchasing a hotel room (the industry accounts) would be defined by the Type I output multipliers. The intergroup effects estimate the impacts on the account where the change is first introduced after "touring" through the other accounts or the "closed-loop" impacts. For example, the intergroup effect of a tourist purchasing a hotel room would be the impacts on the industry accounts resulting from increased household income (the factor accounts) causing an increase in household purchases of goods and services (the institution accounts). The extragroup effects estimate the impacts of the initial change on the other accounts without returning to its starting account or the "open-loop" impacts. For example, the extragroup effect of a tourist purchasing a hotel room would be the impacts of changes in household income (the factor accounts) and in consumption (the institution accounts).

The intragroup, intergroup, and extragroup effects can be seen by rewriting the SAM model using equation (4.36):

$$\begin{bmatrix} x_1^d \\ x_2^d \\ x_3^d \end{bmatrix} = \begin{bmatrix} A_{11} & 0 & A_{13} \\ A_{21} & 0 & 0 \\ A_{31} & A_{32} & A_{33} \end{bmatrix} \cdot \begin{bmatrix} x_1^d \\ x_2^d \\ x_3^d \end{bmatrix} + \begin{bmatrix} f_1 \\ f_2 \\ f_3 \end{bmatrix} \quad (4.36)$$

For notational ease let $x_i^d = x_i$ for $i = 1, 2, 3$. Equation (4.36) can be written as a system of three equations given by equation (4.37):

$$x_1 = A_{11}x_1 + A_{13}x_3 + f_1$$
$$x_2 = A_{21}x_1 + f_2$$
$$x_3 = A_{31}x_1 + A_{32}x_2 + A_{33}x_3 + f_3 \quad (4.37)$$

Solving equation (4.37) for x_i gives equation (4.38):

$$x_1 = (I - A_{11})^{-1} A_{13}x_3 + (I - A_{11})^{-1} f_1$$
$$x_2 = A_{21}x_1 + f_2$$
$$x_3 = (I - A_{33})^{-1} A_{31}x_1 + (I - A_{33})^{-1} A_{32}x_2 + (I - A_{33})^{-1} f_3 \quad (4.38)$$

As Subramanian and Qaim (2009) and Thorbecke (1998) describe, equation (4.38) illustrates the three group effects. Assume a final demand change due to increased government purchases of an industry's output. The intragroup effect is given by $(I - A_{11})^{-1} f_1$ which defines the increased production activity, x_1, and is also the classical I–O model. In addition to the increased production activity, $A_{21}x_1 = x_2$, defines the increase in factor income required from the increased production activity. Given x_1 and x_2, the extragroup effects are illustrated by solving for x_3. This defines the additional income to households and enterprises based on direct sales to industries, A_{31}, distribution of income, A_{32}, and transfer payments, A_{33}. Finally, the intergroup effects are given by $(I - A_{11})^{-1} A_{13}x_3$ as the increased income creates additional production activity.

Example

We will use the supply (make) and use SAM given in Table 3.2 to illustrate how to derive Type I, II, and SAM multipliers. The Type I multipliers will be developed using the supply (make) and use SAM. The Type II multipliers will be developed using a traditional industry-by-industry I–O model. The SAM multipliers will be developed using the supply (make) and use SAM.

Type I multipliers

To develop the Type I multipliers we will make two modifications to the supply (make) and use SAM given in Table 3.2. First, Table 3.2 includes rows and columns defining transactions costs or marketing margins that were distributed across the row elements defining indus-tries' purchases of the commodity transportation. Second, agriculture large-scale and agriculture small-scale were combined into a single row and column. The resulting supply (make) and use SAM is given in Table 4.6.

Table 4.6 can be used to develop an IBT industry-by-industry total requirements matrix, $(I - DB)^{-1}$, as described in Chapter 2 and Table 2.1 where D is the market shares matrix (equation (2.24)) and B is the absorption matrix (equation (2.30)). Using the make and use matrices given in Table 4.6, the market shares matrix is given by Table 4.7. The absorption matrix is given by Table 4.8. Finally, the total requirements matrix is given by Table 4.9.

Type I—output/output

The Type I—output/output multipliers are given by the column sum of the total requirements matrix (equation (4.10)) and are given in Table 4.10.

Table 4.6 Supply and use SAM

	Industries				Commodities				Factors			Households		Ent	Govt	Taxes	S/I	ROW	Total
	1 + 2	3	4	5	6	7	8	9	13	14	15	16	17	18	19	20 + 21 + 22	24 + 25	23	
Industries																			
1 + 2 Agriculture					7,851														7,851
3 Industry						22,733													22,733
4 Transportation							8,263												8,263
5 Other services								15,781											15,781
Commodities																			
6 Agriculture	251	2,697	0	97								1,302	629	0	0	0	−30	2,963	7,909
7 Industry	1,310	5,859	3,075	3,619								5,236	7,255	0	310	0	2,904	2,515	32,083
8 Transportation	1,313	5,050	183	282								604	662	0	169	0	0	0	8,263
9 Other services	745	281	421	1,685								1,913	2,561	0	4,295	0	2,784	1,598	16,283
Factors																			
13 Labor	1,439	2,936	2,446	6,028															12,849
14 Capital	1,979	5,386	1,950	3,524															12,839
15 Land	595	0	0	0															595
Households																			
16 Rural	0	0	0	0					1,605	1,979	595	0	259	5,526	1,113	0	0	102	11,179
17 Urban	0	0	0	0					11,218	127	0	0	0	3,306	346	0	0		14,997
Other institutions																			
18 Enterprise (Ent)	0	0	0	0	0	0	0	0	0	10,733	0			0	1,209	0	0	0	11,942
19 Government (Govt)	0	0	0	0	0	0	0	0	0	0	0			0	0	7,065	0	291	7,356
20 + 21 + 22 Taxes	219	524	188	546	10	1,800	0	51	0	0	0	709	1,351	1,667	0	0	0	0	7,065
24 + 25 Savings investment (S/I)	0	0	0	0	0	0	0	0	0	0	0	1,415	2,280	908	−504	0	−525	1,559	5,133
23 Rest of world (ROW)	0	0	0	0	48	7,550	0	451	26	0	0	0	0	535	418	0	0	0	9,028
Total	7,851	22,733	8,263	15,781	7,909	32,083	8,263	16,283	12,849	12,839	595	11,179	14,997	11,942	7,356	7,065	5,133	9,028	

Source: Table 2.1, Thomas and Bautista (1999)

Table 4.7 The market shares matrix

Market shares (D) = make (V) · total commodity output^{-1} $(\hat{Q})^{-1}$

$$D = V(\hat{Q})^{-1}$$

$$
\begin{bmatrix}
0.99267 & 0 & 0 & 0 \\
0 & 0.70857 & 0 & 0 \\
0 & 0 & 1 & 0 \\
0 & 0 & 0 & 0.96917
\end{bmatrix}
=
\begin{bmatrix}
7851 & 0 & 0 & 0 \\
0 & 22733 & 0 & 0 \\
0 & 0 & 8263 & 0 \\
0 & 0 & 0 & 15781
\end{bmatrix}
\cdot
\begin{bmatrix}
7909 & 0 & 0 & 0 \\
0 & 32083 & 0 & 0 \\
0 & 0 & 8263 & 0 \\
0 & 0 & 0 & 16283
\end{bmatrix}^{-1}
$$

Table 4.8 The absorption matrix

Absorption (B) = use (U) · total industry output^{-1} $(\hat{X})^{-1}$

$$B = U\hat{X}^{-1}$$

$$
\begin{bmatrix}
0.03197 & 0.11864 & 0 & 0.00615 \\
0.16686 & 0.25773 & 0.37214 & 0.22933 \\
0.16724 & 0.22214 & 0.02215 & 0.01787 \\
0.09489 & 0.01236 & 0.05095 & 0.10677
\end{bmatrix}
=
\begin{bmatrix}
251 & 2697 & 0 & 97 \\
1310 & 5859 & 3075 & 3619 \\
1313 & 5050 & 183 & 282 \\
745 & 281 & 421 & 1685
\end{bmatrix}
\cdot
\begin{bmatrix}
7851 & 0 & 0 & 0 \\
0 & 22733 & 0 & 0 \\
0 & 0 & 8263 & 0 \\
0 & 0 & 0 & 15781
\end{bmatrix}^{-1}
$$

Table 4.9 Calculating the **IBT** industry-by-industry total requirements matrix

Total requirements matrix = (identity matrix − market shares matrix · absorption matrix)⁻¹

$$(I - DB)^{-1} = \begin{bmatrix} 1.06488 & 0.16674 & 0.04690 & 0.03840 \\ 0.25746 & 1.36808 & 0.38191 & 0.25733 \\ 0.24292 & 0.34030 & 1.11874 & 0.08563 \\ 0.12606 & 0.05413 & 0.07153 & 1.12752 \end{bmatrix}$$

$$= \left(\begin{bmatrix} 1 & 0 & 0 & 0 \\ 0 & 1 & 0 & 0 \\ 0 & 0 & 1 & 0 \\ 0 & 0 & 0 & 1 \end{bmatrix} - \begin{bmatrix} 0.99267 & 0 & 0 & 0 \\ 0 & 0.70857 & 0 & 0 \\ 0 & 0 & 1 & 0 \\ 0 & 0 & 0 & 0.96917 \end{bmatrix} \cdot \begin{bmatrix} 0.03197 & 0.11864 & 0 & 0.00615 \\ 0.16686 & 0.25773 & 0.37214 & 0.22933 \\ 0.16724 & 0.22214 & 0.02215 & 0.01787 \\ 0.09489 & 0.01236 & 0.05095 & 0.10677 \end{bmatrix} \right)^{-1}$$

Table 4.10 Type I—output/output multiplier

$$O^{(TI-O/O)T} = [1 \ldots 1]^T \cdot (I - DB)^{-1}$$

$$[1.69131 \quad 1.92925 \quad 1.61908 \quad 1.50888] = [1 \ 1 \ 1 \ 1] \cdot \begin{bmatrix} 1.06488 & 0.16674 & 0.04690 & 0.03840 \\ 0.25746 & 1.36808 & 0.38191 & 0.25733 \\ 0.24292 & 0.34030 & 1.11874 & 0.08563 \\ 0.12606 & 0.05413 & 0.07153 & 1.12752 \end{bmatrix}$$

Agriculture	Industry	Transportation	Other services
1.69131	1.92925	1.61908	1.50888

Type I—income/output

The Type I—income/output multipliers are calculated using equation (4.12) and are given in Table 4.11.

Type I—income/income

The Type I—income/output multipliers are calculated using equation (4.15) and are given in Table 4.12.

Type II multipliers

Examining Table 4.6 shows that the make matrix is diagonal. That is each industry produces only one commodity. Furthermore, the diagonal elements of the make matrix are equal to the column sum of the industry accounts. This allows combining the commodity accounts and industry accounts. Finally, the factor and household expenditure accounts can also be combined. Type II multipliers are calculated from an I–O model closed with respect to households (Table 4.1). The resulting industry-by-industry I–O model is illustrated in Table 4.13.

The transactions matrix $(\overline{Z})$, the technical coefficients matrix $(\overline{A})$, and the closed Leontief inverse matrix $(I - \overline{A})^{-1}$ are given in Table 4.14.

Type II—output/output

The Type II—output/output multipliers are given by the column sum of the closed Leontief inverse matrix (equation (4.18)) and are given in Table 4.15.

Type II—income/output

The Type II—income/output multipliers are calculated using equation (4.19) for only the industry accounts of the closed Leontief inverse matrix and are given in Table 4.16.

Type II—output/income

The Type II—income/income multipliers are calculated using equation (4.21) for only the industry accounts of the closed Leontief inverse matrix and are given in Table 4.17.

Table 4.11 Type I—income/output multiplier

$$[\mathcal{H}^{(T1-I/O)}]^T = \omega^T \cdot (I - DB)^{-1}$$

$$[0.34849 \quad 0.32866 \quad 0.41641 \quad 0.49631] = [0.18329 \quad 0.12915 \quad 0.29602 \quad 0.38198] \cdot \begin{bmatrix} 1.06488 & 0.16674 & 0.04690 & 0.03840 \\ 0.25746 & 1.36808 & 0.38191 & 0.25733 \\ 0.24292 & 0.34030 & 1.11874 & 0.08563 \\ 0.12606 & 0.05413 & 0.07153 & 1.12752 \end{bmatrix}$$

Agriculture	Industry	Transportation	Other services
0.34849	0.32866	0.41641	0.49631

Table 4.12 Type I—income/income multiplier

$$[\mathcal{H}^{(T1-I/I)}]^T = [\mathcal{H}^{(T1-I/O)}]^T \cdot (\omega)^{-1}$$

$$[1.90132 \quad 1.79314 \quad 2.27189 \quad 2.70781] = [0.34849 \quad 0.32866 \quad 0.41641 \quad 0.49631] \cdot \begin{bmatrix} 0.18329 & 0 & 0 & 0 \\ 0 & 0.12915 & 0 & 0 \\ 0 & 0 & 0.29602 & 0 \\ 0 & 0 & 0 & 0.38198 \end{bmatrix}^{-1}$$

Agriculture	Industry	Transportation	Other services
1.90132	1.79314	2.27189	2.70781

Table 4.13 Industry-by-industry I-O model

Industries	Industries 1 + 2	3	4	5	HH 13+14+15+16+17	Ent 18	Govt 19	Taxes 20 + 21 + 22	S/I 24 + 25	ROW 23	Total
1 + 2 Agriculture	251	2,697	0	97	1,931	0	0	0	− 30	2,963	7,909
3 Industry	1,310	5,859	3,075	3,619	12,491	0	310	0	2,904	2,515	32,083
4 Transportation	1,313	5,050	183	282	1,266	0	169	0	0	0	8,263
5 Other services	745	281	421	1,685	4,474	0	4,295	0	2,784	1,598	16,283
Factors											
13 Labor	1,439	2,936	2,446	6,028	13,082	8,832	1,459	0	0	102	36,324
14 Capital	1,979	5,386	1,950	3,524	2,106						14,945
15 Land	595	0	0	0	595						1,190
Other institutions											
18 Enterprise (Ent)	0	0	0	0	10,733	0	1,209	0	0	0	11,942
19 Government (Govt)	0	0	0	0	0	0	0	7,065	0	291	7,356
20 + 21 + 22 Taxes	229	2,324	188	597	2,060	1,667	0	0	0	0	7,065
24 + 25 Savings investment (S/I)	0	0	0	0	3,695	908	− 504	0	− 525	1,559	5,133
23 Rest of World (ROW)	48	7,550	0	451	26	535	418	0	0	0	9,028
Total	7,909	32,083	8,263	16,283	52,459	11,942	7,356	7,065	5,133	9,028	

Table 4.14 Transactions, technical coefficients, and closed Leontief inverse matrices

Transactions matrix, $\bar{Z}$

	Ag	Ind	Trans	OS	HH
1 + 2 Agriculture	251	2,697	0	97	1,931
3 Industry	1,310	5,859	3,075	3,619	12,491
4 Transportation	1,313	5,050	183	282	1,266
5 Other services	745	281	421	1,685	4,474
13 Labor	1,439	2,936	2,446	6,028	13,082

Technical coefficients matrix, $\bar{A} = \bar{Z}(\hat{X})^{-1}$

	Ag	Ind	Trans	OS	HH
1 + 2 Agriculture	0.031736	0.08406	0	0.00596	0.03681
3 Industry	0.1656341	0.18262	0.3721409	0.22226	0.23811
4 Transportation	0.1660134	0.1574	0.0221469	0.01732	0.02413
5 Other services	0.0941965	0.00876	0.05095	0.10348	0.08529
13 Labor	0.1819446	0.09151	0.2960184	0.3702	0.24938

Closed Leontief inverse, $(I - \bar{A})^{-1}$

	Ag	Ind	Trans	OS	HH
1 + 2 Agriculture	1.10427	0.14553	0.09465	0.09225	0.11384
3 Industry	0.57001	1.509	0.79097	0.64304	0.60512
4 Transportation	0.29613	0.27815	1.18493	0.15946	0.15897
5 Other services	0.19055	0.08093	0.14776	1.21294	0.17758
13 Labor	0.54791	0.36885	0.65954	0.76185	1.58386

Note: Ag denotes agriculture; Ind denotes industry; Trans denoted transportation; OS denotes other services; HH denotes household expenditures.

SAM multipliers

We will use Table 4.6 illustrate estimating SAM multipliers. Developing SAM multipliers requires closing the interindustry transactions matrix with those accounts to capture all the necessary behavioral and technical relationships of the economic system in a consistent way, or to reflect the circular flow of income that characterizes the process of demand, production, and income distribution (Pyatt and Round 1985; Thorbecke 1985). The transactions matrix, S, the technical coefficients matrix, $S\hat{X}^{-1}$ and SAM total requirements matrix $(I - S\hat{X}^{-1})^{-1}$ are given in Table 4.18.

Table 4.15 Type II—output/output multiplier

$$[O^{(T2-O/o)}]^T = [1 \ldots 1]^T \cdot (I-\bar{A})^{-1}$$

$$[2.16095 \ 2.01361 \ 2.21831 \ 2.10769 \ 1.05551] = [1 \ 1 \ 1 \ 1 \ 1] \cdot \begin{bmatrix} 1.10427 & 0.14533 & 0.09465 & 0.09225 & 0.11384 \\ 0.57001 & 1.50900 & 0.79097 & 0.64304 & 0.60512 \\ 0.29613 & 0.27815 & 1.18493 & 0.15946 & 0.15897 \\ 0.19055 & 0.08093 & 0.14776 & 1.21294 & 0.17758 \\ 0.54791 & 0.36885 & 0.65954 & 0.76185 & 1.58386 \end{bmatrix}$$

Agriculture	Industry	Transportation	Other services	Households
2.16095	2.01361	2.21831	2.10769	1.05551

Table 4.16 Type II—income/output multiplier

$$[\mathcal{H}^{(T2-I/0)}]^T = \omega^T \cdot (I - \bar{A})^{-1}$$

$$[0.41128 \ 0.27687 \ 0.49507 \ 0.57187] = [0.18194 \ 0.09151 \ 0.29602 \ 0.3702] \cdot \begin{bmatrix} 1.10427 & 0.14533 & 0.09465 & 0.09225 \\ 0.57001 & 1.50900 & 0.79097 & 0.64304 \\ 0.29613 & 0.27815 & 1.18493 & 0.15946 \\ 0.19055 & 0.08093 & 0.14776 & 1.21294 \end{bmatrix}$$

Agriculture	Industry	Transportation	Other services
0.41128	0.27687	0.49507	0.57187

Note: Type II—income/output multipliers are only calculated for the industry accounts.

Table 4.17 Type II—income/income multiplier

$$[\mathcal{H}^{(T2-I/I)}]^T = [\mathcal{H}^{(T2-I/O)}]^T \cdot (\omega)^{-1}.$$

$$[2.26046 \quad 3.02546 \quad 1.67242 \quad 1.54474] = [0.41128 \quad 0.27687 \quad 0.49507 \quad 0.57187] \cdot \begin{bmatrix} 0.18194 & 0 & 0 & 0 \\ 0 & 0.09151 & 0 & 0 \\ 0 & 0 & 0.29602 & 0 \\ 0 & 0 & 0 & 0.3702 \end{bmatrix}^{-1}$$

Agriculture	Industry	Transportation	Other services
2.26046	3.02546	1.67242	1.54474

Note: Type II—income/income multipliers are only calculated for the industry accounts.

Table 4.18 Transactions, technical coefficients, and SAM total requirements matrices

Transactions matrix, S

	Ag	Ind	Trans	OS	Labor	Capital	Land	Rural	Urban	Ent
1 + 2 Agriculture	251	2,697	0	97	0	0	0	1,302	629	0
3 Industry	1,310	5,859	3,075	3,619	0	0	0	5,236	7,255	0
4 Transportation	1,313	5,050	183	282	0	0	0	604	662	0
5 Other services	745	281	421	1,685	0	0	0	1,913	2,561	0
13 Labor	1,439	2,936	2,446	6,028	0	0	0	0	0	0
14 Capital	1,979	5,386	1,950	3,524	0	0	0	0	0	0
15 Land	595	0	0	0	0	0	0	0	0	0
16 Rural	0	0	0	0	1,605	1,979	595	0	259	5,526
17 Urban	0	0	0	0	11,218	127	0	0	0	3,306
18 Enterprise	0	0	0	0	0	10,733	0	0	0	0

Technical coefficients matrix, $S\hat{X}^{-1}$

	Ag	Ind	Trans	OS	Labor	Capital	Land	Rural	Urban	Ent
1 + 2 Agriculture	0.03174	0.08406	0	0.00596	0	0	0	0.11647	0.04194	0
3 Industry	0.16563	0.18262	0.37214	0.22226	0	0	0	0.46838	0.48376	0
4 Transportation	0.16601	0.1574	0.02215	0.01732	0	0	0	0.05403	0.04414	0
5 Other services	0.0942	0.00876	0.05095	0.10348	0	0	0	0.17112	0.17077	0
13 Labor	0.18194	0.09151	0.29602	0.3702	0	0	0	0	0	0
14 Capital	0.25022	0.16788	0.23599	0.21642	0	0	0	0	0	0
15 Land	0.07523	0	0	0	0	0	0	0	0	0
16 Rural	0	0	0	0	0.12491	0.15414	1	0	0.01727	0.46274
17 Urban	0	0	0	0	0.87306	0.00989	0	0	0	0.27684
18 Enterprise	0	0	0	0	0	0.83597	0	0	0	0

SAM total requirements matrix, $(I - S\hat{X}^{-1})^{-1}$

	Ag	Ind	Trans	OS	Labor	Capital	Land	Rural	Urban	Ent
1 + 2 Agriculture	1.26707	0.25168	0.23535	0.22949	0.24042	0.22722	0.31744	0.31744	0.22995	0.21055
3 Industry	1.42809	2.07465	1.55991	1.40577	1.40303	1.12868	1.46289	1.46289	1.39772	1.06387
4 Transportation	0.52195	0.42666	1.38577	0.35798	0.36164	0.3009	0.39676	0.39676	0.35745	0.28255
5 Other services	0.44248	0.2469	0.37305	1.43621	0.40961	0.33256	0.4331	0.4331	0.4072	0.31314
13 Labor	0.67954	0.45335	0.73389	0.80806	1.43083	0.35682	0.46941	0.46941	0.42631	0.33523
14 Capital	0.77573	0.56538	0.72853	0.68873	0.46969	1.38932	0.51238	0.51238	0.46467	0.36574
15 Land	0.09532	0.01893	0.01771	0.01726	0.01809	0.01709	1.02388	0.02388	0.0173	0.01584
16 Rural	0.61333	0.39061	0.5176	0.50584	0.47443	0.82442	1.36891	1.36891	0.34756	0.72966
17 Urban	0.78048	0.53224	0.81654	0.87169	1.36255	0.64679	0.53348	0.53348	1.48433	0.65778
18 Enterprise	0.64848	0.47264	0.60903	0.57575	0.39264	1.16143	0.42834	0.42834	0.38845	1.30574

Note: Ag denotes agriculture; Ind denotes industry; Trans denoted transportation; OS denotes other services; Rural denotes rural households; Urban denotes urban households, Ent denotes enterprises.

SAM accounting multipliers

The SAM accounting multipliers are calculated by summing the columns of the SAM total requirements matrix $((I - S\hat{X}^{-1})^{-1}$, Table 4.18) as shown in equations (4.27) and given in Table 4.19. The SAM accounting multipliers are calculated for each industrial activity, primary factor of production, household, and enterprise.

SAM output/output multipliers

SAM output/output multipliers, $SAM^{(O/O)}$, are calculated for only the industry accounts as shown by equation (4.28) and illustrated in Table 4.20.

SAM income/output multipliers

SAM income/output multipliers, $SAM^{(I/O)}$, are calculated for only the industry accounts as shown by equation (4.29) and illustrated in Table 4.21.

SAM value-added/output multipliers

SAM value-added/output multipliers, $SAM^{(VA/O)}$, are calculated for only the industry accounts as shown by equation (4.30) and illustrated in Table 4.22.

SAM income/income multipliers

SAM income/income multipliers, $SAM^{(I/I)}$, are calculated for only the industry accounts as shown by equation (4.33) and illustrated in Table 4.23.

SAM value-added/value-added multipliers

SAM value-added/value-added multipliers, $SAM^{(VA/VA)}$, are calculated for only the industry accounts as shown by equation (4.34) and illustrated in Table 4.24.

Table 4.19 SAM accounting multipliers

SAM—accounting multiplier

$$[SAM^{(AM)}]^T = [1 \ldots 1]^T \cdot (I - S\hat{X}^{-1})^{-1}$$

Ag	Ind	Trans	OS	Labor	Capital	Land	Rural	Urban	Ent
7.25246	5.43305	6.97739	6.89678	6.56293	6.38523	6.9466	5.9466	5.52093	5.28011

Note: Ag denotes agriculture; Ind denotes industry; Trans denoted transportation; OS denotes other services; Rural denotes rural households, Urban denotes urban households, Ent denotes enterprises.

Table 4.20 SAM output/output multipliers

SAM Output/output multipliers, $SAM^{(O/O)}$

$$[SAM^{(O/O)}]^T = [1 \ldots 1]^T \cdot (I - S\hat{X}^{-1})_{Ind}^{-1}$$

$$[3.65958 \quad 2.99989 \quad 3.55409 \quad 3.42945] = [1 \quad 1 \quad 1 \quad 1] \cdot \begin{bmatrix} 1.26707 & 0.25168 & 0.23535 & 0.22949 \\ 1.42809 & 2.07465 & 1.55991 & 1.40577 \\ 0.52195 & 0.42666 & 1.38577 & 0.35798 \\ 0.44248 & 0.24690 & 0.37305 & 1.43621 \end{bmatrix}$$

Agriculture	Industry	Transportation	Other services
3.65958	2.99989	3.55409	3.42945

Note: SAM output/output multipliers, $SAM^{(O/O)}$, are calculated for only the industry accounts (Ind) as designated by $(I - S\hat{X}^{-1})_{Ind}^{-1}$.

Table 4.21 SAM income/output multiplier

SAM income/output multipliers, $SAM^{(I/O)}$

$$[SAM^{(I/O)}]^{\mathrm{T}} = \omega^{\mathrm{T}} \cdot (I - S\hat{X}^{-1})^{-1}_{\mathrm{Ind}}.$$

$$[0.67954 \quad 0.45335 \quad 0.73389 \quad 0.80806] = [0.18194 \quad 0.09151 \quad 0.29602 \quad 0.370201] \cdot \begin{bmatrix} 1.26707 & 0.25168 & 0.23535 & 0.22949 \\ 1.42809 & 2.07465 & 1.55991 & 1.40577 \\ 0.52195 & 0.42666 & 1.38577 & 0.35798 \\ 0.44248 & 0.24690 & 0.37305 & 1.43621 \end{bmatrix}$$

Agriculture	Industry	Transportation	Other services
0.67954	0.45335	0.73389	0.80806

Note: SAM income/output multipliers, $SAM^{(I/O)}$, are calculated for only the industry accounts (Ind) as designated by $(I - S\hat{X}^{-1})^{-1}_{\mathrm{Ind}}$

Table 4.22 SAM value-added/output multiplier

SAM value-added/output multipliers, $SAM^{(VA/O)}$

$$[SAM^{(VA/O)}]^T = v^T \cdot (I - S\hat{X}^{-1})^{-1}_{\text{Ind}}$$

$$v^T = [1 \quad 1 \quad 1] \cdot \begin{bmatrix} 0.18194 & 0.09151 & 0.29602 & 0.37020 \\ 0.25022 & 0.16788 & 0.23599 & 0.21642 \\ 0.07523 & 0.00000 & 0.00000 & 0.00000 \end{bmatrix} = [0.50740 \quad 0.25939 \quad 0.53201 \quad 0.58662]$$

$$[1.55059 \quad 1.03767 \quad 1.48013 \quad 1.51405] = [0.50740 \quad 0.25939 \quad 0.53201 \quad 0.58662] \cdot \begin{bmatrix} 1.26707 & 0.25168 & 0.23535 & 0.22949 \\ 1.42809 & 2.07465 & 1.55991 & 1.40577 \\ 0.52195 & 0.42666 & 1.38577 & 0.35798 \\ 0.44248 & 0.24690 & 0.37305 & 1.43621 \end{bmatrix}$$

Agriculture	Industry	Transportation	Other services
1.55059	1.03767	1.48013	1.51405

Note: SAM value-added/output multipliers, $SAM^{(VA/O)}$, are calculated for only the industry accounts (Ind) as designated by $(I - S\hat{X}^{-1})^{-1}_{\text{Ind}}$ and v^T denotes the column sum of the value added accounts for each industry.

Table 4.23 SAM income/income multiplier

SAM income/income multiplier, $SAM^{(I/I)}$

$$[SAM^{(I/I)}]^T = [SAM^{(I/O)}]^T \cdot \hat{\omega}^{-1}$$

$$[3.73486 \quad 4.95396 \quad 2.47921 \quad 2.18274] = [0.67954 \quad 0.45335 \quad 0.73389 \quad 0.80806] \cdot \begin{bmatrix} 0.18194 & 0 & 0 & 0 \\ 0 & 0.09151 & 0 & 0 \\ 0 & 0 & 0.29602 & 0 \\ 0 & 0 & 0 & 0.37020 \end{bmatrix}^{-1}$$

Agriculture	Industry	Transportation	Other services
3.73486	4.95396	2.47921	2.18274

Note: SAM income/income multipliers, $SAM^{(I/I)}$, are calculated for only the industry accounts (Ind) as designated by $(I - S\hat{X}^{-1})^{-1}_{Ind}$.

Table 4.24 SAM value-added/value-added multiplier

SAM value-added/value-added multipliers, $SAM^{(VA/VA)}$

$$[SAM^{(VA/VA)}]^T = [SAM^{(VA/O)}]^T \cdot \hat{v}^{-1}$$

$$v^T = [1 \quad 1 \quad 1] \cdot \begin{bmatrix} 0.18194 & 0.09151 & 0.29602 & 0.37020 \\ 0.25022 & 0.16788 & 0.23599 & 0.21642 \\ 0.07523 & 0.00000 & 0.00000 & 0.00000 \end{bmatrix} = [0.50740 \quad 0.25939 \quad 0.53201 \quad 0.58662]$$

$$[3.05597 \quad 2.04508 \quad 2.91710 \quad 2.98396] = [1.55059 \quad 1.03767 \quad 1.48013 \quad 1.51405] \cdot \begin{bmatrix} 0.50740 & & & \\ & 0.25939 & & \\ & & 0.53201 & \\ & & & 0.58662 \end{bmatrix}^{-1}$$

Agriculture	Industry	Transportation	Other services
3.05597	2.04508	2.91710	2.98396

Note: SAM value-added/value-added, $SAM^{(VA/VA)}$, are calculated for only the industry accounts (Ind) as designated by $(I - S\hat{X}^{-1})^{-1}_{Ind}$ and v^T denotes the column sum of the value added accounts for each industry.

5 Ecosystem and economic system framework

Introduction

The consensus from the resource, environmental, and ecological economics literature is that the economic system resides inside the eco-system. For example, Daly (1977) describes how the capital and wealth that flows from households to firms takes place due to inputs such as solar energy and matter and then outputs it as waste heat and degraded matter. Hall *et al.* (1986) state that the

> economic processes take place in the physical world and are subject to the same physical laws that operate on and constrain other physical, chemical, and biotic processes. As a result, the economic process ultimately is constrained by the laws of energy, which set limits on the availability and rate of throughput of matter and energy through the economy.

Figure 5.1 represents a systems approach to define the fundamental

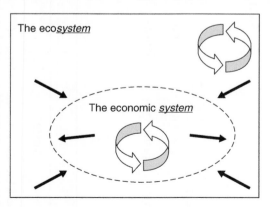

Figure 5.1 A systems approach.

relationship between the ecosystem and the economy system. The ecosystem is described as having physical, chemical, and other biotic processes, which are represented by the circular arrows in the upper right of Figure 5.1. The economic system is also described as having circular flow between production, income distribution, consumption, savings and investment, and trade. Figure 5.1 also defines the interaction between the two systems. Ecosystem services flow from the ecosystem into the economic system across a permeable boundary. These ecosystem services are used in the production of goods and services or for direction consumption. There are also flows from the economic system into the ecosystem across the same permeable boundary. These flows are generally in the form of pollution.

Figure 5.2 depicts the flows between the economic system and the ecosystem of Figure 5.1 in matrix form. It shows how the flows to and from each system are grouped into four basic submatrices. The upper left submatrix depicts flows within the economic system and could be modeled by either an I–O or SAM. The bottom left submatrix depicts flows of ecosystem goods and services from the ecosystem to the economic system. The top right submatrix depicts flows of from the economic system to the ecosystem generally in the form of pollution. The lower right submatrix represents the flows within the ecosystem.

Models vary in the approaches used to depict the flows from the ecosystem to the economic system and vice versa. For example, Proops *et al.* (1993), Bicknell *et al.* (1998), Ferng (2001 and 2002), Hubacek and Giljum (2003), Resosudarmo (2003), McDonald and Patterson (2004), and Wiedmann *et al.* (2006) have used SIOT to analyze the concept of an ecological footprint (EF) or a measure of human demands on

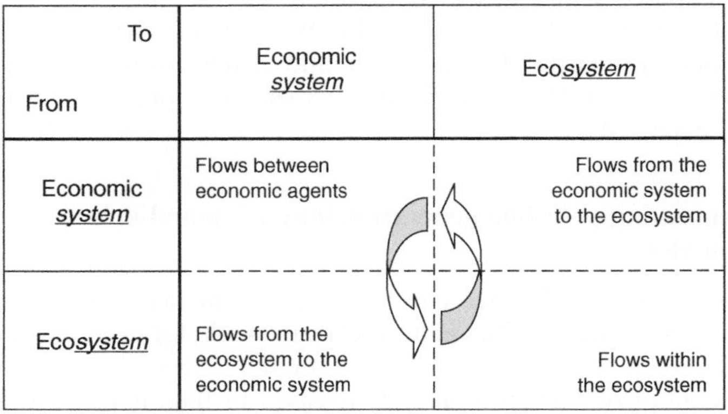

Figure 5.2 A systems approach—resource flows.
Source: Adapted from Daly (1968), Miller and Blair (1985), and Costanza *et al.* (1997b).

ecosystem goods and services. Alcántara (1995), Alcántara and Roca (1995), and Sànchez Chóliz and Duarte (2003a and 2003b) have used SIOT for atmospheric emissions. Carter and Irei (1970), Lofting and McGauhey (1968), Toss and Wiik (1974), Forsund and Stron (1976), Berck *et al.* (1991), Xu *et al.* (1994), Xikang (2000), Hubacek and Sun (2002), Velázquez (2003), Duarte *et al.* (2002) and Sánchez Chóliz and Duarte (2005), Matete and Hassan (2006) have used SIOT for water use and consumption. Leontief (1970), Lee (1982), Rhee and Miranowski (1984), Lowe (1979), Miller and Blair (1985), and Luptáčik and Böhm (1994 and 1999) add a pollution generation and abatement component to an I–O model which is often referred to as the augmented Leontief I–O model. Dobos and Floriska (2007) used a dynamic I–O model to examine the impacts of recycling on the use of non-renewable resources in the economy. Hawkins *et al.* (2007) incorporate physical as well as monetary flows in an I–O model to analyze the life-cycle of materials as they are used throughout the economy. Hawdon and Pearson (1995) use an I–O model to model the interactions of the energy sectors within a regional economy and the deposition of pollution into the environment. Jin *et al.* (2003) use the augmented I–O model to link a costal economy with a marine ecosystem. Rodríguez Morilla *et al.* (2007) augment a SAM to include ecosystem goods and services that flow into the economy and outputs from the economy that flow into the ecosystem.

The purpose of this chapter is to describe some of the approaches used to depict these flows. We will concentrate on those approaches developed using either an I–O or SAM as the foundation. As Miller and Blair (1985) describe, if a linear relationship can be developed between production and any factor (e.g. pollution), then this factor can be included in an I–O model or SAM. We will start with the classical approach of incorporating pollution and abatement into a traditional demand-driven I–O model and then expand to more complex models built on a SAM.

Incorporating pollution generation into a demand-driven I–O model

Leontief (1970: 262) first considered pollution as a by-product of regular economic activities in an I–O framework; for example, the

> quantity of carbon monoxide released in the air bears a definite relationship to the amount of fuel burned by various types of automotive engines, or how the discharge of polluted water into

our streams and lakes is linked directly to the level of output of the steel, the paper the textile and all the water-using industries.

He expanded the I–O model to include the environment in the economy assuming that "pollution and other undesirable—or desirable— external effects of productive or consumptive activities should for all practical purposes be considered part of the economic system" (Leontief 1970: 264). Figure 5.3 illustrates including pollution generation as part of the demand-driven I–O model.

The top half of Figure 5.3 describes the traditional components of a demand-driven I–O model as developed in Chapter 2 (for example, Table 2.1). The pollution generation matrix defines the amount of pollution generated as a result of the production process. The elements ψ_{pj} denote the amount of the pth pollutant emitted by the jth industry, $\psi_{pj} \geq 0$. A row sum of this matrix gives the total amount of the pth pollutant emitted, which is denoted by p_p. This is illustrated by equation (5.1):

$$\psi_{11} + \cdots + \psi_{1p} = p_1$$
$$\vdots \qquad\qquad \vdots$$
$$\psi_{p1} + \cdots + \psi_{pn} = p_p \tag{5.1}$$

The development of a demand-driven predictive model that would include these external effects would follow the same logic as described in Chapter 2. The quantitative dependence of each kind of external output (or input such as natural resources consumption) must be described by an appropriate technical coefficient. This is shown in equation (5.2a):

$$x_1 - a_{11}x_1 - \cdots - a_{1n}x_n = y_1$$
$$\vdots \qquad\qquad \vdots$$
$$x_n - a_{n1}x_1 - \cdots - a_{nn}x_n = y_n$$
$$p_1 - \varphi_{11}x_1 - \cdots - \varphi_{1n}x_n = 0$$
$$\vdots \qquad\qquad \vdots$$
$$p_p - \varphi_{p1}x_1 - \cdots - \varphi_{pn}x_n = 0 \tag{5.2a}$$

where x_j $j = 1, \ldots, n$ denotes the jth industry's total output; a_{ij} denotes the technical coefficients as defined by equation (2.11a); y_j denotes the final demand for the jth industry's output as defined by equation (2.9); and $\varphi_{pj} = \dfrac{\psi_{pj}}{x_j}$ define the amount of the pth pollutant emitted per dollar

Receipts	Expenditures				
	Industry 1 ⋯ n	Final demand		Exports	Total output
Industry 1 ⋮ n	z_{11} ⋯ z_{1n} ⋮ ⋱ ⋮ z_{n1} ⋯ z_{nn}	y_{1H} y_{1G} y_{1In} ⋮ ⋮ ⋮ y_{nH} y_{nG} y_{nIn}		e_1 ⋮ e_n	x_1 ⋮ x_n
Value added	w_{L1} ⋯ w_{Ln} w_{K1} ⋯ w_{Kn}	w_{LH} w_{LG} w_{LIn} w_{KH} w_{KG} w_{KIn}		w_{Le} w_{Ke}	L K
Imports	m_1 ⋯ m_n	m_H m_G m_{In}		m_e	M
Total outlay	x_1 ⋯ x_n	H G In		E	
Pollution generation	ψ_{11} ⋯ ψ_{1n} ⋮ ⋱ ⋮ $\psi_{\rho1}$ ⋯ $\psi_{\rho n}$				p_1 ⋮ p_ρ

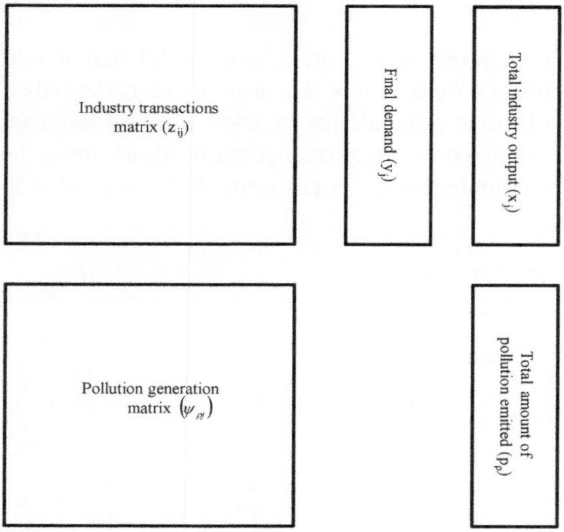

Figure 5.3 Pollution generation included in a demand-driven I–O model.

of jth industry's total output. Equation (5.2b) can be depicted in matrix notation as:

$$
\begin{bmatrix} x_1 \\ \vdots \\ x_n \\ 0 \\ \vdots \\ 0 \end{bmatrix} - \begin{bmatrix} a_{11} & \cdots & a_{1n} & 0 & \cdots & 0 \\ \vdots & \ddots & \vdots & \vdots & \ddots & \vdots \\ a_{n1} & \cdots & a_{nn} & 0 & \cdots & 0 \\ -\varphi_{11} & \cdots & -\varphi_{1n} & 1 & & \\ \vdots & \ddots & \vdots & & \ddots & \\ -\varphi_{\rho 1} & \cdots & -\varphi_{\rho n} & & & 1 \end{bmatrix} \cdot \begin{bmatrix} x_1 \\ \vdots \\ x_n \\ p_1 \\ \vdots \\ p_\rho \end{bmatrix} = \begin{bmatrix} y_1 \\ \vdots \\ y_n \\ 0 \\ \vdots \\ 0 \end{bmatrix}
$$

$$
\begin{bmatrix} x \\ 0 \end{bmatrix} - \begin{bmatrix} A & 0 \\ -P & I \end{bmatrix} \cdot \begin{bmatrix} x \\ p \end{bmatrix} = \begin{bmatrix} y \\ 0 \end{bmatrix}
$$

$$
\begin{bmatrix} I-A & 0 \\ P & -I \end{bmatrix} \cdot \begin{bmatrix} x \\ p \end{bmatrix} = \begin{bmatrix} y \\ 0 \end{bmatrix} \tag{5.2b}
$$

Equations (5.2b) can be solved for the vector $\begin{bmatrix} x \\ p \end{bmatrix}$ giving equation (5.3):

$$
\begin{bmatrix} x \\ p \end{bmatrix} = \begin{bmatrix} I-A & 0 \\ P & -I \end{bmatrix}^{-1} \cdot \begin{bmatrix} y \\ 0 \end{bmatrix}
$$

$$
\begin{bmatrix} x \\ p \end{bmatrix} = \begin{bmatrix} (I-A)^{-1} & 0 \\ P(I-A)^{-1} & -I \end{bmatrix} \begin{bmatrix} y \\ 0 \end{bmatrix} \tag{5.3}
$$

The structure of the 2×2 partitioned matrix inverse in Equation (5.3) defines two components. First is the traditional demand-driven predictive I–O model, $\Delta x = (I-A)^{-1} \Delta y$. Second is a predictive relationship between a change in the jth industry's final demand and the amount of pollution emitted. This is shown in equation (5.4):

$$\begin{bmatrix} \Delta p_1 \\ \vdots \\ \Delta p_\rho \end{bmatrix} = P(I-A)^{-1} \begin{bmatrix} \Delta y_1 \\ \vdots \\ \Delta y_n \end{bmatrix}$$

$$\Delta p = P(I-A)^{-1} \Delta y \tag{5.4}$$

The term $P(I-A)^{-1}$ is a pollution multiplier matrix that converts the direct and indirect effects given in the Leontief inverse $(I-A)^{-1}$ into direct and indirect pollution generation. Miller and Blair (1985) illustrate this using oil and coal consumption, sulfur dioxide and hydrocarbons, and employment using Leontief's (1970) model.

Developing the predictive model in equation (5.3) requires that $(I-A)^{-1}$ and I^{-1} exist and $(I-A)^{-1}$ must be nonnegative. The mathematical conditions that insure $(I-A)^{-1}$ is nonnegative are: (1) $0 < a_{ij} < 1$, (2), $\sum_{i=1}^{n} a_{ij} < 1, j = 1,\ldots,n$, and (3) the A matrix is productive and satisfies the Hawkins–Simon condition (Miller and Blair 1985). Both of these requirements are satisfied. Thus nonnegative changes in final demand will result in nonnegative changes in pollution. While equation (5.3) was developed using pollution as Leontief (1970) describes the P matrix could also denote desirable external effects.

Rodríguez Morilla and Díaz-Salazar (2005) developed an industry-by-industry SAM for Spain that includes CO_2 emissions (Table 5.1a).

Figure 5.3 illustrates how pollution generation can be added to a traditional demand-driven I–O model. The industry transactions matrix (z_{ij}) shown in Figure 5.3 is the upper right submatrix in Table 5.1a delineated by industries 1 through 16. The determination of the final demand vector, y, in Figure 5.3 is described by equation (2.9) in Chapter 2. In Table 5.1a the final demand vector would be the row sum of the institutions and exports for the 16 industries. The total industry output vector, x, in Figure 5.3 is the first 16 rows of the total column in Table 5.1a. The pollution generation matrix in Figure 5.3 is in this case a vector given by the first 16 elements of the row entitled CO_2 emissions in Table 5.1a. The total tons of CO_2 emitted is given by last element in that row.

Table 5.1b is the pollution generation inverse given in equation (5.3).

As can be seen the inverse is nonnegative. Table 5.1b also contains the Type I output/output multipliers. This information can be used to predict both the change in total industry output and CO_2 emissions given and change in final demand. For example, a 50 million euro change in final demand for food, beverage, and tobacco (6) would result in a 114.99 million euro change in total industry output and generate an additional 50.28 tons of CO_2 emissions. Using the Type I output/output multiplier, the change in total industry output is $114.99 = 50*2.29$. The additional tons of CO_2 emitted is $50.28 = 50*1.005$.

A closer examination of Table 5.1a reveals two interesting details. The first deals with pollution generation. Based on the system described in Figure 5.3 only industries generate pollution. However, according to Table 5.1a, households also contribute to CO_2 emissions. Following Thorbecke's (1985) statement that the interindustry transaction submatrix should be closed to contain all the necessary behavioral and technical relationships of the economic system in a consistent way, the interindustry transactions submatrix should be closed with respect to households (21). Households receive their income from labor (17) and capital (20). This draws attention to the second detail: Some of the industries are paying a negative amount in taxes or they are receiving a subsidy from the government. Including both labor and capital in the closure would imply that the column sum of technical coefficients for the food, beverage, and tobacco industry (6) would be greater than 1.

Incorporating pollution generation and abatement into a demand-driven I–O model

Building on the system described in Figure 5.3 and equation (5.2), pollution generation and abatement can be included in the traditional demand-driven I–O model. Figure 5.4 illustrates this system as described by Leontief (1970), Lowe (1979), Lee (1982), Miller and Blair (1985), and Luptáčik and Böhm (1994 and 1999).

As with Figure 5.3 the industry transactions matrix and final demand and total industry output vectors are the same as those defined in Chapter 2 (Table 2.1). The pollution generation matrix defines the amount of the ρth pollutant emitted by the jth industry, $p_{\rho j}$. As Leontief (1970) describes, the abatement transactions matrix is composed of industries whose purpose is to reduce the level of the pollution generated as the result of production. The elements of this matrix, $\tilde{z}_{i\rho}$, denotes the purchase of inputs from the ith industry by the ρth pollution abatement industry. If these pollution abatement industries also generate pollution, this is captured in the pollution generated by abatement industry matrix. The elements of this matrix, $\tilde{\psi}_{\rho\rho}$, denotes the amount of the ρth pollutant emitted by the ρth pollution abatement industry. A row sum of these two matrices defines to total amount of the ρth pollution generated. The final demand vector for pollution abatement, $p_{\rho(fd)}$, defines society's demand for abating the ρth pollutant or the

Table 5.1a Spanish industry-by-industry SAM including CO_2 emissions, 2002

		1	2	3	4	5	6	7	8	9	10	11	12	13
Industries	1	2439	0	0	0	36	18757	397	633	72	0	0	181	0
	2	7	1	11	101	1125	10	7	0	0	10	111	187	0
	3	11	1	9	0	20	12	0	0	131	1189	233	185	0
	4	379	25	79	252	862	68	30	27	755	304	142	211	27
	5	670	89	203	343	1856	885	375	590	1067	970	1744	415	543
	6	4373	0	0	0	0	13076	229	21	127	0	0	0	0
	7	77	4	4	0	53	1575	617	43	355	37	120	406	478
	8	196	29	17	0	167	1525	224	6726	1162	509	504	615	205
	9	809	45	132	4	175	1743	836	733	4214	527	1981	1194	2870
	10	42	7	25	0	71	546	7	10	87	1246	358	301	224
	11	887	64	146	100	680	764	334	694	1262	1007	13085	2694	5515
	12	12	1	2	0	136	19	8	0	0	46	804	1780	491
	13	96	2	2	0	33	39	8	0	39	69	48	200	3438
	14	8	0	2	0	33	10	7	40	0	9	458	198	0
	15	161	14	31	19	218	111	43	129	87	154	276	262	115
	16	3044	197	649	1343	2136	9346	2863	4628	6542	4378	10019	4854	3753
Factors	17	3041	715	566	859	3825	11715	5318	6416	8082	4694	14832	5280	8350
	18	– 151	– 1	94	560	– 457	– 7177	201	182	1786	601	417	404	348
	19	– 494	– 3	– 4	4	7	– 48	12	18	12	15	– 4	1	6
	20	17134	411	708	2790	10410	8886	1854	3752	4465	3301	6843	2017	3480
Institutions	21	0	0	0	0	0	0	0	0	0	0	0	0	0
	22	0	0	0	0	0	0	0	0	0	0	0	0	0
	23	0	0	0	0	0	0	0	0	0	0	0	0	0
	24	0	0	0	0	0	0	0	0	0	0	0	0	0
	25	0	0	0	0	0	0	0	0	0	0	0	0	0
Imports	26	2139	43	139	11953	3159	5250	5582	7004	13711	1159	13574	1163	21634
CO_2 emissions		55370	1413	562	17640	92318	4782	2051	7376	15899	42483	19415	624	1257

Source: Adapted from Rodríguez Morilla and Llanes Díaz-Salazar (2005b).

Notes: Transactions are measured in millions of euros. CO_2 emissions are measured in tons.

Industries
1 Agriculture cattle, hunting, and silviculture; 2 Energy extraction; 3 Extraction of other minerals; 4 Coal and nuclear fuel; 5 Electricity, gas, and water; 6 Food, beverage, and tobacco 7 Clothing industry; 8 Wood and cork industry; 9 Chemical industry; 10 Other mineral production (not metal); 11 Metal industry; 12 Electric, electronic, and optical equipments 13 Transportation materials; 14 Other manufacturing industries; 15 Building sector; 16 Trade and repair

14	15	16	17	18	19	20	21	22	23	24	25	26	Total
32	414	1442	0	0	0	0	2374	0	0	0	89	8014	34880
0	0	74	0	0	0	0	0	0	0	0	0	0	1644
17	446	64	0	0	0	0	0	0	0	0	− 56	553	2815
4	307	3036	0	0	0	0	6007	0	0	0	− 46	5859	18328
107	385	7897	0	0	0	0	6366	0	0	0	40	0	24545
0	0	14713	0	0	0	0	22850	0	0	0	224	10081	65694
251	202	1682	0	0	0	0	8457	0	0	0	495	5514	23952
919	2190	6803	0	0	0	0	4448	0	0	0	31	4376	31646
391	1948	3804	0	0	0	0	4469	0	0	3203	305	14573	43956
66	11705	940	0	0	0	0	92	0	0	0	305	4193	20225
910	7134	2453	0	0	0	0	1968	0	0	0	6646	19202	65545
24	1972	629	0	0	0	0	1599	0	0	37	4773	10215	22548
43	121	4881	0	0	0	0	5329	0	0	0	3773	33356	51477
437	217	684	0	0	0	0	4458	0	0	0	3645	2949	13155
32	15780	14169	0	0	0	0	2385	0	0	0	79137	0	113123
257	15862	115112	0	0	0	0	238992	0	4298	102894	19388	32818	585373
204	28233	200965	0	0	0	0	0	0	0	0	0	691	306786
101	1319	21087	0	0	0	0	30684	0	0	246	9143	197	59584
− 25	541	2861	0	0	0	0	0	0	0	0	0	1631	4530
129	14504	159756	0	0	0	0	0	0	0	0	0	0	241440
0	0	0	305939	0	0	126294	18555	44707	690	80369	0	41765	618319
0	0	0	0	0	0	105508	28193	56940	66	15315	0	13982	220004
0	0	0	0	0	0	229	3401	429	146	828	0	776	5809
0	0	0	0	59584	4530	9409	127841	23129	105	609	0	4528	229735
0	0	0	0	0	0	0	42790	74110	356	19736	0	19869	156861
256	9843	22321	847	0	0	0	57061	20689	148	6498	28969		235142
278	3794	53236	0	0	0	0	63216	0	0	0	0	0	382714

Factors
17 Labor 18 Net taxes on products; 19 Other taxes; 20 Capital accounts

Institutions
21 Households; 22 Firms; 23 Non-profit institutions; 24 Government; 25 Saving

Import/exports
26 Rest of the world

Table 5.1b The pollution generation inverse or total requirements matrix for the Spanish SAM including CO_2 emissions

$$\begin{bmatrix} (I-A)^{-1} & 0 \\ P(I-A)^{-1} & -I \end{bmatrix}$$

1	2	3	4	5	6	7	8	9	10	11	12	13	14	15	16	
1.13266	0.00354	0.00545	0.00144	0.00443	0.40841	0.03332	0.03295	0.00784	0.00616	0.00467	0.01717	0.00312	0.01229	0.01013	0.01741	0
0.00197	1.0039	0.00847	0.00669	0.05043	0.00222	0.0019	0.00169	0.00195	0.00443	0.00442	0.01139	0.00147	0.00139	0.00165	0.00129	0
0.0011	0.00153	1.00473	0.00015	0.00165	0.00172	0.00056	0.00059	0.00387	0.06379	0.00554	0.0113	0.00141	0.00252	0.01316	0.00085	0
0.01582	0.0199	0.03538	1.01551	0.04113	0.01042	0.00555	0.00497	0.02245	0.02381	0.00733	0.01676	0.00425	0.0045	0.00928	0.00834	0
0.03269	0.06608	0.09015	0.02298	1.09084	0.03772	0.03	0.03336	0.03671	0.07159	0.0443	0.04007	0.02258	0.0238	0.02283	0.02204	0
0.18336	0.00674	0.01197	0.00341	0.00564	1.32285	0.02832	0.01467	0.01294	0.01249	0.00966	0.01544	0.00589	0.01216	0.01108	0.043	0
0.00537	0.00487	0.00462	0.00057	0.00447	0.00763	1.30834	0.00417	0.01313	0.00534	0.00556	0.02929	0.01529	0.02846	0.00578	0.00563	0
0.01914	0.02885	0.01856	0.00232	0.01534	0.0506	0.02313	1.27751	0.04293	0.04455	0.02207	0.05309	0.01359	0.20085	0.04211	0.02281	0
0.03923	0.03641	0.0607	0.0021	0.01494	0.05627	0.05638	0.03851	1.1127	0.04331	0.0483	0.07963	0.07514	0.04816	0.03666	0.01432	0
0.00531	0.00748	0.01389	0.00087	0.00621	0.01504	0.00268	0.00313	0.00451	1.07037	0.01022	0.02105	0.00762	0.00867	0.13133	0.00696	0
0.04544	0.05739	0.07783	0.00945	0.04614	0.04224	0.03102	0.04251	0.0466	0.08237	1.2616	0.1795	0.15233	0.10365	0.11166	0.0155	0
0.00181	0.00242	0.00332	0.00049	0.00776	0.00212	0.00159	0.00141	0.00138	0.00515	0.01778	1.08958	0.01366	0.0043	0.02458	0.00269	0
0.0053	0.00328	0.00425	0.00097	0.0032	0.00516	0.00282	0.00263	0.00337	0.00749	0.00386	0.01431	1.07339	0.00666	0.00491	0.01167	0
0.00097	0.00084	0.00196	0.00024	0.00217	0.00118	0.00102	0.0024	0.00078	0.00182	0.00975	0.01187	0.00149	1.03586	0.00388	0.00183	0
0.01256	0.01667	0.02448	0.00446	0.01671	0.01504	0.01026	0.01441	0.01036	0.02208	0.01517	0.02798	0.00879	0.01366	1.17327	0.03678	0
0.1861	0.19043	0.34514	0.1009	0.15382	0.32126	0.23147	0.26356	0.23921	0.35909	0.27637	0.38471	0.15747	0.30455	0.295	1.27893	0
2.0128	1.20808	0.70202	1.08751	4.24465	1.00569	0.34912	0.5412	0.63468	2.65253	0.63214	0.41593	0.23007	0.3606	0.51557	0.27124	−1

Type I output/output multiplier

1.68881	1.45033	1.71091	1.17255	1.46488	2.29988	1.76836	1.73848	1.56073	1.82382	1.7466	2.00316	1.55748	1.81148	1.8973	1.49005

Source: Based on the information contained in Figure 5.1a.

Receipts	Industry 1 $\cdots$ n	Abatement industries	Final demand	Exports	Total output
Industry 1 $\vdots$ n	z_{11} $\cdots$ z_{1n} $\vdots$ $\ddots$ $\vdots$ z_{n1} $\cdots$ z_{nn}	$\tilde{z}_{11}$ $\cdots$ $\tilde{z}_{1\rho}$ $\vdots$ $\ddots$ $\vdots$ $\tilde{z}_{n1}$ $\cdots$ $\tilde{z}_{n\rho}$	y_{1H} y_{1G} y_{1In} $\vdots$ $\vdots$ $\vdots$ y_{nH} y_{nG} y_{nIn}	e_1 $\vdots$ e_n	x_1 $\vdots$ x_n
Value added	w_{L1} $\cdots$ w_{Ln} w_{K1} $\cdots$ w_{Kn}		w_{LH} w_{LG} w_{LIn} w_{KH} w_{KG} w_{KIn}	w_{Le} w_{Ke}	L K
Imports	m_1 $\cdots$ m_n		m_H m_G m_{In}	m_e	M
Total outlay	x_1 $\cdots$ x_n		H $\quad$ G $\quad$ In	E	
Pollution generation	ψ_{11} $\cdots$ ψ_{1n} $\vdots$ $\ddots$ $\vdots$ $\psi_{\rho1}$ $\cdots$ $\psi_{\rho n}$	$\tilde{\psi}_{11}$ $\cdots$ $\tilde{\psi}_{1\rho}$ $\vdots$ $\ddots$ $\vdots$ $\tilde{\psi}_{\rho1}$ $\cdots$ $\tilde{\psi}_{\rho\rho}$	$-p_{1(fd)}$ $\vdots$ $-p_{p(fd)}$		p_1 $\vdots$ p_p

Column header spanning Industry 1...n through Exports: **Expenditures**

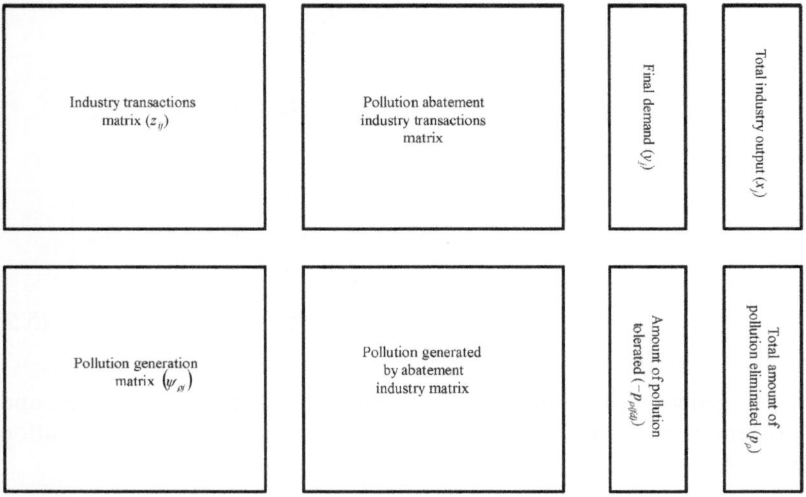

Figure 5.4 Pollution generation and abatement included in a demand-driven I–O model.

amount of the ρth pollutant emitted. The convention is to define the final demand or the amount of the ρth pollutant emitted as $-p_{\rho(fd)}$ (Lowe 1979, Miller and Blair 1985, and Luptáčik and Böhm 1999). Thus the total amount of the ρth pollutant eliminated, p_ρ, is the row sum of the pollution generation and the pollution generated by abatement industry matrices plus the final demand for pollution abatement vector.

Figure 5.4 illustrates an I–O transactions table similar to Table 2.1d described in Chapter 2. The development of a predictive model requires creating technical coefficients for the matrices in Figure 5.4. The technical coefficients are generated by equation (5.5):

$$
\begin{bmatrix} Z & \tilde{Z} \\ \Psi & \tilde{\Psi} \end{bmatrix} \cdot
\begin{bmatrix}
x_1 & 0 & \cdots & & & 0 \\
0 & \ddots & \ddots & & & \\
 & \ddots & x_n & 0 & & \vdots \\
\vdots & & 0 & p_1 & \ddots & \\
 & \ddots & & \ddots & \ddots & 0 \\
0 & \cdots & & & 0 & p_\rho
\end{bmatrix}^{-1}
$$

$$
=
\begin{bmatrix}
a_{11} & \cdots & a_{1n} & \tilde{a}_{11} & \cdots & \tilde{a}_{1n} \\
\vdots & \ddots & \vdots & \vdots & \ddots & \vdots \\
a_{n1} & \cdots & a_{nn} & \tilde{a}_{n1} & \cdots & \tilde{a}_{nn} \\
\varphi_{11} & \cdots & \varphi_{1n} & \tilde{\varphi}_{11} & \cdots & \varphi_{1n} \\
\vdots & \ddots & \vdots & \vdots & \ddots & \\
\varphi_{\rho 1} & \cdots & \varphi_{\rho n} & \tilde{\varphi}_{\rho 1} & \cdots & \varphi_{\rho n}
\end{bmatrix} \quad (5.5)
$$

A generalized system that includes pollution generation and abatement is given in equation (5.6a) and in matrix form in equation (5.6b):

$$
\begin{aligned}
x_1 - a_{11}x_1 - \cdots - a_{1n}x_n - \tilde{a}_{11}p_1 - \cdots - \tilde{a}_{1\rho}p_\rho &= y_1 \\
&\vdots \\
x_n - a_{n1}x_1 - \cdots - a_{nn}x_n - \tilde{a}_{n1}p_1 - \cdots - \tilde{a}_{n\rho}p_\rho &= y_n \\
p_1 - \varphi_{11}x_1 - \cdots - \varphi_{1n}x_n - \tilde{\varphi}_{1\rho}p_1 - \cdots - \tilde{\varphi}_{1\rho}p_\rho &= -p_{1(fd)} \\
&\vdots \\
p_\rho - \varphi_{\rho 1}x_1 - \cdots - \varphi_{\rho n}x_n - \tilde{\varphi}_{\rho 1}p_\rho - \cdots - \tilde{\varphi}_{\rho\rho}p_\rho &= -p_{\rho(fd)} \quad (5.6a)
\end{aligned}
$$

$$
\begin{bmatrix} x_1 \\ \vdots \\ x_n \\ p_1 \\ \vdots \\ p_\rho \end{bmatrix} - \begin{bmatrix} a_{11} & \cdots & a_{1n} & \tilde{a}_{11} & \cdots & \tilde{a}_{1\rho} \\ \vdots & \ddots & \vdots & \vdots & \ddots & \vdots \\ a_{n1} & \cdots & a_{nn} & \tilde{a}_{n1} & \cdots & \tilde{a}_{n\rho} \\ \varphi_{11} & \cdots & \varphi_{1n} & \tilde{\varphi}_{11} & \cdots & \tilde{\varphi}_{1\rho} \\ \vdots & \ddots & \vdots & \vdots & \ddots & \vdots \\ \varphi_{\rho 1} & \cdots & \varphi_{\rho n} & \tilde{\varphi}_{\rho 1} & \cdots & \tilde{\varphi}_{\rho\rho} \end{bmatrix} \cdot \begin{bmatrix} x_1 \\ \vdots \\ x_n \\ p_1 \\ \vdots \\ p_\rho \end{bmatrix} = \begin{bmatrix} y_1 \\ \vdots \\ y_n \\ -p_{1(fd)} \\ \vdots \\ -p_{\rho(fd)} \end{bmatrix}
$$

$$
\begin{bmatrix} x \\ p \end{bmatrix} - \begin{bmatrix} A & \tilde{A} \\ P & \tilde{P} \end{bmatrix} \cdot \begin{bmatrix} x \\ p \end{bmatrix} = \begin{bmatrix} y \\ -p_{(fd)} \end{bmatrix}
$$

$$
\begin{bmatrix} I-A & -\tilde{A} \\ -P & I-\tilde{P} \end{bmatrix} \cdot \begin{bmatrix} x \\ p \end{bmatrix} = \begin{bmatrix} y \\ -p_{(fd)} \end{bmatrix} \tag{5.6b}
$$

where

$a_{ij} = \dfrac{z_{ij}}{x_j}$ is the jth industry's technical coefficient as defined in Chapter 2

$\varphi_{\rho j} = \dfrac{\psi_{\rho j}}{x_j}$ defines the amount of the ρth pollutant emitted per dollar of jth industry's total output with $\varphi_{\rho j} > 0$

$\tilde{a}_{i\rho} = \dfrac{z_{i\rho}}{p_\rho}$ is the technical coefficient for the ρth pollution abatement industry with $0 \leq \tilde{a}_{i\rho} < 1$ for all i and ρ

$\tilde{\varphi}_{\rho\rho} = \dfrac{\tilde{\psi}_{\rho\rho}}{p_\rho}$ define the amount of the ρth pollutant emitted per dollar of ρth abatement industry's total output $0 \leq \tilde{\varphi}_{\rho\rho} < 1$ for all ρ

$p_{\rho(fd)}$ defines society's final demand for the ρth pollutant, $p_{\rho(fd)} \geq 0$.

p_ρ defines the total amount of the ρth pollution eliminated. The total physical amount of the ρth pollutant generated is $p_\rho + p_{\rho(fd)}$ for all ρ.

Equations (5.6a) and (5.6b) are commonly referred to as the augmented Leontief model (Leontief 1970).

Luptáčik and Böhm (1999) solve equation (5.6b) for the vector $\begin{bmatrix} x \\ p \end{bmatrix}$

based on the 2×2 partition inverse given by Miller and Blair (1985: 385–87):

$$
\begin{bmatrix} x_1 \\ \vdots \\ x_n \\ p_1 \\ \vdots \\ p_\rho \end{bmatrix} = \begin{bmatrix} (I-A)^{-1}\left[I + \tilde{A}\Omega P(I-A)^{-1}\right] & (I-A)^{-1}\tilde{A}\Omega \\ \Omega^{-1}P(I-A)^{-1} & \Omega^{-1} \end{bmatrix} \cdot \begin{bmatrix} y_1 \\ \vdots \\ y_n \\ -p_{1(fd)} \\ \vdots \\ -p_{\rho(fd)} \end{bmatrix} \quad (5.7)
$$

where $\Omega = [I - \tilde{P} - P(I - A)^{-1} \tilde{A}]$. As noted by Lowe (1979), Miller and Blair (1985), and Luptáčik and Böhm (1999), the system given by equation (5.7) presents some challenges. First, the dimension of A and P are $n \times n$ and $\rho \times n$, respectively, this implies that the dimension of $\tilde{A}$ is $n \times \rho$. Given the dimensions of $\tilde{A}$, this implies the dimensions of $\tilde{P}$ are $\rho \times \rho$. Thus there are ρ emissions and ρ industries and each industry will abate one type of pollutant. This is consistent with the one-to-one correspondence between industries and commodities in the traditional demand-driven I–O model. Second, the traditional I–O model presented in Chapter 2 resulted in the predictive model giving a non-negative total industry output vector [x] if the change in final demand [y] was nonnegative. The mathematical conditions that insured this result are: (1) $0 < a_{ij} < 1$, (2) $\sum_{i=1}^{n} a_{ij} < 1$, j = 1, . . . ,n, and (3) the A matrix is productive and satisfies the Hawkins–Simon condition (Miller and Blair 1985). In the case of the augmented Leontief model given in equation (5.7) two more conditions must be included so that a non-negative change in final demand $\begin{bmatrix} y \\ -P_{(fd)} \end{bmatrix}$ will give a nonnegative change in $\begin{bmatrix} x \\ p \end{bmatrix}$: (1) $P(I - A)^{-1}y \geq p_{(fd)}$, and (2) $\tilde{P} + P(I - A)^{-1} \tilde{A}$ is productive and satisfy the Hawkins–Simon condition (Luptáčik and Böhm 1994 and 1999). The first condition requires that the amount of pollution generated from direct and indirect production must be greater than the amount of pollution left untreated. The second condition insures that Ω^{-1} exists and the augmented Leontief inverse given in equation (5.7) is nonnegative.

The 2×2 partitioned inverse in equation (5.7) allows two equations to be developed. One showing the impacts on total industry output and the second showing the amount of pollution eliminated given changes in final demand and society's demand for pollution levels. Equation (5.8a) shows the effect of pollution and the abatement industries on the traditional demand-driven predictive I–O model:

$$
\begin{bmatrix} x_1 \\ \vdots \\ x_n \end{bmatrix} = (I-A)^{-1}\left[I + \tilde{A}\Omega P(I-A)^{-1}\right] \cdot \begin{bmatrix} y_1 \\ \vdots \\ y_n \end{bmatrix} + (I-A)^{-1}\tilde{A}\Omega \cdot \begin{bmatrix} -p_{1(fd)} \\ \vdots \\ -p_{\rho(fd)} \end{bmatrix} \quad (5.8a)
$$

The first term to the right of the equal sign determines the impact of the pollution and abatement industries on total industry output given a change in final demand. For example if the P, $\tilde{P}$, and $\tilde{A}$ matrices are zero filled, the result is the traditional demand-driven I–O model. The second term determines the impact on total industry output of society's demand for levels of untreated pollution or levels of pollution emitted. The Leontief inverse, $(I-A)^{-1}$, can be factored from equation (5.8a) giving equation (5.8b):

$$
\begin{bmatrix} x_1 \\ \vdots \\ x_n \end{bmatrix} = (I-A)^{-1}\left\{\left[I + \tilde{A}\Omega P(I-A)^{-1}\right]\cdot \begin{bmatrix} y_1 \\ \vdots \\ y_n \end{bmatrix} + \tilde{A}\Omega\begin{bmatrix} -p_{1(fd)} \\ \vdots \\ -p_{\rho(fd)} \end{bmatrix}\right\}
$$

$$
\begin{bmatrix} x_1 \\ \vdots \\ x_n \end{bmatrix} = (I-A)^{-1}\left\{\begin{bmatrix} y_1 \\ \vdots \\ y_n \end{bmatrix} + \left[\tilde{A}\Omega P(I-A)^{-1}\right]\cdot \begin{bmatrix} y_1 \\ \vdots \\ y_n \end{bmatrix} + \tilde{A}\Omega\begin{bmatrix} -p_{1(fd)} \\ \vdots \\ -p_{\rho(fd)} \end{bmatrix}\right\}
$$

$$
\begin{bmatrix} x_1 \\ \vdots \\ x_n \end{bmatrix} = (I-A)^{-1}\left\{\begin{bmatrix} y_1 \\ \vdots \\ y_n \end{bmatrix} + \tilde{A}\Omega\left[P(I-A)^{-1}\begin{bmatrix} y_1 \\ \vdots \\ y_n \end{bmatrix} + \begin{bmatrix} -p_{1(fd)} \\ \vdots \\ -p_{\rho(fd)} \end{bmatrix}\right]\right\} \quad (5.8b)
$$

The terms in the brackets defined the final demand vector, y, and the final demand created by the abatement industries mitigating $[P(I-A)^{-1}y - p_{(fd)}]$ level of pollution as a result of increased production.

Equation (5.9) shows the amount of pollution eliminated

$$\begin{bmatrix} p_1 \\ \vdots \\ p_\rho \end{bmatrix} = \Omega^{-1} P (I-A)^{-1} \begin{bmatrix} y_1 \\ \vdots \\ y_n \end{bmatrix} + \Omega^{-1} \begin{bmatrix} -p_{1(fd)} \\ \vdots \\ -p_{\rho(fd)} \end{bmatrix}$$

$$\begin{bmatrix} p_1 \\ \vdots \\ p_\rho \end{bmatrix} = \Omega^{-1} \left\{ P(I-A)^{-1} \begin{bmatrix} y_1 \\ \vdots \\ y_n \end{bmatrix} + \begin{bmatrix} -p_{1(fd)} \\ \vdots \\ -p_{\rho(fd)} \end{bmatrix} \right\} \tag{5.9}$$

The term in the brackets is also depicted in equation (5.8b).

Demand-driven ecosystem-economic I–O models

In the previous models the flow was from the economic system into the ecosystem in the form of pollution. Table 5.2 illustrates a system in which there are input flows from the ecosystem into the production process and flows from the economic system into the ecosystem, generally in the form of pollution.

As with the previous approaches, these flows could be described in physical or monetary terms.

The approach to develop a predictive model again follows the same recipe: Developing technical coefficients matrices of the flow matrices. Equations (5.10) and (5.11) define these technical coefficients matrices for input flows from the ecosystem and output flows from the economic system respectively:

$$\tilde{\varepsilon} = \begin{bmatrix} \varepsilon_{11} & \cdots & \varepsilon_{1n} \\ \vdots & \ddots & \vdots \\ \varepsilon_{k1} & \cdots & \varepsilon_{kn} \end{bmatrix} \cdot \begin{bmatrix} 1/x_1 & & \\ & \ddots & \\ & & 1/x_n \end{bmatrix} = \varepsilon \cdot (\hat{X})^{-1} \tag{5.10}$$

$$P = \psi^T \cdot (\hat{X})^{-1} = \begin{bmatrix} \psi_{11} & \cdots & \psi_{n\rho} \\ \vdots & \ddots & \vdots \\ \psi_{\rho1} & \cdots & \psi_{n\rho} \end{bmatrix} \cdot (\hat{X})^{-1} \tag{5.11}$$

Table 5.2 Ecosystem-economic I–O model

Receipts	Expenditures				Total output	Economic system output
	Industry 1 ... n	Final demand H G In	Exports			
Industry 1 ⋮ n	z_{11} ... z_{1n} ⋮ ⋱ ⋮ z_{n1} ... z_{nn}	y_{1H} y_{1G} y_{1In} ⋮ y_{nH} y_{nG} y_{nIn}	e_1 ⋮ e_n		x_1 ⋮ x_n	ψ_{11} ... ψ_{1p} ⋮ ⋱ ⋮ ψ_{n1} ... ψ_{np}
Value added	w_{L1} ... w_{Ln} w_{K1} ... w_{Kn}	w_{LH} w_{LG} w_{LIn} w_{KH} w_{KG} w_{KIn}	w_{Le} w_{Ke}		L K	
Imports	m_1 ... m_n	m_H m_G m_{In}	m_e		M	
Total outlay	x_1 ... x_n	H G In	E			
Ecosystem input	ε_{11} ... ε_{1n} ⋮ ⋱ ⋮ ε_{k1} ... ε_{kn}					

Source: Adapted from Miller and Blair (1985).

Equation (5.10) defines the amount of the kth ecosystem input required per dollar of the jth industry's output. Equation (5.11) defines the amount of the ρth pollutant emitted per dollar of the jth industry's output.

The technical coefficients matrices given in equations (5.10) and (5.11) can be multiplied by the Leontief inverse to determine the direct and indirect ecosystem inputs requirements and the pollution emitted given changes in final demand for the jth industry's output. These relationships are given in equations (5.12) and (5.13) respectively:

$$\begin{bmatrix} \varepsilon_1^* \\ \vdots \\ \varepsilon_k^* \end{bmatrix} = \tilde{\varepsilon}(I - A)^{-1} \cdot \begin{bmatrix} \Delta y_1 \\ \vdots \\ \Delta y_n \end{bmatrix}$$

(5.12)

$$\begin{bmatrix} p_1 \\ \vdots \\ p_\rho \end{bmatrix} = P(I - A)^{-1} \cdot \begin{bmatrix} \Delta y_1 \\ \vdots \\ \Delta y_n \end{bmatrix}$$

(5.13)

The reader will notice that equation (5.13) is also part of the previous two models. Equations (5.10) through (5.13) reinforce Miller and Blair's (1985) conclusion that if a linear relationship can be developed between production and any ecosystem input and economic system output then they can be included in an I–O model (and as we shall see a SAM also).

The definition of ecosystem inputs can be described as water, energy, air, and land, etc. For example, Proops *et al.* (1993), Bicknell *et al.* (1998), Ferng (2001 and 2002), Hubacek and Gilgum (2003), Reso-sudarmo (2003), McDonald and Patterson (2004), Wiedmann *et al.* (2006), and McDonald and Patterson (2004) have used this approach to examine the EFs of economies. The basic idea of an EF is to estimate the land (or sea) area necessary to sustain current levels of resource consumption for a given region's population (Bicknell *et al.* 1998). To estimate the EF, the land area (measured in hectares or acres) used by each industry is determined. This defines an ecosystem input vector. A matrix of land use technical coefficients is calculated using equation (5.14):

$$\tilde{L} = \begin{bmatrix} l_1 & & \\ & \ddots & \\ & & l_n \end{bmatrix} \cdot (\hat{X})^{-1}$$

(5.14)

where l_i denotes the amount of land area used by the ith industry. Each element of the $\tilde{L}$ matrix determines the amount of land used to produce a dollar of the ith industry's output. Equation (5.15) is used to determine the direct and indirect land use requirements of each industry given the final demands for their outputs:

$$
\begin{bmatrix} l_1^* \\ \vdots \\ l_n^* \end{bmatrix} = \tilde{L}(I - A)^{-1} \cdot \begin{bmatrix} y_1 \\ \vdots \\ y_n \end{bmatrix}
$$

(5.15)

where $\tilde{L}(I - A)^{-1}$ denotes the direct and indirect land input requirements or a land use multiplier matrix. The EF of each industry is determined by dividing each element of $\begin{bmatrix} l_1^* \\ \vdots \\ l_n^* \end{bmatrix}$ by the region's population. The region's EF is the sum of all the per capita total land use requirements.

The development of a diagonal matrix would imply that all land is identical. For example, Lofting and McGauhey (1968) used a diagonal matrix to determine the consumption of water resources. However, Ferng (2001) noted that not all land is identical. Ferng (2001) developed a land use matrix composed of different type of land (e.g. agricultural, forest, commercial, and degraded lands) as well as the land use from other regions as resulting from importing intermediate inputs. This level of detail adds to the complexity in terms of the matrix algebra. Nonetheless, the basic approach to the analysis as described would not change.

Use and make matrix ecosystem-economic system models

The approaches presented so far used a demand-driven I–O model as the foundation for developing ecosystem-economic system models. The demand-driven I–O model is defined as an industry-by-industry model. However, as discussed in Chapter 2, industries may produce more than one commodity or product. Accounting for this possibility requires describing the economic system using use and make (supply) matrices or SUTs. Building on Table 2.13, Table 5.3 illustrates Figures 5.1 and 5.2 using SUT to describe the economic system.

An additional row is added to show the flows from the ecosystem into the economic system in terms of ecosystem inputs used in the

Table 5.3 Ecosystem-economic system use and make (supply) matrix model

	Commodity 1 … c	Industry 1 … n	Final demand H G In E	Total output	Economic system outputs to ecosystem
Commodity 1 ⋮ c		$u_{11} \cdots u_{1n}$ ⋮ $u_{c1} \cdots u_{cn}$	$f_{1H}\ f_{1G}\ f_{1In}\ e_1$ ⋮ $f_{cH}\ f_{cG}\ f_{cIn}\ e_c$	$q_1 \cdots q_c$	$\psi^c_{11} \cdots \psi^c_{1p}$ ⋮ $\psi^c_{c1} \cdots \psi^c_{cp}$
Industry 1 ⋮ n	$v_{11} \cdots v_{nc}$ ⋮ $v_{n1} \cdots v_{nc}$			$x_1 \cdots x_n$	$\psi_{11} \cdots \psi_{1p}$ ⋮ $\psi_{n1} \cdots \psi_{np}$
Payments		$w_{L1} \cdots w_{Ln}$ / $w_{K1} \cdots w_{Kn}$ / $m_1 \cdots m_n$	$w_{LH}\ w_{LG}\ w_{Ln}\ e_L$ / $w_{KH}\ w_{KG}\ w_{Kn}\ e_K$ / $m_H\ m_G\ m_{In}\ m_e$	L K M	
Total input	$q_1 \cdots q_c$	$x_1 \cdots x_n$	H G In E		
Ecosystem inputs to economic system 1 ⋮ n	$r^c_{11} \cdots r^c_{1c}$ ⋮ $r^c_{k1} \cdots r^c_{kc}$	$r_{11} \cdots r_{1n}$ ⋮ $r_{k1} \cdots r_{kn}$			

	Commodity 1 ⋮ c	Industry 1 … n	Final demand	Total output	Economic system outputs to ecosystem
Commodity 1 ⋮ c		U	f_c	q_c	ψ_c
Industry 1 ⋮ n	V			x_n	ψ
Payments 1 ⋮ n		w^{T}	α	β	
Total input	q_c^{T}	x_n^{T}	β		
Ecosystem inputs to economic system	R_c	R			

production of commodities, R_c, and the ecosystem inputs used by industries, R. The flow of ecosystem inputs could also be defined as those coming from within the region or imported. An additional column is added to show the flows from the economic system into the ecosystem in terms of pollution generated by the production of commodities, ψ_c, and of pollution generated by industries, ψ.

The driver, as with the demand-driven I–O models, is the economic system. Flows into the economic system (ecosystem) from the ecosystem (economic system) are tied to changes that occur in the economic system. If these flows are defined using a linear relationship with respect to production, then changes in the economic system (modeled using either an I–O model, SUT, or SAM) can be used to estimate impacts on the ecosystem. For example, equation (5.3) describes this generic process succinctly: The economic system impacts are given by $\Delta x = (I - A)^{-1}\Delta y$ and the ecosystem impacts are given by $\Delta p = P(I - A)^{-1}\Delta y = P\cdot\Delta x$. Equations (5.7), (5.12), and (5.15) all illustrate the same process.

A SAM allows for flexibility in modeling the impacts of the economic system given the use and make (supply) matrices.[1] Table 5.4 summarizes the four different total requirements matrices that can be developed to estimate the impacts of the economic system given either an IBT or a CBT assumption.

Given Table 5.3, flows from the ecosystem into the economic system can be described in terms per dollar commodity or industry output. These are given in equations (5.16) and (5.17) respectively:

$$\widetilde{R}_c = R_c\left(\hat{Q}\right)^{-1} \tag{5.16}$$

$$\widetilde{R} = R\left(\hat{X}\right)^{-1} \tag{5.17}$$

In a similar manner flows from the economic system into the ecosystem can be described in terms of per dollar commodity or industry output. These are given in equations (5.18) and (5.19) respectively:

$$P_c = \psi_c\left(\hat{Q}\right)^{-1} \tag{5.18}$$

$$P = \psi\left(\hat{X}\right)^{-1} \tag{5.19}$$

Given Table 5.3, Table 5.4, and equations (5.16) to (5.19), eight different SAM economic system-ecosystem models could be develop. These are described in Tables 5.5a through 5.5d.

Table 5.4 Summary of total requirement matrices

	Industry-based technology	Commodity-based technology
Commodity-by-commodity	$(I - BD)^{-1}$	$(I - BG^{-1})^{-1}$
Commodity-by-industry	$(I - BD)^{-1} D^{-1}$ or $D^{-1}(I - BD)^{-1}$	$(I - BG^{-1})^{-1}G$ or $G(I - G^{-1}B)^{-1}$
Industry-by-commodity	$D(I - BD)^{-1}$ or $(I - DB)^{-1}D$	$G^{-1}(I - BG^-)^{-1}$ or $(I - G^{-1}B)^{-1}G^{-1}$
Industry-by-industry	$(I - DB)^{-1}$	$(I - G^{-1}B)^{-1}$

Source: Adapted from Miller and Blair (1985).

Notes: Assume that the number of commodities equals the number of industries.
IBT definitions:
  Absorption matrix (B) = $U(\hat{X})^{-1}$
  Market shares matrix (D) = $V(\hat{Q})^{-1}$
CBT definitions:
  By-products matrix (G) = $V^{T}(\hat{X})^{-1}$

Table 5.5a IBT economic system-ecosystem direct and indirect impacts: flows from the ecosystem to the economic system

	Economic system	Ecosystem inputs to the economic system
Commodity-by-commodity	$\Delta q_c^c = (I - BD)^{-1} \Delta f_c$	$\tilde{R}_c \Delta q_c^c$
Commodity-by-industry	$\Delta q_c = (I - BD)^{-1} D^{-1}\Delta y$ or $\Delta q_c = D^{-1}(I - DB)^{-1}\Delta y$	$\tilde{R}\Delta q_c$
Industry-by-commodity	$\Delta x_c = D(I - BD)^{-1} \Delta f_c$ or $\Delta x_c = (I - DB)^{-1} D\Delta f_c$	$\tilde{R}_c \Delta x_c$
Industry-by-industry	$\Delta x = (I - DB)^{-1} \Delta y$	$\tilde{R}\Delta x$

Wiedmann *et al.* (2006) develops an EF model based on the industry-by-commodity model given in Table 5.2a. The economic system was modeled using $x_c = (I - DB)^{-1} D \cdot f_c$. They defined the EF per industry output which they term the direct intensity matrix EF^{dir} which is analogous to R_c defined in Table 5.3. The resulting model $EF^{tot} = EF^{dir} (I - DB)^{-1} D \cdot f_c$ results in the total intensity matrix, EF^{tot}, which represents the total direct and indirect EF of industrial activities arising

Table 5.5b IBT economic system-ecosystem direct and indirect impacts: flows
from the economic system to the ecosystem

	Economic system	*Economic system outputs to the ecosystem*
Commodity-by-commodity	$\Delta q_c^c = (I - BD)^{-1} \Delta f_c$	$\tilde{R}_c \Delta q_c^c$
Commodity-by-industry	$\Delta q_c = (I - BD)^{-1} D^{-1} \Delta y$ or $\Delta q_c = D^{-1}(I - DB)^{-1} \Delta y$	$\tilde{R} \Delta q_c$
Industry-by-commodity	$\Delta x_c = D(I - BD)^{-1} \Delta f_c$ or $\Delta x_c = (I - DB)^{-1} D \Delta f_c$	$\tilde{R}_c \Delta x_c$
Industry-by-industry	$\Delta x = (I - DB)^{-1} \Delta y$	$\tilde{R} \Delta x$

Table 5.5c CBT economic system-ecosystem direct and indirect impacts: flows
from the ecosystem to the economic system

	Economic system	*Ecosystem inputs to the economic system*
Commodity-by-commodity	$\Delta q_c^c = (I - BG^{-1})^{-1} \Delta f_c$	$P_c \Delta q_c^c$
Commodity-by-industry	$\Delta q_c = (I - BG^{-1})^{-1} G \Delta y$ or $\Delta q_c = G(I - G^{-1}B)^{-1} \Delta y$	$P \Delta q_c$
Industry-by-commodity	$\Delta x_c = G^{-1}(I - BG^{-1})^{-1} \Delta f_c$ or $\Delta x_c = (I - G^{-1}B)^{-1} G^{-1} \Delta f_c$	$P_c \Delta x_c$
Industry-by-industry	$\Delta x = (I - G^{-1}B)^{-1} \Delta y$	$P \Delta x$

through the entire industrial supply chain to provide one unit of final
demand.

Ecosystem-economic system SAM models

As has been described in Chapter 3, a SAM gives a comprehensive
picture of the flow of income among households, primary factors of
production, and economic institutions. Thus a SAM is best described
as a socioeconomic model as it includes not only flows among the
actors involved in production but also the interdependence of production with the rest of society (Thorbecke 1998). Using a SAM as

Table 5.5d CBT economic system-ecosystem direct and indirect impacts: flows from the economic system to the ecosystem

	Economic system	Economic system outputs to the ecosystem
Commodity-by-commodity	$\Delta q_c^c = (I - BG^{-1})^{-1} \Delta f_c$	$P_c \Delta q_c^c$
Commodity-by-industry	$\Delta q_c = (I - BG^{-1})^{-1} G\Delta y$ or $\Delta q_c = G(I - G^{-1}B)^{-1} \Delta y$	$P\Delta q_c$
Industry-by-commodity	$\Delta x_c = G^{-1}(I - BG^{-1})^{-1} \Delta f_c$ or $\Delta x_c = (I - G^{-1}B)^{-1} G^{-1}\Delta f_c$	$P_c \Delta x_c$
Industry-by-industry	$\Delta x = (I - G^{-1}B)^{-1} \Delta y$	$P\Delta x$

the foundation allows for a better representation of the economic system and for more description in terms of the flows between the economic system and the ecosystem. The complexity of these systems is limited by one's imagination and data.

Sánchez-Chóliz and Duarte (2007) describe at least three practical reasons for expanding the ecosystem-economic system depicted in Figures 5.1 and 5.2 to SAM models as shown in Table 5.6.

1   Not all the ecosystem-economic system implications and relationships can be captured through a simple interindustry transaction table or even using a SUT. As Matete and Hassan (2006) show, since many ecosystem resources and services are usually not traded in the market and can be used by other economic actors (e.g. institutions), the structure of a SAM is able to capture these ecosystem-economic system interactions. This is the case for example in developing countries or in many areas where households use a natural resource such as the water from a river directly.

2   An ecosystem-economic system SAM allows the inclusion of pollution and natural resource consumption by households directly (Sánchez Chóliz and Duarte 2007). In fact, Sánchez Chóliz and Duarte (2007) suggest changes in household expenditure patterns (e.g. diet changes, reduction in the use of private cars, increase in the use of private heating systems) can represent change in the natural resource use and pollutant emissions.

3   An ecosystem-economic system SAM can be used to examine the welfare implications of natural resource use restriction (Castellano

Table 5.6 Ecosystem-economic system SAM model

Receipts	Expenditures					
	(1) Industry	(2) Factors	(3) Institutions	(4) Exports	(5) Total output	(6) Economic system outputs to ecosystem
Industry	S_{11}		S_{13}	S_{14}	x_1^d	S_{16}
Factors	S_{21}			S_{24}	x_2^d	
Institutions	S_{31}	S_{32}	S_{33}	S_{34}	x_3^d	S_{36}
Imports	S_{41}	S_{42}	S_{43}	S_{45}	x_4^d	
Total outlay	x_1^{sT}	x_2^{sT}	x_3^{sT}	x_4^{sT}		
Ecosystem inputs to economic system	S_{61}		S_{63}			

Notes:

Matrices

S_{11}—Interindustry transactions matrix; S_{21}—Value-added matrix; the sum of all the elements of this matrix define gross regional product; S_{31}—Sales and taxes matrix; S_{41}—Industry imports; S_{61}—Ecosystem inputs used by industries regardless of commodities produced; S_{32}—Distribution of factor payments to institutions matrix; S_{42}—Factor imports; S_{13}—Final demand purchases by institutions; S_{33}—Transfer payments among institutions; S_{43}—Institutional imports; S_{63}—Ecosystem inputs used by institutions; S_{14}—Industry export matrix; S_{24}—Factor export matrix; S_{34}—Institutional export matrix; S_{44}—Transshipment matrix; S_{16}—Flow from industries into the ecosystem usually in the form of pollution regardless of commodities produced; S_{36}—Flow from institutions into the ecosystem as the result of consumption

Row totals

x_1^d—Column vector of the sum of the row elements of the industry accounts (1). Total industry output; x_2^d—Column vector of the sum of the row elements of the factor accounts (3). Total factor income; x_3^d—Column vector of the sum of the row elements of the institutional accounts (4). Total institutional income; x_4^d—Column vector of the sum of the row elements of the import accounts (5). Total imports; *Column totals*; x_1^{sT}—Row vector of the sum of the column elements in the industry accounts (1). Total industry expenditures or outlay; x_2^{sT}—Row vector of the sum of the column elements of the factor accounts (3). Total factor expenditures; x_3^{sT}—Row vector of the sum of the column elements of the institution accounts (4). Total institution expenditures; x_4^{sT}—Row vector of the sum of the column elements of the export accounts (5). Total exports *et al.* 2008) or level of pollutants (Sánchez Chóliz and Duarte 2004).

Therefore, ecosystem-economic system SAM models can facilitate the understanding of how the pollution (or any other natural resource consumed such as water, timber, CO_2 produced) can "circulate" throughout the economy. It can help us relate concepts of scarcity, sustainability, depletion, or pollution. The key is determining the most appropriate manner to close the ecosystem-economic system SAM; namely which accounts are defined as endogenous versus exogenous. As Thorbecke (1985) states, the interindustry transaction submatrix, S_{11}, should be closed to contain all the necessary behavioral and technical relationships of the economic system in a consistent way. For example, Table 3.5 in Chapter 3 shows the endogenous accounts included the industry, S_{11}, and factor, S_{21}, accounts plus the household and enterprise components of the institution accounts. The exogenous accounts were composed of the government and capital investment components of the institution accounts plus imports/exports. This definition of endogenous and exogenous accounts would allow ecosystem-economic system impacts to be driven by changes in government expenditures. This approach can be illustrated using the industry-by-industry SAM for Spain that includes CO_2 emissions developed by Rodríguez Morilla and Díaz-Salazar (2005b) shown in Table 5.1a. We will define the endogenous accounts, S, to include industries (1 through 16), labor (17), and households (21). Table 5.7 defines the SAM total requirements matrix, $(I - S\hat{X}^{-1})^{-1}$.

Table 5.7 also contains the SAM accounting multipliers and the SAM output/output multipliers.

Equation (5.20) defines the economic system impacts:

$$\Delta x = \left(I - S\hat{X}^{-1}\right)^{-1} \Delta y \tag{5.20}$$

Equation (5.21) defines the ecosystem impacts in terms of CO_2 emissions:

$$\Delta p = P\left(I - S\hat{X}^{-1}\right)^{-1} \Delta y = P \cdot \Delta x \tag{5.21}$$

where P is defined as the CO_2 emissions per total industry output for sectors 1 through 16 and CO_2 emissions per total household expenditures for sector 21 (see Table 5.7). This information can be used to predict both the change in total industry output and CO_2 emissions

Table 5.7 The total requirements matrix for the Spanish SAM including CO_2 emissions

	1	2	3	4	5	6	7	8	9	10	11	12	13	14	15	16	17	21
1	1.10036	0.0227	0.01887	0.0047	0.01391	0.40896	0.04655	0.04529	0.01898	0.02164	0.01929	0.03397	0.01341	0.02774	0.02679	0.03361	0.03515	0.03525
2	0.07915	1.00644	0.01046	0.00718	0.05188	0.0315	0.00586	0.00552	0.00384	0.00671	0.0065	0.01462	0.00292	0.00411	0.00436	0.00446	0.00419	0.0042
3	0.0027	0.002	1.00507	0.00023	0.00189	0.00259	0.00095	0.00096	0.00416	0.06417	0.0059	0.01174	0.00166	0.00291	0.01358	0.00127	0.00084	0.00084
4	0.01069	0.0303	0.0427	1.01729	0.0463	0.01517	0.01306	0.012	0.02856	0.03225	0.01528	0.02603	0.00985	0.01299	0.0184	0.01729	0.01901	0.01906
5	0.03609	0.08301	0.10209	0.02589	1.09928	0.04966	0.04255	0.04512	0.04671	0.08535	0.05727	0.0553	0.03171	0.03771	0.03773	0.03676	0.03087	0.03095
6	0.05908	0.05314	0.04434	0.01127	0.02848	1.30766	0.05909	0.04331	0.03968	0.04983	0.04498	0.05554	0.03077	0.04918	0.05111	0.08164	0.08536	0.08559
7	0.19145	0.02403	0.01861	0.00399	0.01446	0.08649	1.32748	0.02239	0.02538	0.02145	0.02056	0.04878	0.02581	0.04571	0.02378	0.02459	0.03389	0.03398
8	0.02305	0.04548	0.03029	0.00518	0.02364	0.06253	0.03547	1.28908	0.05276	0.05807	0.03481	0.06806	0.02256	0.21452	0.05677	0.03728	0.03032	0.03041
9	0.02989	0.04973	0.07006	0.00438	0.02156	0.06135	0.06593	0.04745	1.12051	0.05411	0.05848	0.09147	0.08231	0.059	0.04831	0.02574	0.02436	0.02442
10	0.03118	0.01116	0.01655	0.00152	0.00811	0.02664	0.00609	0.00637	0.00681	1.07343	0.01308	0.02467	0.00963	0.0119	0.13472	0.01048	0.00656	0.00658
11	0.02601	0.06891	0.08589	0.01142	0.05184	0.04257	0.03897	0.04992	0.0533	0.09167	1.27039	0.1896	0.15852	0.11294	0.12167	0.02524	0.02112	0.02118
12	0.03313	0.00626	0.0061	0.00117	0.00975	0.01578	0.00526	0.00489	0.0038	0.00836	0.02077	1.09341	0.01576	0.0077	0.02814	0.00641	0.00682	0.00683
13	0.00808	0.0137	0.0116	0.00276	0.00841	0.01276	0.01056	0.00989	0.00953	0.01597	0.01185	0.0237	1.07901	0.01523	0.0141	0.02074	0.019	0.01905
14	0.0075	0.00708	0.00637	0.00132	0.00529	0.00747	0.00579	0.00688	0.00449	0.00691	0.01454	0.01756	0.00486	1.04103	0.00941	0.00732	0.01135	0.01138
15	0.01387	0.03141	0.03487	0.00699	0.02406	0.02484	0.02115	0.02461	0.01906	0.03406	0.02646	0.04122	0.01673	0.02576	1.18624	0.04957	0.02689	0.02696
16	0.31286	0.57437	0.61602	0.16681	0.34552	0.60979	0.51743	0.53163	0.46636	0.67146	0.5706	0.73079	0.36456	0.62044	0.63344	1.61329	0.69974	0.70167
17	0.33522	0.71625	0.50558	0.12303	0.35785	0.57366	0.53614	0.50277	0.42425	0.58302	0.54907	0.64684	0.38644	0.59012	0.63199	0.625	1.30482	0.30566
21	0.44354	0.73841	0.52148	0.12691	0.36915	0.62653	0.55538	0.52096	0.43787	0.60134	0.56622	0.66806	0.3985	0.60919	0.65215	0.64558	1.34463	1.34835
CO_2	2.14755	1.45118	0.87368	1.12928	4.36616	1.20792	0.53166	0.71241	0.77878	2.85047	0.81853	0.63573	0.36126	0.56107	0.7302	0.48364	0.44275	0.44398

SAM—accounting multiplier

3.74387	4.02972	5.11989	5.27208	6.75436	8.76576	9.20219	10.1453	10.9039	12.2955	13.1908	14.5265	14.8701	16.2889	17.4086	17.9957	18.0555	22.0584

SAM—output/output multiplier

1.9651	2.02972	2.11989	1.27208	1.75436	2.76576	2.20219	2.14531	1.90394	2.29545	2.19075	2.52646	1.87009	2.28888	2.40856	1.99569

Source: Based on the information contained in Table 5.1a.

given and change in final demand. For example, a 50 million euro change in final demand for food, beverage, and tobacco (6) would result in a 138.288 million euro change in total industry output and generate an additional 60.40 tons of CO_2 emissions. Using the SAM output/output multiplier, the change in total industry output is 138.288 = 50*2.76576. The additional tons of CO_2 emitted is 60.40 = 50*1.20792. Comparing these results with the previous analysis shows that including the labor (17) and household (21) accounts resulted in estimating an additional economic impact of 23.294 million euro change in total industry output and an additional 10.12 tons of CO_2 emissions.

Sánchez Chóliz and Duarte (2007) describe an alternative approach. They define the exogenous accounts to include only households. The endogenous account would include everything else. This allowed Sánchez Chóliz and Duarte (2007) to examine the ecosystem-economic system impacts resulting from households changing their consumption behaviors. Table 5.8 illustrates the ecosystem-economic system SAM with only households exogenous.

Let $\bar{S}$ represent the endogenous accounts. The economic system model would then be given by equation (5.22):

$$\Delta x = \left(I - \bar{S}\hat{X}^{-1}\right)^{-1} \Delta h \tag{5.22}$$

where Δh represents a change in household expenditure patterns. As households are defined as exogenous, the ecosystem model would need to contain two components. The ecosystem effects resulting from increased production due to a change in household expenditures is given by equation (5.23):

$$\Delta p = P\left(I - \bar{S}\hat{X}^{-1}\right)^{-1} \Delta h = P \cdot \Delta x \tag{5.23}$$

The ecosystem effects resulting from the change in household expenditures is given by equation (5.24):

$$\Delta p_h = P_h \cdot \Delta h \tag{5.24}$$

where P_h represents the ecosystem effects per dollar of household expenditures. The elements of $(P_h)_{i\rho}$ denote the ρth ecosystem effect of a household consuming the ith industry's output. Thus the total ecosystem effects are given by equation (5.25):

$$\Delta p^{total} = \Delta p + \Delta p_h \tag{5.25}$$

Table 5.8 Sánchez Chóliz and Duarte's ecosystem-economic system SAM model

| Receipts | Endogenous accounts | | | Exogenous account | (5) | (6) |
	(1) Industry	(2) Factors	(3) Institutions plus exports	(4) Households	Total output	Economic system outputs to ecosystem
Industry	S_{11}		S_{13}	S_{14}	x_1^d	S_{16}
Factors	S_{21}		S_{23}		x_2^d	
Institutions plus imports	S_{31}	S_{32}	S_{33}	S_{34}	x_3^d	S_{36}
Households	S_{41}	S_{42}	S_{43}	S_{45}	x_4^d	S_{46}
Total outlay	x_1^{sT}	x_2^{sT}	x_3^{sT}	x_4^{sT}		
Ecosystem inputs to economic system	S_{61}		S_{63}	S_{64}		

Source: Sánchez Chóliz and Duarte (2007).

While Sánchez Chóliz and Duarte (2007) examined flows from the economic system into the ecosystem as shown by equations (5.22) through (5.25), this approach could also be used to examine flows from the ecosystem into the economic system.

Multiregional ecosystem-economic system models

The previous ecosystem-economic system models were for examining a single region. These can be expanded to describe multiregional ecosystem-economic system interactions. We will use a two-region model to illustrate this approach. Let A_{ij} define the technical coefficients matrices for endogenous accounts of a SAM or an I–O model with i, j = 1, 2. The economic system model is given by equation (5.26):

$$\begin{bmatrix} x_1 \\ x_2 \end{bmatrix} = \begin{bmatrix} A_{11} & A_{12} \\ A_{21} & A_{22} \end{bmatrix} \begin{bmatrix} x_1 \\ x_2 \end{bmatrix} + \begin{bmatrix} y_1 \\ y_2 \end{bmatrix} \tag{5.26}$$

where A_{11} and A_{22} represent the economic system of regions 1 and 2 respectively; A_{21} represents the economic flows from region 2 into region 1; A_{12} represent the economic flows from region 1 into region 2; x_1 and x_2 define the total output of the endogenous accounts; and y_1 and y_2 define the exogenous accounts.

A predictive model can be developed by solving for $\begin{bmatrix} x_1 \\ x_2 \end{bmatrix}$ given by equation (5.27):

$$\begin{bmatrix} x_1 \\ x_2 \end{bmatrix} = \begin{bmatrix} I - A_{11} & - A_{12} \\ - A_{21} & I - A_{22} \end{bmatrix}^{-1} \cdot \begin{bmatrix} y_1 \\ y_2 \end{bmatrix} \tag{5.27}$$

However, the multiregional model given in equation (5.26) allows delineating intraregional effects from interregional effects by decomposing A into two matrices:

$$\begin{bmatrix} A_{11} & A_{12} \\ A_{21} & A_{22} \end{bmatrix} = \begin{bmatrix} A_{11} & 0 \\ 0 & A_{22} \end{bmatrix} + \begin{bmatrix} 0 & A_{12} \\ A_{21} & 0 \end{bmatrix} \tag{5.28}$$

Thus equation (5.26) can be re-written to reflect the intraregional and interregional effects:

$$\begin{bmatrix} x_1 \\ x_2 \end{bmatrix} = \begin{bmatrix} A_{11} & 0 \\ 0 & A_{22} \end{bmatrix} \cdot \begin{bmatrix} x_1 \\ x_2 \end{bmatrix} + \begin{bmatrix} 0 & A_{12} \\ A_{21} & 0 \end{bmatrix} \cdot \begin{bmatrix} x_1 \\ x_2 \end{bmatrix} + \begin{bmatrix} y_1 \\ y \end{bmatrix}$$

$$\begin{bmatrix} x_1 \\ x_2 \end{bmatrix} = A_1 \cdot \begin{bmatrix} x_1 \\ x_2 \end{bmatrix} + A_2 \cdot \begin{bmatrix} x_1 \\ x_2 \end{bmatrix} + \begin{bmatrix} y_1 \\ y \end{bmatrix} \tag{5.29}$$

Using the solution technique described by Stone (1985), equation (5.29) can be solved for $\begin{bmatrix} x_1 \\ x_2 \end{bmatrix}$:

$$\begin{bmatrix} x_x \\ x_2 \end{bmatrix} = \left[I - (I - A_1)^{-1} A_2 \right]^{-1} (I - A_1)^{-1} \begin{bmatrix} y_1 \\ y_2 \end{bmatrix}$$

$$\begin{bmatrix} x_x \\ x_2 \end{bmatrix} = \begin{bmatrix} I & -(I - A_{11})^{-1} A_{12} \\ -(I - A_{22})^{-1} A_{21} & I \end{bmatrix}^{-1}$$
$$\cdot \begin{bmatrix} (I - A_{11})^{-1} & 0 \\ 0 & (I - A_{22})^{-1} \end{bmatrix} \cdot \begin{bmatrix} y_1 \\ y_2 \end{bmatrix}$$

$$\begin{bmatrix} x_x \\ x_2 \end{bmatrix} = M_2 M_1 \begin{bmatrix} y_1 \\ y_2 \end{bmatrix} \tag{5.30}$$

where M_1 represents the intraregional multiplier matrix and shows the effect that result from linkages wholly within each region and M_2 is the interregional multiplier matrix and captures all the repercussions between regions. Matete and Hassan (2006) used this approach to develop a two-region model for evaluating inter-basin water transfers.

As with all the preceding analyses, an ecosystem model can be developed:

$$\begin{bmatrix} p_1 \\ p_2 \end{bmatrix} = \begin{bmatrix} P_{11} & 0 \\ 0 & P_{22} \end{bmatrix} \cdot M_2 M_1 \cdot \begin{bmatrix} y_1 \\ y_2 \end{bmatrix} \tag{5.31}$$

where P_{11} and P_{22} define the flows from the economic system into the ecosystem per dollar total expenditure. This approach could also be used to examine flows from the ecosystem into the economic system.

Other ecosystem-economic system approaches

There are other approaches to analyzing the interactions between the ecosystem and the economic system. We will very briefly highlight just a select few. Inoperability input output analysis examines the interconnectedness of critical infrastructures within a region's economy (e.g. Leung *et al.* 2007, Percoco 2006, Santos and Haimes 2004). This approach can be used to examine the impacts on consumers in addition to industries of a shortage of natural resources or a collapse of an economic sector due to an environmental accident. Constrained fixed price multiplier introduced into a SAM can relate levels of air pollutants with the social structure of an economy including health effects and cost of these effects (Resosudarmo and Thorbecke 1996). The ecosystem-economic system, I–O, SUT, and SAM models presented are classified as linear models. As such they can be formulated as a constrained linear optimization problem. A standard solution technique that can be employed to solve these types of constrained linear optimization problems is linear programming. Lowe (1979) and Luptáčik and Böhm (1994 and 1999) describe this approach to examining ecosystem-economic system interactions.

6 The accounting of sustainability in a SAM

Introduction

An ESAM provides a framework for describing the structure of an economy in terms of links between production, income distribution, and demand within a region's economy, and also provides a concise framework for synthesizing and displaying the data on a region's economy. Chapter 5 showed some frameworks that included linkages to the environment. Introducing not only the environment but also sustainability into an ESAM is an attempt to improve on past regional economic models. This chapter proposes models of how to account for sustainability in order to include it into an ESAM.

In order to build these models, forests are used as environmental accounts. Forests are a renewal resource and provide different environmental services, from timber to CO_2, sinks, and clean water. They can also be managed in different ways providing different market and non-market values. Forests can be used to understand different kinds of relationship between sustainable management of the resources, the environment, and the economy. This complexity provides an adequate example for building sustainable ESAM frameworks and defines basic premises to account for sustainability into the models.

Background

Daly (1968 and 1977), Victor (1972), and Isard (1968) described I–O models that include flows from the ecosystem to the economic flow and vice versa. Unfortunately, those models could not incorporate ecological functions as economical values but only as physical relationships. Kigyossy-Schmidt (1989) suggested a method for introducing environmental services into an I–O model. Leatherman and Marcouiller (1999a, 1999b, and 1996), Marcouiller (1998), Marcouiller and Deller (1997 and 1996), and Marcouiller *et al.* (1995) modified a SAM to examine how timber production impacts value-added and household income. These modified SAMs only capture the flow from the environment to the economy. Kim (1993) assessed sustainability issues for Mexico by incorporating environmental stock values of forest resources into a SAM. Atkinson (1996) modified a SAM to obtain a corrected measure of environmental income and Rodríguez Morilla *et al.* (2007) build a multisectorial model of economic and environmental performance, orientated to calculate the domestic social accounting matrix and environmental accounts (SAMEA) multipliers.

In this chapter an accounting system able to capture the flow from the environment to regional economy and the flow from the regional economy to the environment is presented. The first is accounted by considering the role of natural resources in the production, income distribution, consumption of goods and services, saving and investments, and trade. The second is done by considering the pollution produced by some economic activities and the restoring role of some others into the environment. An accounting system that puts together these two components can be used to introduce a concept of sustainability in an ESAM.

The ESAM is developed by expanding a SAM to include accounts specific to the forest in order to establish monetary links between the economic agents and the different kinds of profit and expenditures that come from a forest. The proposed ESAM incorporates the forest as a component in a larger model of how the economy and environment of areas interact. The ESAM entails adding extra rows and columns to the SAM, which capture the economic contributions of the forest's timber and, conversely, how economic activities affect the forest in general. ESAMs allow for investigating the strategies that would have the most impact on the forest or, alternatively, the changes in the forest base that would affect income from forest-based activities such as tourism or the lumber industry.

The general approach is to first build the SAM, second modify the structure of the SAM to assess impacts on household income due to changes in natural resource policy (Leatherman and Marcouiller 1996, 1999a and 1999b, Marcouiller 1998, Marcouiller and Deller 1997 and 1996, and Marcouiller *et al.* 1995), third make the modified SAM consistent with already existing frameworks for forest accounting (Vincent 1999, Van Dieren 1995, United Nations 2000), and fourth, include Hicksian income agroforestry economic accounting systems (Campos 1999a and 1999b, Campos *et al.* 2001, Caparrós *et al.* 2001a and 2001b).

This ESAM provides a framework to assess who gains and loses when reductions in the natural capital stock take place below a safe minimum standard. Sustainability is defined as a non-declining utility and a constant underlying capital stock (Pearce and Atkinson 1995). The concept of sustainability is introduced in the ESAM through the concepts of Hicksian income (Hicks 1946) and natural capital (Pearce and Turner 1990, Folke *et al.* 1994). The Hicksian total sustainable income of forestlands is defined as the monetary flow generated in the accounting period which, when totally spent within the period, leaves the agents at the end of the period with the same forestland economic wealth (capital) that they had at the beginning in real terms (Hicks 1946). Natural capital has life-support functions that are not produced by man-made capital such as the maintenance of the stock of biological resources. Environmental or ecological services that provide a wide range of ecosystem processes and functions are the flows that result from natural capital (Folke *et al.* 1994). These flows when sustainable are accounted for as Hicksian income.

ESAM accounting framework premises

In order to study the effects of the forest on the economic system and vice versa, these effects are introduced as endogenous and exogenous components in a SAM. In order to provide a system for valuing forests compatible with the SAM framework, forests are assessed according to six fundamental premises.

First premise

Sustainability can be described in biophysical and economic terms but translating between them can be problematic. We will define sustainability in economic terms. The notion of sustainability generally includes the concept that the stock of renewable resources should not decline over time (Prato 1998; Pearce and Turner 1990). If a resource is over-exploited or the assimilative capacity of an ecosystem is overwhelmed, the stock of renewable resources is depleted. Consequently, given a non-declining renewable resource stock, the annual growth rate or the annual assimilative capacity rate defines the maximum rate at which a renewable resource can be sustainably harvested or a pollutant can be put into the ecosystem in a sustainable manner (Prato 1998; Pearce and Turner 1990). However, resources not used in one year may be used in other years; resources overexploited in one year can be restored using other natural or man-made resources either in the present year or future years. This sustainability can have different interpretations. The notion of "strong sustainability" is that harvest (physical units) must be less than or equal to growth (physical units). A strong sustainability condition would require that some natural assets be held constant or increasing:

$$dK_N/dt \geq 0 \tag{6.1}$$

where, natural capital, K_N, is defined as the stock of environmental resources (Pearce and Turner 1990). If biophysical values or quantity are multiplied by constant prices, sustainability can be described in economic terms and a "weak sustainability" rule can be applied: some substitution is possible between certain elements of natural and man-made capital. Man-made capital, K_M, includes machines, buildings, and roads. A weak sustainability rule assumes a constant capital rule. The value of the net change in the total capital must be greater than or equal to zero:

$$dK/dt = d(K_M + K_N)/dt \geq 0 \text{ where } K = f(K_M + K_N) \tag{6.2}$$

We will define sustainability using equation (6.2). Turning physical values into economic ones is problematic when the constant price assumption is not reasonable. In most cases, physical growth can be different than the economic value of growth and the physical removals can be different than the economic value of the removals because prices associated with the growth are normally different than the price associated with the removals. For example, a cubic meter of growth in older trees generally has a greater economic value than a cubic meter of growth in younger trees as older trees are generally more economically valuable than younger trees. Thus the economic value of a cubic meter of growth is relative not absolute. A similar argument can be made for a cubic meter of removals. Thus the economic value of the growth could be less than the economic value of the removals and the physical growth could be greater than the physical removals or vice versa. When building an ESAM that accounts for sustainability, strong or weak sustainability conditions must be carefully defined. For instance, if resources values are defined in economic terms in order to apply a weak sustainability condition that allows substitution between natural and man-made capital, specific restrictions must be presented. The simplest example is to consider prices as a constant for growth and removals. More sophisticated accounting systems can be used also in an ESAM. For example, the agroforestry accounting system developed by Campos

(1999a and 1999b), Campos *et al.* (2001) or Caparrós *et al.* (2001a and 2001b), based on the European Framework for Integrated Environmental and Economic Accounting for Forests (IEEAF), could be a framework for more complex ESAM models. Also other authors such as Bergen (1999 and 2001), Campos (1999a and 1999b), Kriström (1999a, 1999b) Skanberg and Kriström (2001), Merlo and Jöbstl (1999), Merlo and Boschetti (2001), Nordhaus and Kokkelenberg (1999), Peyron (1998), Vanoli (1998), and Vincent (1999) have developed several methodologies to include market and non-market economic values into a single accounting framework.

Second premise

The biophysical concept of sustainability can be described using the Pearce and Atkinson (1995) concept of environmental stock and the concept of Hicksian income. A sustainable ecosystem is analogous to a bank that gives yearly dividends to its costumers unless they deplete their capital. Capital is defined as the land and the forest. Hicksian income for timber is equal to the economic value of the annual growth, G, of the forest. Removals, R, are defined as the economic value of the harvest. If $G = R$, then the forest is harvested at the sustainable level and the natural income that forests provide are non-decreasing with the time. If $G > R$, then the forest is harvested at less than the sustainable level and the residual $(G - R)$ is an addition to future income. If $G < R$, then the harvest is not sustainable and the residual $(R - G)$ is a reduction of natural capital.

Third premise

The penalty for $G < R$ is defined as the cost of restoring the land and forest to pre-harvest conditions plus the profits the forest would have generated had there been no damage. If $G \geq R$, the penalty costs are zero. However, if $G < R$, the penalty costs increase as the G/R ratio decreases. The first part of this premise is consistent with the concept of environmental capacity proposed by United Nations (2000). Restoration costs can be divided into four steps according to the "damage valuation" concept defined by the United Nations (2000). This concept is based on the ability to reach sustainable targets through assessing the damage caused by current or past activities measuring them by steps defined as "distances" (United Nations 2000). The second can be established with annuity formulas for forestry incomes discounted to present accounting year equivalents. Because the forest is a dynamic system, it will be necessary to review the state of the forest each time the penalty is estimated. Given that SAMs are time invariant, building a new SAM is required for each time period. Penalty costs will decrease if the forest tends to regenerate by itself or will increase if the forest tends to degenerate. This concept of a penalty cost is similar to the definition of a replacement cost discussed by Prato (1998).

Fourth premise

The economic value of the timber resource will be divided into Hicksian income and natural capital accounts. The forest resources accounts will be divided into market and non-market accounts. Commercial Hicksian income is the market value of the Hicksian income from the timber resource. Non-market Hicksian income is the non-market part of the Hicksian income from timber resource. Natural commercial stock is the market value of the natural capital. Non-market natural capital is the non-market natural capital not included in the natural commercial stock. Natural Hicksian income and natural commercial stock subaccounts are commercial flows that are disaggregated in the SAM model. Non-market Hicksian income and non-market natural capital are subaccounts added to the receipts and expenditures of a SAM. These accounts make possible to introduce concepts such as net domestic product (NDP) or environmental net product (ENP) into the ESAM. Although these concepts have been proposed for a SAM (Atkinson 1996) and a forestry accounting system (Vincent 1999), both concepts have not been included in the same accounting system.

Fifth premise

Land and the forest will be considered as factors of production owned by the institutions when identified as receipts. Land and the forest will be considered as flows from institutions to activities or institutions that do the restoration when identified as expenditures. Institutions that own the resources and those that restore them do not have to be the same. Market accounts are already registered in the SAM. Non-market subaccounts are added in order to keep the SAM structure in the ESAM.

Figure 6.1 describes the circular flow of the economy and the interactions with the forest resource proposed in the model. Solid lines represent market flows accounted in traditional SAM models and represent the direction of the money flow, $, where markets or transactions exist. Arrows represent non-market flows between forests and

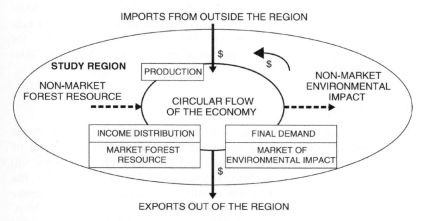

Figure 6.1 Circular flow of the economy inside an ecosystem

society. Dashed lines represent a SAM non-accounted flow of wealth. Non-market forest resources account for the wealth provided by forests and which is not accounted for in the circular flow of the economy. Non-market environmental impact accounts for the wealth lost and not accounted for in the circular flow.

Sixth premise

Sustainability defined by Prato (1998) and Pearce and Turner (1990) implies that future generations will have the ability to fulfill their needs as well as the present generation. Regional economic flows to measure this can go beyond the regional economic time-constricted scope of a SAM. In order to incorporate the sustainability target in the proposed accounting system, we will assume that the rest of the "environmental debt" up to the sustainable target not accounted for or not even suffered by the present and local inhabitants of the region must be assigned to the rest of the world account.

In order to include the concept of sustainability in the ESAM, we will assume that foreign institutions would suffer and therefore would be willing to pay to restore nature to its sustainable level for the equivalent amount of money not accounted for by local activities and institutions. Among foreign institutions, theoretically willingness to pay off future generations discounted to its net present value could also be included. In fact, this premise is equivalent to assuming that future generations would suffer the cost of "insustainability", the amount of money that they would be willing to pay is exactly equal to the difference between the "sustainability target" and the present and local generation "environmental debt." This premise makes the ESAM natural column account consistent with the "environmental capacity" for an accounting period concept proposed by the United Nations (2000) and the ESAM third premise.

ESAM example

In order to provide a framework where the relationships between the forest and economy can be described in monetary terms instead of physical units, the Hicksian income and natural capital concepts will be added to the SAM as additional rows and columns. In Table 3.1, the factors row will be broken down into commercial Hicksian income (CHI), natural commercial stock (NCS), and rest of factors. Non-market Hicksian income (NMHI) and non-market natural capital (NMNC) rows will be added to Table 3.1. Institutions column will be broken down into commercial Hicksian income (CHI), natural commercial stock (NCS), and rest of institutions. Also, non-market Hicksian income (NMHI) and non-market natural capital (NMNC) columns will be added to Table 3.1. Table 6.1 illustrates the proposed ESAM.

The Hicksian income rows describe the total sustainable income available. The commercial and non-commercial values of the Hicksian income are the values of the annual growth. Forests are owned by local institutions, but timber from those forests can be harvested by local firms, local institutions, or foreign companies. The ESAM could also account for other market and non-market income such as mushrooms or firewood. Non-market valuation techniques can provide estimations of those values. Campos (1999a) provides a system to integrate them into Hicksian income. However, accounting for non-market values is beyond the scope of this book.

The natural capital rows account for the ecological use value of the land and forest. Reductions in natural capital can occur due to harvesting more than growth. This reduction can be used locally by industries or institutions or can also be exported. Increases in natural capital can generate additions to future incomes or to the stock of natural capital. These additions can be accounted for as income or capital.

The Hicksian income column is divided into two subaccounts. CHI accounts for the investments made in the forest over the sustainable level. NMHI accounts for economic losses due to harvesting more than growth or gains due to harvesting less than growth. The natural capital column is divided into two subaccounts. The NMNC column describes additions or reductions to the land and forest. Additions are accounted for as "environmental debt", according to the definitions by the United Nations (2000) as stated in the third premise. In the ESAM, "environmental debt" is a measure of the environmental damage suffered. Loss of wealth corresponding to decrease of sustainability harvest level can be suffered by local institutions or activities according to the third premise or by the "rest of the world" according to the sixth premise.

Damage reductions can occur due to investing by activities, harvesting less than growth, investing or subsidizes by foreign institutions. These are accounted for in the submatrix "investments in natural capital" and are the monies institutions pay to local activities for restoration. This is the reason why the intersection between CHI and NCS columns and institutions row is zero. Institutions can also invest in natural capital outside the market through direct actions. These actions, such as reforestations or voluntary activities, are accounted for as "non-market investments in natural capital", and they must not be accounted as part of the circular flow of the economy. This is due to the fact that they are made for free and, therefore, they do not reflect any movement of money.

Industries invest in natural capital; for example, silvicultural activities such as site preparation, planting, thinning, or a regeneration harvest. The costs of the intermediate and primary factors of production of these examples are accounted for in SIC 08 (Forestry) and SIC 2411 (Logging). These are man-made capital activities and therefore are accounted for in the interindustry submatrix accounts and are not accounted for in any of the "sustainable harvest" submatrices (such as "sustainable harvest to activities" or "sustainable harvest to institutions" in the Hicksian income row). These submatrices only capture the value of the flow that results from natural capital (Folke *et al.* 1994) and not the change in value of the forest as a result of the silvicultural activities. Industries can also behave as final demand institutions as far as they represent a social demand of environmental need by making money transfers for nature restoration, for example, to non-governmental organizations. This can be done by having industries pay themselves for nature restoration or improvements. This payment is registered into a fictitious "institutions" row account. This "institution account" spends this money in natural capital restoration as it is described through an extra column inside of NCS (institutions and activities account) in order to keep the SAM double-entry book structure.

Table 6.2 illustrates how to estimate the Hicksian income and natural capital rows and column according to the growth and removals of timber.

Table 6.1 The proposed ESAM accounting framework

Receipts	Expenditures							
	Activities	Factors	Institutions	Hicksian income		Natural capital		Exports	Total
				CHI (institutions/ activities account)	NMHI	NCS (institutions/ activities account)	NMNC		
Activities	Interindustry transactions	0	Final demand	Forest improvement investments	Future income lost for activities	Investment in natural capital by activities	Environmental debt from activities	Activity exports	Total industry output
Factors	Value added	0	0	0	0	0	0	Factor exports	Total factor income
Institutions	Sales and taxes	Distribution	Transfers	0	Future income lost for institutions	0	Environmental debt from institutions	Institutional exports	Total institutional income
Hicksian income — CHI (factors account)	Sustainable harvest to activities	0	Sustainable harvests to institutions	0	0	0	0	Sustainable harvest to exports	Total commercial Hicksian income
Hicksian income — NMHI	Non-market profits from harvest to activities	0	Non-market profits from forests to institutions	0	Additions to future incomes from non harvested forests	0	0	Non-market profits from harvest to exports	Total non-commercial Hicksian income

Natural capital	NCS (factors account)	Non-sustainable commercial forest profits to activities	0	Non-sustainable commercial forest profits to institutions	0	0	0	0	Non-sustainable commercial forest profits	Total commercial natural capital
Natural capital	NMNC	Non-commercial stock reductions (activities)	0	Non-commercial stock reductions (institutions)	0	Additions/subtractions to future incomes	(Non-market investments in natural capital)	Additions/subtraction to natural capital		Total non-commercial natural capital
Imports		Activity imports	Factor imports	Institution imports	Forest improvement investments (rest of world)	Future income lost for the rest of the world	Inv. in natural capital by the rest of the world	Environmental debt (up to sustainability target)	Transshipments	Total imports
Total		Total activity outlay	Total factor outlay	Total institution outlay	Total forest improvement investments	Future incomes balance	Total inv. in natural capital	Natural capital damage balance	Total exports	

Table 6.2 SAM including the Hicksian income and natural capital

Column groups under **Expenditures**: *SAM accounts*; *Hicksian income* (CHI, NMHI); *Natural capital* (NCS, NMNC); *Total* (SAM, SAM (+ non market values)).

Receipts	SAM accounts	CHI	NMHI	NCS	NMNC	SAM	SAM (+ non market values)
SAM accounts — Activities	S'	If G ≥ R, then I = 0; If G < R, then I = 0	If G ≥ R then $f(G/R)$ = 0; If G < R, then $f_i(G/R)$ < 0	If G ≥ R, then I = 0; If G < R, then I ≥ 0	If G ≥ R then $f(G/R)$ = 0; If G < R, then $f_c(G/R)$ < 0	X^{DT} + I	X^{DT} + I
Factors						X^{DT} + I	X^{DT} + I − $f_r(G/R)$
Institutions	If G ≥ R, then R; If G < R, then G	0				**R**	**R**
Import/export						**G**	**G**
Hicksian income — CHI						**0**	**G − R**
NMHI			If G ≥ R, then (G − R); If G < R, then 0			**0**	**0**
Natural capital — NCS	If G ≥ R, then 0; If R < G, then (R − G)					**0**	**0**
NMNC		If G ≥ R, then (I_{nm}); If G < R, then 0	If G ≥ R, then T_1; If G < R, then 0	If G ≥ R, then 0; If G < R, then (I_{nm})	If G ≥ R, then T_2; If G < R, then 0	**R − G**	**R − G**
Total — SAM	X^{ST} + R	I	0	0	0		**0**
SAM (+ non market values) (If G ≥ R and if G < R)	X^{ST} + R; X^{ST} + G	I + I_{nm}; 0	G − R + T_1 − $f_i(G/R)$	0; I + I_{nm}	T_2; −$f_c(G/R)$	**0**	**T_1 + T_2 + I_{nm}** / **I_{nm}**

Notes: G = value of the annual growth. R = value of the timber harvest. I = investment in land and forest. T_1 and T_2 silvicultural assigned values of non-harvested stock that becomes yield in the next harvest. I_{nm} non-market natural capital investments made by institutions. X^{ST} and X^{DT} are total receipt and expenditures SAM values. $f_c(G/R)$ is the environmental debt or penalty cost and $f_i(G/R)$ the future income lost function. $f_r(G/R) = f_c(G/R)−$

In the ESAM shown in Table 6.2, light grey shows market values, and dark grey shows non-market values. Matrices with no shading show original SAM values with natural resources substracted (they are now accounted for in the new ESAM rows and columns). When SAM values and non-market values (light grey matrices in Table 6.2) are considered, total row and column vectors are allocated slightly different than on the original SAM. The disaggregation of market values of investment in land and forest and the value of the timber harvest allow these final values to be allocated into the new Hicksian income and natural capital accounts. In this case, the vector of total sum of the columns of the SAM is equal to the total ESAM column sum vector, and the sum of total receipts is equal to the sum of total expenditures in both models. When non-market values are included (dark grey matrices in Table 6.2), differences from a SAM start to appear and the total sum of column and row vectors of the ESAM become different than the SAM values. This is due to the fact that non-market values are new elements that are not included in a traditional SAM. It also means that the new ESAM that we are building cannot be considered as a SAM, but a SAM with satellite accounts.

To illustrate these calculations, we will assume initially that the forests are owned locally. As can be seen in Table 6.3, the estimate of each submatrix depends on growth relative to removal. The intersection of the SAM accounts column and the Hicksian income and natural capital rows define the value of the timber harvest. If $G \geq R$, then the harvest value is $R = R + 0$.

The intersection of the Hicksian income row and the Hicksian income column can define natural additions to future incomes from non-harvested forests. If $G \geq R$, then $(G - R)$ defines the natural additions to natural capital. If $G < R$, then there are no natural additions to future Hicksian incomes. The intersection of the natural capital row and the Hicksian income and natural capital columns defines the growth of the forest. If $G \geq R$, then T_1 and T_2 define the natural additions to future sustainable incomes (T_1) and to natural capital (T_2) according to the silvicultural model prescribed. T_1 and T_2 will be greater than zero except if natural disasters (such as a fire) happen. If $G < R$, then there are no natural additions to natural capital or income. In this case, natural disasters should be accounted by f_c and $f_i(G/R)$ functions.

The intersection of the SAM accounts row and the natural capital column defines investments in natural capital and income; denoted as "I", this can occur regardless of harvest level. If $G \geq R$, then investments are made over the sustainable level and are accounted for as increases in income. If $G < R$, then investments are accounted for as natural capital. If $G \geq R$, the environmental debt $f(G/R) = 0$. If $G < R$, the environmental debts $f(G/R) < 0$. The natural capital column defines the state of improvement, conservation, or depreciation of the value of the natural resources. This number defines the nature state index (NSI). If $G \geq R$, then $NSI = T_2$. This implies that, if there are no natural disasters, $NSI \geq 0$ and it reflects a non-declining renewable resource stock and indicates that the economic flow is based on a sustainable management. If $G < R$, then $NSI = I + I_{nm} - f(G/R) < 0$. If $I \geq f(G/R)$, then $NSI \geq 0$. However, if $I < f(G/R)$, then $NSI < 0$ and reflects a decline in the renewable resource stock. The NSI provides an estimation of the non-sustainability of the region under the current management regime. Natural capital column plus Hicksian income define the state of capitalization of a forest. This number defines the nature state capitalization (NSC). If $G \geq R$, then $NSC = I + I_{nm} + G - R + T_1 + T_2$. This implies $NSI \geq 0$ and it reflects an increasing capitalization of the forest resource. It also indicates that the economic flow, based on a sustainable management can provide increasing incomes in the future.

If $f_c(G/R)$ is defined as the environmental debt or penalty cost and $f_i(G/R)$ as the future income lost function, then:

$$f_T(G/R) = f_c(G/R) + f_i(G/R) \tag{6.3}$$

If $G < R$, then $NSC = I + I_{nm} - f_i(G/R) - f_c(G/R) < 0$. If $I_T \geq f_T(G/R)$, then $NSC \geq 0$. However if $I_T < f_T(G/R)$, then $NSC < 0$ and it reflects a decline in the future wealth. The NSC provides an estimation of the state of future economic flows from the resources to the region under the current management regime.

According to Table 3.1, vector x_r^{sT} ($r = 1$ to 4) can be understood as the total expenditure vector of the SAM and x_r^d as the total receipt vector.

Let us define X^{ST} as a number made of the total sum of the elements of the x_r^{sT} row vectors made of the column sum of all SAM expenditures:

$$X^{ST} = \sum_{r=1}^{4} \sum_{k=1}^{4} \sum_i \left(S_{kr} \right)_{ij} \tag{6.4}$$

And let us define X^{DT} as a number made of the total sum of the elements of the x_r^d column vectors made of the row sum of all SAM receipts:

$$X^{DT} = \sum_{R=1}^{4} \sum_{g=1}^{4} \sum_j \left(S_{rg} \right)_{ij} \tag{6.5}$$

By definition to balance, expenditures must equal receipts in a SAM ($x^{sT}_r = x^d_r$), therefore X^{DT} equals XST.

Let us define X'^{ST} and X'^{DT} as X^{ST} and X^{DT} minus the values that will be included in the Hicksian income and natural capital new accounts (expenditures and receipts) or the final total receipt and expenditures value of the SAM included into an ESAM.

Hicksian income and natural capital values are divided into market and non-market values. If only market values are considered, in the ESAM proposed (Table 6.11) then $X^{ST} = (X'^{ST} + R)$ and $X = (X'^{DT}) + I$ and:

$$(X'^{ST} + R) + I = (X'^{DT} + I) + R \text{ for } G \geq R \tag{6.6}$$

$$(X'^{ST'} + R) + I = (X'^{DT} + I) + G + R - G \text{ for } G < R \tag{6.7}$$

This condition is feasible only if X' had already discounted R from a factor row and I from an institutions column. But this is not the case when non-market values are included.

If an ESAM includes the satellite non-market total accounts values individual accounts may not balance, while the total expenditures will equal total receipts:

$$(X'^{ST} + R) + (I + I_{NM}) + (G - R + T_1) + T_2$$
$$= (X'^{DT} + I) + R + (G - R) + T_1 + T_2 + I_{NM}, \text{ for } G \geq R \tag{6.8}$$

and

$$X'^{ST} + G - f_i(G/R) + I + I_{NM} - f_C(G/R)$$
$$= X'^{DT} + I - f_T(G/R) + G + R - G + I_{NM}, \text{ for } G < R \tag{6.8}$$

The intersection of the SAM accounts row and the non-market natural capital column defines the "environmental debt" matrices. The intersection of the SAM accounts column with the natural capital row defines the "non-sustainable commercial forest profits" (NSCFP) and "non-commercial stock reductions" (NCRS) matrices. These matrices accounts for receipts or expenditures made by activities, institutions, and rest of the world. Comparing these row and column matrices, it can be assessed who gains and who loses when natural resources are unsustainably managed. This information can be a useful tool for policy makers in order to establish fair distributions for abating costs of environmental damages. For example, if the intersection of the activities column and the value of NSCFP + NCSR is greater than the intersection between environmental debt and institutions, policy makers could suggest industries that use unsustainable management compensate institutions for the damage suffered through added taxes to pay for restoration costs.

Up to this point, only the timber produced in a forest has been considered. However, forests can provide other goods or services. In many areas, forests are the basis of the tourism industry. As far as hikers prefer to walk in a forest rather than in a clear-cut area, or the scenic value of a view changes with the silvicultural treatment, it seems that both uses are at some point incompatible for the same areas. In addition, forests also have an important role as pollution sinks: they provide a "cleaning service" by converting the CO_2 into fixed carbon at the same time that they release O_2. The economic values of those functions could also be included in the model by creating new Hicksian income and natural capital rows and columns. Different techniques could be used in order to estimate the value that a forest has for tourism or for cleaning the atmosphere. This value could be included in the model. These estimations are beyond the scope of this simple example. Finally, the ESAM has been developed for timber only; other renewable resources could use this same model.

Numerical example

Consider a forest managed to produce an annual growth of 5 cubic meters/year. The owner decides to cut 5.5 cubic meters. Given a price of $1.00/cubic meter, he or she will have $5.50 of revenue. The penalty cost of over harvesting 0.5 cubic meters is $0.70. Finally, the money spent on restoration (MSR) is $0.40 dollars. In this example, the G < R (5 < 5.5). Table 6.3 illustrates the example.

The intersection of the SAM accounts column and the Hicksian income and inventory column equals 5.5 and defines the flow from ecosystem to the economy system. The NSI = NSC = 0.4 – 0.7 = – 0.3. This indicates a non-sustainable renewable resource use based on economic flow and, therefore, it indicates a potential problem in the regional economy. Comparing NMNC + NCS rows with NMNC column it can be appreciated how over harvesting has profited 0.5 while some sectors have suffered from that 0.7 over-cut. Based on this information, policy makers could establish fair environmental compensations among different sectors.

Now assume a harvest of 4.2 cubic meters, which implies additions to natural capital of 0.8 cubic meters. In this case, G ≥ R and an NSI = 0.8

Table 6.3 Example of ESAM accounting

Receipts		Expenditures					
		SAM accounts	Hicksian income		Natural inventory		Total
							SAM	SAM
			CHI	NMHI	NCS	NMNC	SAM	+ (NMV)
SAM accounts		S'			0.4	−0.7	S' + 0.4	S − 0.3
Hicksian income	CHI	5.0					5	5
	NMHI							
Natural capital	NCS	0.5					0.5	0.5
	NMNC							
Total SAM + (NMV)	SAM	S' + 5.5		0.4		0		
		S + '5.5		0.4		0.7		

Note: NMV = non-market values.

and NSC = 1.2. This indicates a sustainable renewable resource use based on economic flow and an increasing capitalization of the forest resource.

Gross and net regional product

Closely related to a SAM are the national or regional income and production accounts. Various techniques have been described to include the use and non-use values of renewable and non-renewable resources in these accounts (Prato 1998). These changes allow gross regional product (GRP) and net regional product (NRP) to reflect these use and non-use values. Vincent (1999) provides a framework for including forestry-related adjustments to the national income accounts. This framework is internally consistent and theoretically sound while it simultaneously avoids double-counting and other problems. Vincent develops a Hamiltonian equation using six state equations—two address the depreciation of human-made capital; two are concerned with the net value of converting land from forestry to other uses; one relates growth to removals; and one addresses the capacity of the forest environment to assimilate pollution. The state equations are described as the first derivative of each state with respect to time.

Vincent (1999) defines an adjusted NRP as GRP plus non-market values associated with the forest minus depreciation of human-made capital plus net accumulations of natural capital. Net accumulation of natural capital is defined as the net value of land conversions plus growth minus harvest plus the value of the assimilative capacity of the forest (Vincent 1999). The ESAM illustrated in Tables 6.11 and 6.12 describe a methodology of incorporating the relationship between growth and harvest that is consistent with Vincent (1999). Non-market values associated with the forest are defined in the "non-commercial stock reductions" and "non-market profits from harvest" matrices. Growth minus harvest is also defined in the ESAM. The NSC is an equivalent concept to Vincent's definition of the net accumulation of natural forest capital within a region. NSC can be used to adjust GRP to reflect the sustainable harvest of a forest. Net timber regional product (NTRP) will be defined for the ESAM as NTRP = GRP + NSC. It is a first approximation of NRP. This is a first step in modifying a SAM to better reflect the links between a forest and a regional economy. Other values related to the assimilative capacity of the forest or the net value of converting land from forestry to other uses should be added as extra rows and columns to the ESAM in order to account for all of Vincent's values. Also, to calculate the adjusted NRP as defined by Vincent, depreciation of human-made capital accounts should be added as a satellite account to the ESAM.

Building environmental SAMs

Once sustainability accounts have been described, they must be integrated into an ESAM. Four different forms of the ESAM can be used to illustrate different points. The ESAMs must be based on three fundamental premises:

1   Environmental resources provide goods and services as primary factors of productions to industries and to institutions.
2   The profits of those factors of production are distributed among the institutions.
3   Institutions pay the restoration costs.

According to these premises, the environmental economic paradigm can be described as follows (Figure 6.2).

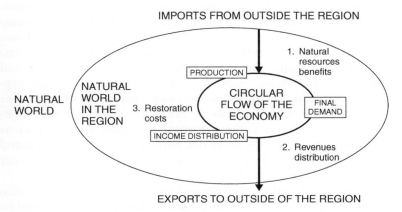

Figure 6.2 Environmental and economic paradigm.

The circular flow of this environmental economic model is similar to a closed circular flow considered in a SAM model: production to value added to income distribution among institutions and finally back to production. Consequently, there are three steps:

1   *Flow from industries to factors of production*: nature provides good and services to industries and institutions. Those good and services are paid as factors of production by the industries and institutions.
2   *Flow from factors of production to institutions*: the revenues from the factors of production can be distributed among their owners: low-, medium-, and high-income households for example, and enterprises and government agencies.
3   *Flow from institutions to the production sector*: the institutions make investments in restoration—or should do so—in order to keep the system producing in a sustainable manner. The restoration costs are paid to the restoration firms and government agencies.

ESAM Form 1

The ESAM Form 1 disaggregates some of the basic SAM accounts into environmental and non-environmental accounts. The following accounts are disaggregated:

1   *Factors of production*: for each renewable resource used, a "natural dividend" and "natural inventory" row and column are added. Natural dividend and natural inventory factor of production rows

enumerate the services provided to industries and the government. Natural dividend and inventory factor of production columns enumerate how the revenues are distributed among the institutions.

2   *Institutions*: each institution (e.g. households and governments) includes a "natural inventory" and "natural dividends" row and column. Institutional natural dividend columns define the payments made in the restoration processes. They can be interpreted as the environmental liabilities of firms, governments, and households. Institutional natural inventory columns define additions to inventory from resources not harvested. Institutional natural inventory and dividend rows define the subsidies received in order to increase or improve the state of the renewable resources.

3   *Industry*: restoration firms should be separated from the "retail and services account." Also governmental agencies dedicated to restoration should be separated from the account "government production."

The resulting ESAM Form 1 is reflected in Table 6.4.

The ESAM Form 1 can be used to accurately identify all the economic flows that deal with the environment, to describe industries' dependence on renewable resources, to determine who profits and who pays from renewable resources benefits and receipts, and to account for the environmental taxes and subsidies. It can also determine the part of the GRP that depends directly on renewable resources as well as how this dependence takes place.

ESAM Form 2

The ESAM Form 2 is developed by isolating some of the environmental accounts and aggregating other non-environmentally relevant accounts. Isolating the accounts dealing directly with the use and state of renewable resources is given below:

1   *Factors of production*: all the "natural dividends" rows and "natural inventory" rows of the different renewable resources can be aggregated into two single accounts. These accounts reflect the total sustainable and non-sustainable value of the renewable resources provided to industries. "Natural dividend" and "natural inventory" columns are aggregated with the rest of non-environmental factor of productions.

2   *Institutions*: "natural dividend" rows and "natural inventory" rows are added to the natural inventory and dividend rows from the

Table 6.4 ESAM Form 1

			EXPENDITURES									
			Industry production			Factors of production			Institutions			Rest of the world
			Restoration agencies	Restoration industries	Other accounts	Natural dividend	Natural inventory	Other factors	Natural dividend	Natural inventory	Other	
RECEIPTS	Industry production	Restoration agencies										
		Restoration industries										
		Other accounts										
	Factors of production	Other factors										
		Natural inventory										
		Natural dividend										
	Institutions	Other liabilities										
		Natural inventory										
		Natural dividend										
	Rest of the world											

factors of production accounts. Revenues from the renewable resources sold to industries and subsidies received for improving renewable resource quality are included in the same rows. "Natural dividend" columns of the different renewable resources are aggregated into a single account. This account reflects the total investments made by industries in restoration. "Natural inventory" columns of the different renewable resources are also aggregated into a single account. This account defines the restoration cost that should be made. The column sum of the natural inventory and natural dividend defines the NSI.

3 *Industry*: restoration firms are aggregated with the "retail and services" account. Also governmental agencies dedicated to restoration are aggregated with the "government production" account.

Table 6.5 shows the resulting ESAM Form 2. Only subaccounts that deal directly with the management and restoration of renewable resources are enumerated. The resulting natural resource accounts are the "natural dividend" and "natural inventory" rows and column.

These natural resource accounts could be further disaggregated into several subaccounts that considered each renewable resource—for example forests or rivers etc.—or aspects of those resources, the tourist, timber, or aesthetic functions of a forest. In that case, such as both natural dividend and natural inventory should also be defined for each resource.

Table 6.6 shows the definitions for each of the submatrices of the ESAM Form 2.

The ESAM Form 2 includes two submatrices not explicitly considered in the model of Table 6.4. The intersection of institutions and nature accounts allows for enumerating the environmental taxes used

Table 6.5 ESAM Form 2

		EXPENDITURES					
		Industry production	Factors of production	Institutions	Nature		Rest of the world
					Natural inventory	Natural dividend	
RECEIPTS	Industry production						
	Factors of production						
	Institutions						
	Nature — Natural inventory						
	Natural dividend						
	Rest of the world						

Table 6.6 ESAM Form 2 including the definitions for each of the submatrices

		EXPENDITURES					
		Industries	Factors of production	Institutions	Nature	Exports	Total
RECEIPTS	Industries	*Industry production*		*Institutions consumption*	*Replacement costs* S_{1n}		
	Factors of production	*Purchases by industries*					
	Institutions		*Distribution of value added among households*		*Replacement costs (environmental taxes)* S_{3n}		
	Nature	*Natural resources and services* S_{n1}		*Nature resources and services (environmental subsidies)* S_{n3}	*Value of the ecosystem flows* S_{nn}	S_{n4}	s_n
	Imports				S_{4n}		
	Total				$s^T_n = NSI$		

for restoration purposes and subsidies for the protection and improvement of renewable resources.

Description of the ESAM Form 2 submatrices

The nature submatrices defined in the ESAM are:

Natural resources provided to industries submatrix (S_{n1}): this submatrix defines the flow from nature to industries, or the value of the renewable resources used by industries. For each renewable resource, the natural dividend row represents the value of the sustainable part of the harvest. Natural inventory rows represent the value of the non-sustainable part of the harvest. Natural dividend plus natural inventory represents the total value of the harvest.

Natural resources subsidies provided to institutions submatrix (S_{n3}): this submatrix defines the flow of subsidies. It accounts for the preservation or improvement of renewable resources by governments or other institutions.

Natural resources export submatrix (S_{n4}): this submatrix defines the flow from the nature resource accounts to exports or the value of the nature removed and sold outside of the region to foreign industries or agents. Natural dividend, inventory, and capital rows define the sustainable or non-sustainable levels of harvesting. It enumerates the flow of funds paid by foreign agencies to improve and preserve renewable resources.

Natural resources industry investments submatrix (S_{1n}): this submatrix defines the flow from industries to the nature resource accounts. It contains the MSR by the institutions that own the renewable resources. This money is received by the restoration agencies or industries. Each element of the submatrix represents "receipts" from each industry to nature.

Natural resources institutions investments submatrix (S_{3n}): this submatrix defines the flow of taxes that are used for restoration processes. It accounts for the money paid as environmental taxes from institutions to the government.

Natural resources foreign investments submatrix (S_{4n}): this submatrix defines the flow from foreign industries to nature resource accounts. It contains the MSR processes by the institutions that own the resources to foreign restoration agencies or industries. Each element of the submatrix represents "receipts" from foreign industries to nature.

Natural resources transfer submatrix (S_{nn}): this submatrix represents the value of the flow among different elements and uses of renewable resources. For each resource, the intersection between its natural inventory column and the natural dividend column represents the values of the renewable resources not removed or used in the present year that contribute to the sustainability of the system by leaving them for future years. This is denoted by a positive number. The intersection between the natural inventory column and the natural inventory row represents the replacement costs of the resources removed that exceed the sustainable level. This is denoted by a negative number. The intersection between natural dividend column and natural dividend and inventory columns enumerates the economic value of the natural growth or decay of the renewable resources. The intersection between the natural dividends and inventory of different resources can account for the value of the alternative uses of a natural resource. A forest used in past years for harvesting and used in the present as a tourist attraction will decrease its inventory and dividend as a provider of timber but will increase these accounts as a provider of amenity values.

Total natural resources provided by nature (S_n): this column vector represents the row sum of natural dividends and natural inventory values of each resource or from each use of the resource considered.

Total natural resource index (S^T_n): this row vector represents the column sum of natural dividends and natural inventory values of each resource considered. S^T_n defines the NSI for each resource. S^T_n does not have to equal S_n. If the sustainable harvest level is not exceeded, investments in the renewable resource are not needed. If the sustainable harvest level is exceeded, the replacement cost functions and the investments can have different values from those provided by the use of the resource.

ESAM Form 3

An ESAM Form 3 is built in order to estimate multipliers. An ESAM Form 3 is built using the ESAM Form 2 by eliminating the addition to the natural inventory column and aggregating the natural inventory and natural dividend rows.

I–O models are constructed with observed data from a particular economic area. Those data are the monetary flows or products from each of the sectors (Miller and Blair 1985); therefore, accounts that do not describe actual monetary flows – such as willingness to pay – should be excluded. As the natural inventory column includes subtractions and additions to the natural inventory that are not considered in the actual economic flow, this column is to be excluded in the ESAM Form 3. Only the natural dividend column is accounted for.

On the other hand, both natural inventory columns and rows estimate inputs from nature to the economy. The distinction between inventory and dividend does not provide any relevant information to the economic flow because once the resources are harvested, both sustainable and non-sustainable parts of it are equally consumed. Therefore, the rows can be aggregated into a single row. The resulting natural resource subaccount includes the natural dividend and inventory rows.

By doing these two steps, a square matrix is obtained and the multipliers can be found by inverting its corresponding Leontief matrix. Table 6.7 shows the resulting ESAM Form 3.

ESAM Form 4

In order to develop the intra-group, extra-group and inter-group multiplier matrices defined by Stone (1985), an ESAM Form 4, which is

Table 6.7 ESAM Form 3

			EXPENDITURES				
		Industry production	Factors of production	Institutions	Natural resources	Natural dividend	Rest of the world
RECEIPTS	*Industry production*						
	Factors of production						
	Institutions						
	Natural resources	Natural inventory plus natural dividend					
	Rest of the world						

a simplification of the ESAM Form 3, is used. Only the accounts that relate directly with the natural resources use and restoration are considered.

The submatrix S_{n1} of ESAM Form 2 enumerates the flows from the ecosystem to the economy. The natural resources industry investments submatrix, S_{1n}, defines expenditures to improve the quality of the renewable resources. Environmental taxes as well as environmental subsidies do not deal directly with the environment and, therefore, they are aggregated into the transfer submatrix. With this simplification the role of the resources as provider of goods and services as well as the impact of their restoration can be easily studied. The natural resources submatrix, S_{nn}, defines the transfers between the dividends from the natural resources row and the natural inventory columns which do not have an actual economic flow; therefore, the S_{nn} is equal to a zero matrix. Table 6.8 shows the resulting ESAM Form 4.

Study case

An ESAM Form 2 based on the 1990 MicroIMPLAN database was built using as the study area 101 forested counties of Michigan,

Table 6.8 ESAM Form 4

Receipts \ Expenditures	1 Production	2 Factors (value added)	3 Institutions	4 Natural resources (Natural dividend)	5 Rest of world
1 Production	S_{11} Interindustry transaction submatrix	0	S_{13} Final demand submatrix	S_{1n} Natural resources industry investments submatrix	S_{14} Activity export submatrix
2 Factors or value added	S_{21} Value-added submatrix	0	0	0	S_{24} Factor export submatrix
3 Institutions	S_{31} Sales and taxes submatrix	S_{32} Distribution submatrix	S_{33} Transfer submatrix		S_{34} Institutional exports submatrix
4 Natural resources (Natural dividend plus natural inventory)	S_{n1} Natural resources provided to industries submatrix	0	**0**	S_{nn} Natural resources transfer submatrix	S_{n4} Natural resources export submatrix
5 Rest of world	S_{41} Activity import submatrix	0	S_{43} Institutional imports submatrix	**0**	S_{44} Transshipment submatrix

Minnesota, and Wisconsin (northern part of Great Lake States). The activities subaccounts are agricultural products (Ag), timber productions and services (Timber), manufacturing (Manu), food processing (Food), wood processing (Wood), retail services (Retail), finance, investment, and real estate (FIRE), and government production (GP). The primary factors of production subaccounts are employee compensation (EC), proprietary income (PI), and other property income (OPI). The institution subaccounts are household (HH), corporations and enterprises (Ent), governments (Gov't), and capital (Capital). The export/import accounts describe trade flows into and out of the region. The value of the timber production (1993/4 growth and removals) was provided by the source North Central FIA. Prices are determined by price data from Wisconsin Stumpage Price Reports (Wisconsin Price Reports 1996).

Data from growth and removals of the 101 counties of the Lake States came from the US Forest Service (USFS). Hicksian income and natural capital values were obtained by multiplying the different species stumpage prices by the volume harvested. Sustainability limits were found by comparing the mean of the removals with the growth data. Table 6.9 allocates growth and removals in million cubic feet. Table 6.10 allocates removals economic value (Marcouiller and Deller 1997). They show how growth was higher than removals. Total removals value was 175,423 thousand dollars. This value was considered as Hicksian income (factor of production), given that growth is greater than removals. This timber was sold to the wood processing industry. "Hicksian income" and "natural capital" values were discounted from the "proprietor income" and "other property income" accounts (Table 6.11). "Additions to future incomes" represent the part of the sustainable resource not harvested and left as an inventory for following periods. Values were found estimating the difference between

Table 6.9 Average net annual growth and average annual removals of growing stock on timberland by species group

Species group	Growth (million cubic feet)	Removals (million cubic feet)
Total softwoods	473.7	183.3
Total hardwoods	1,152.3	630.2
All species	1626.0	813.5

Source: North Central FIA, St Paul, MN.

Table 6.10 Timber removals values

Removals value	All owners	Forest industry	National forest	Other public	Other private
Softwood sawtimber	47,393,857	7,338,644	10,765,828	13,196,521	16,102,177
Hardwood sawtimber	79,230,424	12,709,424	9,516,416	16,919,812	40,092,598
Softwood pulp	19,047,600	2,534,400	6,237,000	5,445,000	4,831,200
Hardwood pulp	29,751,037.5	3,312,150	4,525,050	9,551,587.5	12,338,925
Total	175,422,918.5	25,894,618	31,044,294	45,112,920.5	73,364,900

Source: North Central FIA, St Paul, MN.

the total growth of the resource and the harvest assuming equal prices. "Environmental debt" and "investment in natural capital" were zero. When nature state capitalization (NSC = 350,630.00 thousand dollars) was added to the gross regional product (GRP = 82,707.93 thousand dollars) the net timber regional product (NTRP = 83,338.56 thousand dollars) increased the accounted regional product.

Other models

Integrating green national accounting within the agents of the circular flow above described and depicted in SAMs can confer the advantage of linking environmental data with conventional accounting information of all relevant economic agents in a consistent manner inside of a matrix (Atkinson, 1996). This integration started with the National Accounting Matrix including Environmental Accounts (NAMEA) created by the Dutch Central Bureau of Statistics (CBS) and was adopted as one part of the framework for a European Union green accounting program (De Boo *et al.* 1991) whose last version is the system environmental and economic accounting (SEEA03). This SEEA03 was also based on the "National Accounts System of United Nations, 1993" (NAS93), where it appeared, for the first time, that the national system of accounts was extended to environmental accounting.

In a NAMEA, the environment was introduced via the addition of new accounts to the matrix: the "environmental agents" and the "changes in environmental assets." The former referred to pressure-type indicators such as waste emissions, while the latter described effects

Table 6.11 ESAM for the 101 counties of the Lake States

	Agriculture	Timber production	Manufactures	Food/fiber process	Wood processing	Retail/services	FIRE	Government production	Employee compensation income	Proprietors Income
Agriculture	224.27	0.46	58.68	1,133.03	21.49	26.31	13.34	2.39	0.00	0.00
Timber production	48.14	20.82	0.67	0.25	171.42	0.48	0.00	0.00	0.00	0.00
Manufactures	193.04	19.37	4,804.10	224.48	1,093.20	1,369.26	642.28	417.75	0.00	0.00
Food/fiber process	13.34	5.90	11.71	975.79	2.08	261.26	0.38	9.14	0.00	0.00
Wood processing	11.07	0.23	551.35	91.93	1,087.19	30.16	1.07	4.57	0.00	0.00
Retail/services	96.08	5.23	2,779.90	233.30	673.20	1,183.22	409.19	148.71	0.00	0.00
FIRE	90.07	12.87	770.02	26.44	110.11	609.36	934.22	102.50	0.00	0.00
Government production	2.90	0.50	125.06	7.85	42.78	104.30	113.35	35.15	0.00	0.00
Employee compensation income	374.88	46.60	8,091.75	579.83	2,207.17	10,717.7	1,343.27	7,084.59	0.00	0.00
Proprietors income	104.05	24.26	790.28	7.72	**38.37**	1,604.31	154.35	5.01	0.00	0.00
Other property income	832.95	38.25	4,549.53	513.73	**1,106.6**	3,156.62	3,508.16	57.41	0.00	0.00
Enterprises	0.00	0.00	0.00	0.00	0.00	0.00	0.00	0.00	0.00	0.00
Low-income households 8.87%	0.00	0.00	0.00	0.00	0.00	0.00	0.00	0.00	1,998.48	245.82
Medium-income households 55.9%	0.00	0.00	0.00	0.00	0.00	0.00	0.00	0.00	12,596.9	1,549.50
High-income households 35.2%	0.00	0.00	0.00	0.00	0.00	0.00	0.00	0.00	7,935.35	976.09
Government transfers	40.71	4.80	619.93	31.32	159.11	1,880.8	1,390.0	15.93	3,900.9	2,220.5
Inventory	204.39	0.00	81.32	16.10	18.58	0.00	0.00	59.20	0.00	0.00
Capital formation	0.00	0.00	0.00	0.00	0.00	0.00	0.00	0.00	4,014.1	2,034
Hicksian income — **CHI**	0.00	0.00	0.00	0.00	175,42	0.00	0.00	0.00	0.00	0.00
Hicksian income — **NMHI**	0.00	0.00	0.00	0.00	0.00	0.00	0.00	0.00	0.00	0.00
Natural capital — **NCS**	0.00	0.00	0.00	0.00	0.00	0.00	0.00	0.00	0.00	0.00
Natural capital — **NMNC**	0.00	0.00	0.00	0.00	0.00	0.00	0.00	0.00	0.00	0.00
Rest of the world	10,60.1	76.66	11,018	1,376.6	2,456.0	4,001.5	2,229.0	517.58	0.00	0.00
Total	3,358.0	264.96	34,252.	5,218.4	9,384.1	24,945.0	10,938.	8,459.9	30,445.	2,957.8

Note: Values in bold type represent different values from the original SAM.

Enterprises	Low-income households	Medium-income households	High income households	Government transfers	Inventory	Capital formation	Hicksian income		Natural capital		Exports	Total
							CHI	NMHI	NCS	NMCS		
0.00	62.30	108.82	51.97	31.43	18.87	0.15	0.00	0.00	0.0	0.00	1,393.3	3,358.04
0.00	2.66	7.19	4.33	0.01	2.90	0.00	0.00	0.00	0.0	0.00	6.10	264.96
0.00	223.82	319.84	308.09	2,147.79	63.96	5,894.28	0.00	0.00	0.0	0.00	16,120	34,252.9
0.00	255.13	432.88	200.93	51.91	3.63	0.01	0.00	0.00	0.0	0.00	2,993.3	5,219.43
0.00	17.92	43.15	30.43	21.46	115.24	51.38	0.00	0.00	0.0	0.00	7327.0	9,384.12
0.00	3,470.55	7,896.06	4,212.30	710.23	56.29	302.76	0.00	0.00	0.0	0.00	2768.4	24,945.4
0.00	1,050.25	2,473.24	1,433.89	247.06	0.00	35.07	0.00	0.00	0.0	0.00	3043.6	10,938.7
0.00	301.58	713.52	518.24	5,944.99	0.11	0.88	0.00	0.00	0.0	0.00	348.70	8,459.92
0.00	0.00	0.00	0.00	0.00	0.00	0.00	0.00	0.00	0.0	0.00	0.00	30,445.8
0.00	0.00	0.00	0.00	0.00	0.00	0.00	0.00	0.00	0.0	0.00	0.00	2,808.35
0.00	0.00	0.00	0.00	0.00	0.00	0.00	0.00	0.00	0.0	0.00	0.00	13,765.2
0.00	0.00	0.00	0.00	0.00	0.00	0.00	0.00	0.00	0.0	0.00	0.00	8,437.99
700.70	0.00	0.00	0.00	5,614.40	0.00	0.00	0.00	0.00	0.0	0.00	0.00	8,846.97
1,863.7	0.00	0.00	0.00	3,592.00	0.00	0.00	0.00	0.00	0.0	0.00	0.00	21, 414.7
5,093.0	0.00	0.00	0.00	1509.30	0.00	0.00	0.00	0.00	0.0	0.00	0.00	16,655.5
0.00	564.30	2663.2	3049.2	0.00	0.00	0.00	0.00	0.00	0.0	0.00	3,230.1	19,870
0.00	0.00	0.00	0.00	0.00	0.00	261,35	0.00	0.00	0.0	0.00	0.00	641.07
0.00	278.66	1,313.2	1,510.2	0.00	0.00	0.00		0.00	0.0	0.00	0.00	7,094.3
0.00	0.00	0.00	0.00	0.00	0.00	0.00	0.00	350.63	0.0	0.00	0.00	175,423 / 536.053
0.00	0.00	0.00	0.00	0.00	0.00	0.00	0.00	0.00	0.0	0.00	0.00	
0.00	0.00	0.00	0.00	0.00	0.00	0.00	0.00	0.00	0.0	0.00	0.00	0.00
0.00	0.00	0.00	0.00	0.00	0.00	0.00	0.00	0.00	0.0	0.00	0.00	
780.59	2,619.8	5,243.6	5,336.0	0.00	378.06	547.54	0.00	0.00	0.0	0.00	0.00	37.641
8,437.9	21,414.	21,414.	16,655.	19,870.	641.07	7,094.3	0.00	(350.6)	0.0		37,642	

in the form of ecosystem damage. According to Atkinson (1996), in this system although the two accounts, waste emissions and damage environmental assets, overlapped, what they were intended to show was a flow of effects where, for example, household activities could lead to waste emissions which in turn would pollute the environment leading to a loss of household welfare.

Atkinson (1996) improved NAMEA by including the additional new accounts into a social accounting framework to make a "green" SAM. He kept the SAM structure, which requires that the sum of the contents in each column is equal to the sum of the contents of each row, and added two "new" accounts, namely resources and environment.

The resulting SAMEA for Atkinson is shown in Table 6.12. It shows how each account—including "resources" and "environment"—has a corresponding residual balancing item.

Atkinson's model stresses the components of a measure of genuine saving. It indicates the extent to which sales or liquidation of assets are being exchanged for other assets (e.g. sale of resources to finance investment in produced assets) as the residual, Sg, of the saving accounts. Table 6.12 tells how much of saving is genuine: i.e. not made to offset loss of other assets which is absolutely necessary if flow accounts are to be linked to wealth accounts (balance sheets) such that policies for sustainable development can be evaluated.

According to Atkinson (1996), including this information into a SAM format increases the policy usefulness of SAM and NAMEA accounts in three ways: First, it does this by emphasizing the detail of green accounts; second, it emphasizes the productive aspects of resources and environment (i.e. growth of resources and dissipation of pollution); and third, policy use lies in the modeling of linkages between environment and economy.

Rodríguez Morilla and Llanes Díaz-Salazar (2007) propose a new SAMEA simplifying Atkinson's model by considering the environmental and resource accounts as exogenous to the SAM. Their SAMEA integrates physical water circular flow and emissions to the atmosphere of greenhouse effect gasses (GE), together with the economic flow sourced from the Spanish National Accounting System. Their SAMEA is especially designed to obtain the domestic production multipliers, emissions of greenhouse effect gasses and consumption of water associated as they were described in Chapter 5.

Rodríguez Morilla *et al.*'s (2007) SAMEA follows the structure proposed in the SEEA03, the NAS93 as well as the EAS95 and contains the elements described in Table 6.13. Their model contains from an economic point of view a SAM, where the flows related to production

Table 6.12 Atkinson's SAMEA including resources and environment

Disposition / Supply	Production	Factors	Institutions	Saving	Rest of world	Resources	Environment	Totals
Production			C	I	X			Total disposition of good and services
Factors	NDP							Net disposition of good and services
Institutions		NDP				NRP	NEP	Disposition of welfare
Saving	δK		Sg				$\sigma.e$	Total disposition of saving (investment finance)
Rest of world	M			(X – M)				Total disposition to rest of the world
Resources				n.g				Gross resource product
Environment			$p_B.B$	$\sigma.d$				Gross environmental product
Totals	Total supply of human-made goods and services	Net supply of human-made goods and services	Supply of welfare (MEW)	Total supply of saving	Total supply to rest of the world	Total supply of resources	Total supply of environmental benefits	

Source: Atkinson (1996).

Notes: Account balance:

1 Production account: $C + I + (X - M) = NDP + \delta K = GDP; \rightarrow NDP = C + (I - \delta K) + (X - M) =$ net domestic product

2 Institutions account: $C + Sg + p_B.B = NDP + NRP + NEP = MEW =$ measure of welfare

3 Savings account: $I + (X - M) + n.g + \sigma.d = Sg + \delta K + n.R + \sigma.e \rightarrow [I + (X - M) + n.g + \sigma.d] - [\delta K + n.R + \sigma.e] = Sg$

4 Resource account: $n.g = NRP + n.R \rightarrow NRP = n.g - n.R =$ net resource product

5 Environment account: $p_B.B + \sigma.d = NEP + \sigma.e \rightarrow NEP = p_B.B + \sigma(d - e) =$ net environmental product

Table 6.13 Structure of a SAMEA according to Rodríguez Morilla and Llanes Díaz-Salazar

SAMEA	National economy	Rest of the world economy	Total	National environment	Rest of the world environment
National economy	S (SAM flows of product, income distribution, final consumption, and capital formation)	e_i (i = 1, 2 3)	x_i^d (i = 1,2,3)	Residual by resident	Residuals by resident to the rest of the world
Rest of the world economy	m_j^T (j = 1,2,3)	m_4^T		Residual by non-resident	
Total	x_j^{sT} (j = 1,2,3)	x_4^{sT}	x_4^4		
National environment	Natural resources inputs	Natural resource exports			
Rest of the world environment	Natural resources from the rest of the world				
National residuals	Residual reabsorbed				Cross boundary residual outflows
Rest of the world residuals	Residual reabsorbed			Cross boundary residual inflows	

Source: Rodríguez Morilla and Llanes Díaz-Salazar (2007).

Table 6.14 Exogenous and endogenous accounts in Rodríguez Morilla *et al.*'s SAMEA

SAMEA	National economy	Rest of the world economy	Total	Environment accounts
National economy	S (Endogenous)	e_i (i = 1,2 3) Exogenous	x_i^d (i = 1,2,3)	(Endogenous)
Rest of the world economy	m_j^T (j = 1,2,3) (Exogenous)	m_4^T	x_4^4	
Total	x_j^{sT} (j = 1,2,3)	x_4^{sT}		
Environment accounts	(Endogenous)			

Source: Rodríguez Morilla *et al.* (2007).

Table 6.15 Rodríguez Morilla et al.'s specific SAMEA layout

	1 Production	2 Factors/ value added	3 Institutions	4 Rest of world	Total	NATIONAL ENVIRONMENT		
						Waste waters by environmental protection services	Water return	Net flow from environment to national economy
1 Production	S_{11} Interindustry transaction matrix or industry by industry (I × I) matrix	0	S_{13} Final demand matrix	S_{14} Activity export matrix	x_1^d Total industry output or production	Discharge of waste waters	Discharge of waste waters	Apparent water consumption
2 Factors or value added	S_{21} Value-added matrix	0	0	S_{24} Factor export matrix	x_2^d Total factor output receipt vector			
3 Institutions	S_{31} Sales and taxes matrix	S_{32} Distribution matrix	S_{33} Transfer matrix	S_{34} Institutional exports matrix	x_3^d Total institutional expenditures/ receipt	Discharge of waste waters		Apparent water consumption
4 Rest of world	S_{41} Activity import matrix	S_{42} Factor import matrix	S_{43} Institutional imports matrix	S_{44} Transshipment matrix	x_4^d Total imports vector			Apparent water consumption

	x_1^s Total industry outlay or production	x_2^T Total factor outlay vector	x_3^s Total institutional expenditures/receipt vector	x_4^T Total export vector		Discharge to public sewage	Direct return	Apparent water consumption incorporated to economy
Total								
NATIONAL ENVIRONMENT — Abstraction of surface and groundwaters	Abstraction of surface water and groundwater				Abstraction of water			Total abstraction water
Consumption of water: abstractions and distributions	Recycling, re-use, and treatment of waste water				Waste water treatment			Return to nature
Recycling, re-use and treatment of waste water	Consumptions of water		Consumptions of water by households		Total water consumption			

Source: Rodríguez Morilla *et al.* (2007).

activity, consumption, and distribution, and from an ecological point of view, two matrices expressed in physical units. In the first one, the flows of natural resources show what the productive system uses as inputs (in this case, they refer to receptions of water resources) or the reabsorbed residuals that are picked up and processed. The second one shows how recycled water is picked up by nature once it has been used by the production process, household consumption, and the emission of greenhouse effect gasses.

The Rodríguez Morilla *et al.* (2007) model can be easily used to establish environmental linear, fixed price multipliers as in Chapter 5. To do this, information has to be divided into endogenous and exogenous accounts (Table 6.14). Table 6.15 shows how their final model can be adapted to the SAM as it was defined in Chapter 3.

Notes

1 Basic concepts in natural resource economics

1 Held values have been defined by Rescher (1968) as the *underlying values* or *values proper*, which is also loosely the base for Rokeach's "value" definition. They are modes of conduct, end-states, or qualities that could possibly be desirable.

2 See the section "The total economic value of natural renewable resources" (p. 6).

3 TEV is the sum of consumer and producer surplus (TEV = consumer surplus + producer surplus).

4 Some other complexities related to the distribution of the natural goods that must be taken into account when studying a regional economy are:

- Establishing who pays and who profits from the market and non-market natural resource inputs.
- The distribution of benefits by household income level (Wear and Hyde 1992).
- The consideration of the different combinations of land, labor, financial capital, and growing stock inputs that alternative forest management regimes use (Marcouiller and Deller 1997).
- The consideration of the different natures of the goods produced. Management choice of input combination determines output levels of both private goods (timber stumpage) and public goods (recreational values, aesthetics, biodiversity, spatial disturbance patterns, etc.). A public good is defined as a good that has no congestion in its consumption: one person's consumption has no effect on the consumption of that good by others (Rideout and Hesseln 1995).

2 Regional I–O economic models

1 If the export vector in Table 2.1d or in the hypothetical example shown in Table 2.2 is defined as net exports (i.e. exports—imports) then the payments vector, w^T, would only include the value-added components or the primary factors of production.

5   Ecosystem and economic system framework

1   The following discussion draws heavily on the material contained in Chapters 2 and 3.

6   The accounting of sustainability in a SAM

1   This study only focuses on harvesting the renewable resource timber. The analysis of non-renewable resources is beyond the scope of this research.

2   IIEAF is based on the European System of Accounts (ESA95), EURO-STAT System of Forestry Accounts (EUROSTAT 1996, 1997, 1999a, 1999b, and 2000).

3   The physical volume removed from the forest cut in a sustainable fashion can be considered as a non-declining income if prices are held constant. Constant prices are an assumption of SAMs. In this case, the assumption has also been applied to ESAMs as a restriction in order to make possible a definition of weak sustainability. Other restrictions can be defined in more sophisticated ESAMs.

4   The term $R - G > 0$ defines a reduction in natural capital. An additional assumption of using either a SAM or ESAM is that they are not time variant predictive models. Therefore, a harvest level defined as $G < R$ is not sustainable.

5   United Nations (1993) elaborated a framework to systematically account for the stocks and flows of environmental resources of the System of Integrated Environmental and Economic Accounting (SIEEA) consistent with the System of National Accounts (SNA). Based on this self-proclaimed "interim version" framework, United Nations (2000) distinguish among four environmental "distances" or "types of damages with specific methods for its valuation" to achieve an "environmental capacity" level during an accounting period. These different damages are measured as the cost of restoring environmental quality to sustainability standards incurred by damages in the past and present and borne by present and future generations (United Nations 2000).

6   According to Vincent's (1999) accounting framework, the value of agricultural land λ_a is the discounted sum of future agricultural land rents (net economic returns). In this case (forest land) future lost incomes can be accounted according to

$$\lambda_a = \int_t^\infty e^{-r(s-t)} \, pQf_F^Q \, ds$$

where f_F^Q is the marginal product of forest land (timber in the ESAM), r the interest rate, p_Q is the price and s the restoration time required.

7   SIC stands for standard industrial classification. The SIC codes for forestry and logging are based on the *Standard Industrial Classification Manual* (Office of Management and Budget 1987).

8   If the local forests are owned by foreign institutions or foreign institutions subsidize investment in local forests, then "I" is the sum of local investment and foreign investments.

9 Gross domestic product and net national income are usually reserved for national-level accounting while gross regional product and net regional product are used for sub-national regions. GRP can be defined using an income, expenditure, or output approach (Pearce 1992). Using the expenditure approach:

$$GRP = C + G + In + (E - M)$$

where C is consumer consumption, G is government expenditures on goods and services, In is investment, E are exports, and M are imports, NRP can be defined as GRP minus depreciation on human-made capital (Pearce 1992).

10 Given that ESAM Form 4 is based on ESAM Form 3, S_{nI} submatrix contains aggregated the natural dividend and the natural inventory rows and S_{in} submatrix only contains the natural dividend column.

Bibliography

Alcántara, V. (1995) *Economía y contaminación atmosférica: hacia un nuevo enfoque desde el análisis input–output*. Doctoral thesis, University of Barcelona.

Alcántara, V. and Roca, J. (1995) "Energy and CO_2 emissions in Spain. Methodology of analysis and some results for 1980–90." *Energy Economics* 17 (3): 221–30.

Allan, J.A. (1996) *Water, Peace and the Middle East: Negotiating Resources in the Jordan Basin*. New York: St Martin's Press.

—— (1998) "Virtual water: a strategic resource, global solutions to regional deficits." *Ground Water* 36: 545–46.

Alward, G. and Lofting E.M. (1985) "Opportunities for analyzing the economic impacts of recreation and tourism expenditure using IMPLAN." Paper delivered at the annual meeting of the Regional Science Association, Philadelphia.

Alward, G., Siverts, E., Taylor, C., and Winter, S. (1993) *Micro INPLAN User's Guide*. Fort Collins, CO: United Department of Agriculture.

Andrews, R.B.M. and Waits, M.J. (1978) *Environmental Values in Public Decisions: A Research Agenda*. Ann Arbor, MI: Ann Arbor School of Natural Resources, University of Michigan.

Arrow, J. and Fisher, A.C. (1974) "Preservation, uncertainty, and irreversibility." *Quarterly Journal of Economics* 88 (2): 312–19.

Atkinson, G. (1995) "Social accounting, genuine saving and measures of economic welfare." CSERGE Working Paper GEC 95–23 University College London and University of East Anglia.

—— (1996) "Sustainable development: theory, measurement and policy." Spanish translation. *Información Comercial Española* 751: 23–26.

Augusztinovics, M. (1970) "Methods of international and intertemporal comparison of structure." In A.P. Carter and A. Brody (eds) *Applications of Input-Output Analysis* (2 vols). Amsterdam: North Holland Publishing Company, pp. 249–69.

Becerril, J.G., Dyer, J.E., Taylor, J.E., and Yúnez-Naude, A. (1996) *Elaboración de Matrices de Contabilidad Social para poblaciones agropecuarias: El caso de El Chante, Jalisco*. Working Paper September. El Colegio de México.

Berck, P., Robinson, S., and Goldman, G.E. (1991) "The use of computable general equilibrium models to assess water policies." In A. Dinar, and D. Zilberman (eds) *The Economics and Management of Water and Drainage in Agriculture*. Boston: Kluwer Academic, pp. 489–509.

Bergen, V. (1999) "Framework and empirical content of forestry reporting in Germany." In C.S. Roper and A. Park (eds) *The Living Forest: Non-market Benefits of Forestry*. London: Forestry Commission, pp. 387–92.

—— (2001) "Forest public goods in national accounts." *Sistemas y Recursos Forestales* (special issue on New Forestlands Economic Accounting: Theories and Applications) 10 (1): 7–26.

Bergstrom, J.C., Cordell, G.A., and Watson, A.E. (1990) "Economic impact of recreational spending in rural areas: a case of study." *Economic Development Quarterly* 4 (1): 29–39.

Bicknell, K.B., Ball, R.J., Cullen, R., and Bigsby, H.R. (1998) "New methodology for the ecological footprint with an application to the New Zealand economy." *Ecological Economics* 27 (2): 149–60.

Black, P. (1995) "The critical role of 'unused' resources." *Water Resources Bulletin* 31 (4): 589.

Bohlin, L. and Widell, L. (2006) "Estimation of commodity-by-commodity input–output matrices." *Economic Systems Research* 18 (2): 205–15.

Bostedt, G. and Mattsson, L. (1995) "The value of forest for tourism in Sweden." *Annals of Tourism Research* 22 (3): 671–80.

Boulding, K.E. (1956) "Some contributions of economics to the general theory of value." *Philosophy of Science* 23 (1): 1–14.

Braidant, M. (2002) "Transformation of supply and use tables to symmetric input–output tables." Paper presented at the XIVth International Conference on Input-Output Techniques. Reference number MSS/2.1. October 10–15, Montréal, Canada.

Brown, T.C. (1984) "The concept of value in resource allocation." *Land Economics* 60 (3): 231–46.

Bulmer-Thomas, V. (1982) *Input-Output Analysis in Developing Countries*. New York: John Wiley and Sons, Inc.

Burgess, J., Clark, J., and Harrison, C. (1995) *Valuing Nature: What Lies Behind Responses to Contingent Valuation Surveys?* London: University College London.

Campos, P. (1999a) "An agroforestry economic accounting system." In M. Merlo, H. Jöbstl, and L. Venzi (eds) *Institutional Aspects of Managerial Economics and Accounting in Forestry*. Viterbo, Italy: IUFRO, pp. 9–19.

—— (1999b) "Hacia la medición de la renta de bienestar del uso múltiple de un bosque." *Investigación Agraria: Sistemas y Recursos Forestales* 8 (2): 407–22.

Campos, P., Rodríguez, Y., and Caparrós, A. (2001) "Towards the Dehesa total income accounting: theory and operative Monfragüe study cases." *Investigación Agraria: Sistemas y Recursos Forestales* 10 (1): 45–69.

Caparrós, A., Campos, P., and Montero, G. (2001a) "Applied multiple use forest accounting in the Guadarrama pinewoods (Spain)." *Sistemas y*

Recursos Forestales (special issue on New Forestlands Economic Accounting: Theories and Applications) 10 (1): 93–110.

—— (2001b) "An operative framework for total Hicksian income accounting: application to a multiple use forest." *EAERE Annual Conference*, June 28–30, Southampton.

Carter, H.O. and Irei, D. (1970) "Linkage of California–Arizona input–output models to analyze water transfer pattern." In A.P. Carter and A. Brody (eds) *Application of Input–Output Analysis*. Amsterdam: North Holland Publishing, pp. 139–68.

Castellano, E., Martínez de Anguita, P., Elorrieta, J.I., Pellitero, M., and Rey, C. (2008) "Estimating a socially optimal water price for irrigation versus an environmentally optimal water price through the use of Geographical Information Systems and Social Accounting Matrix." *Environmental and Resource Economics* 39 (3): 331–56.

Costanza, R. (1992) *Ecological Economics: The Science and Management of Sustainability*. New York: Columbia University Press.

Costanza, R., d'Arge R., de Groot, R., Farber, S., Grasso, M. et al. (1997a) "The value of the world's ecosystem services and natural capital." *Nature* 387 (6230): 253–60.

Costanza, R., Cumberland, J., Daly, H., Goodland, R., and Norgaard, R. (1997b) *An Introduction to Ecological Economics*. Boca Raton, FL: St Lucie Press.

Daly, H.E. (1968) "On economics as a life science." *Journal of Political Economy* 76 (3): 392–406.

—— (1977) *Steady-state Economics: The Economics of Biophysical Equilibrium and Moral Growth*. San Francisco: Freeman.

—— (1990) "Towards an environmental macroeconomics." Paper presented at the Conference on The ecological economics of sustainability: Making local and short term goals consistent with global and long terms goals, held at the International Society for Ecological Economics, Washington D.C., May.

—— (1991) "Elements of environmental macroeconomics." In R. Costanza (ed.) *Ecological Economics: The Science and Management of Sustainability*. New York: Columbia University Press, pp. 1–20.

Darr, D.R. and Fight, R.D. (1974) "Douglas County Oregon: potential economic impacts of a changing resource base." *USDA Forest Service Research Paper* PNW-179.

Dean, G.W., Carter, H.O., Nickerson, E.A., and Adams, R.M. (1973) "Structure and projection of Humboldt County economy: economic growth versus environmental quality." Giannini Foundation Research Report No. 318, University of California, Berkeley.

De Boo, A., Bosch, P., Gortner C., and Keuning, S. (1991) *An Environmental Module and the Complete System of National Accounts NA/46*. Voorburg: Netherlands Central Bureau of Statistics.

Dietzenbacher, E. (1997) "In vindication of the Gosh model: a reinterpretation as a price model." *Journal of Regional Science* 37: 629–51.

Dixon, K., Taniguchi, H., Wattenbach, A., and Tanyeri-Arbu, A. (eds)

(2004) *Smallholders, Globalization and Policy Analysis*. Rome: Agricultural Management, Marketing and Finance Service (AGSF), Agricultural Support Systems Division, Food and Agriculture Organization of the United Nations.

Dobos, I. and Floriska, A. (2007) "The resource conservation effect of recycling in a dynamic Leontief model." *International Journal of Production Economics* 108: 334–40.

Duarte, R., Sánchez Chóliz, J., and Bielsa, J. (2002) "Water use in the Spanish economy: an input–output approach." *Ecological Economics* 43(1): 71–85.

Ehrlich, P. and Erhlich, A. (1990) *The Population Explosion*. New York: Doubleday.

English, D.B., Bowder, J.M., Bergstrom, H., and Cordell, K. (1995) *Estimating the Economic Impact of Recreation Response to Resource Management Alternatives*. Athens, GA: USDA Forest Service General Technical Report SE-91, Southern Research Station.

Eurostat (1996) *European System of Accounts (ESA-95)*. Brussels/ Luxemburg: Eurostat.

—— (1997) *Manual on Economic Accounts for Agriculture and Forestry (Rev. 1) (EAA/EAF)*. Luxemburg: Eurostat.

—— (1999a) *The European Framework for Integrated Environmental and Economic Accounting for Forests: Results of Pilot Applications*. Luxemburg: Eurostat.

—— (1999b) *The European Framework for Integrated Environmental and Economic Accounting for Forests (IEEAF)*. Luxemburg: European Communities.

—— (2000) *Valuation of European Forests. Results of IEEAF Test Applications*. Luxemburg : European Communities.

Faucheux, S. and O'Connor, M. (1998) "Weak and strong sustainability." In S. Faucheix and M. O'Conors (eds) *Valuation for Sustainable Development: Methods and Policy Indicators*. Cheltenham (UK) and Lyme, CT (US): Edward Elgar.

Ferng, J.J. (2001) "Using composition of land multiplier to estimate ecological footprints associated with production activity." *Ecological Economics* 37 (2): 159–72.

—— (2002) "Toward a scenario analysis framework for energy footprints." *Ecological Economics* 40 (1): 53–69.

Field, B.C. and Field, M.K. (2006) *Environmental Economics: An Introduction* (fourth edition). New York: McGraw Hill Companies.

Fletcher, J.E. (1989) "Input-output analysis and tourism impact studies." *Annals of Tourism Research* 16: 514–29.

Flick, W.A., Trenchi III, P., and Bowers, J.R. (1980) "Regional analysis of forest industries: input–output methods." *Forest Science* 26 (4): 548–60.

Folke, C., Hammer, H., Costanza, R., and Jansson, A.M. (1994) "Investing in natural capital—why, what, and how?" In A.M. Jansson, S. Koskoff, R. Costanza, C. Folke, and M. Hammer (eds) *Investing in Natural Capital. The Ecological Economics Approach to Sustainability*. Washington D.C.: Island Press, pp. 1–20.

——, Kautsky, N., Berg, H., Jansson, A. and Troell, M. (1998) "The ecological footprint concept for sustainable seafood production: a review." *Ecological Applications* 8 (1): 63–71.

Forsund, F.R. and Strom, S. (1976) "The generation of residual flows in Norway: an input–output approach." *Journal of Environmental Economics and Management* 3 (2): 129–41.

Ghosh, A. (1958) "Input-output approach in an allocation system." *Economica* 25 (97): 58–64.

Goodland, R. and Daly, H.E. (1990) "The missing tools (for sustainability)." In C. Mungall and D.J. McLaren (eds) *Planet Under Stress: The Challenge of Global Change.* Oxford: Oxford University Press.

Goodstein, E.S. (1995) *Economics and the Environment.* Englewood Cliffs, NJ: Prentice Hall, Inc.

Gowdy, J.M. (1997) "The value of biodiversity: markets, society and ecosystems." *Lands Economics* 73 (1): 25–41.

Greber, B. (1994) "Economic assessment of FEMAT options." *Journal of Forestry* 92 (4): 36–40.

Guo, J., Lawson, A., and Planting, M. (2002) "From make-use to symmetric I–O tables: an assessment of alternative technology assumptions." Working Paper WP2002–03, Bureau of Economic Analysis, US Department of Commerce, Washington, D.C.

Hall, C.A.S., Cleveland, C., and Kauffman. R. (1986) *Energy and Resource Quality: The Ecology of the Economic Process.* New York: Wiley & Sons.

Hannon, B. (1973) "The structure of ecosystems." *Journal of Theoretical Biology* 41 (3): 535–46.

—— (1990) "Biological time value." *Mathematical Biosciences* 110: 115–40.

—— (2001) "Ecological pricing and economic efficiency." *Ecological Economics* 36: 19–30.

Hannon, B. and Joiris, C. (1987) "A seasonal analysis of the southern North Sea ecosystem." *Ecology* 70 (6): 1916–34.

Hannon, B., Costanza, R., and Ulanowicz, R. (1991) "A general accounting framework for ecological systems: a functional taxonomy for connectivist ecology." *Theoretical Populaltion Biology* 40 (1): 78–104.

Hawdon, D. and Pearson, P. (1995) "Input-output simulations of energy, environment, economy interactions in the UK." *Energy Economics* 17 (1): 73–86.

Hawkins, T., Hendrickson, C., Higgins, C., Matthews, H.S., and Suh, S. (2007) "A mixed-unit input–output model for environmental life-cycle assessment and material flow analysis." *Environmental Science and Technology* 41: 1024–31.

Heilbroner, R.L. and Thurow, L.C. (1981) *Five Economic Challenges.* Englewood Cliffs, NJ, Prentice Hall.

Heng, T.M. and Low, L. (1990) "Economic impact of tourism in Singapore." *Annals of Tourism Research* 17: 246–69.

Henry, C. (1974) "Option values in the economics of irreplaceable assets." *Review of Economic Studies* 41: 89–104.

Hicks, J. (1946) *Value and Capital* (second edn). Oxford: Oxford University Press.

Hodge, I. (1994) "Rural amenity: property rights and policy mechanisms." In *The Contribution of Amenities to Rural Development*. Paris: Organization for Economic Cooperation and Development.

Hotvedt, J.E., Busby, R.L., and Jacob R.E. (1988) "Use of IMPLAN for regional input–output studies." Paper presented at the annual meeting of the Southern Forest Economics Association, Buena Vista, FL.

Hubacek, K. and Giljum, S. (2003) "Applying physical input–output analysis to estimate land appropriation (ecological footprints) of international trade activities." *Ecological Economics* 44 (1): 137–51.

Hubacek, K. and Sun, L. (2002) "Changes in China's economy and society and its effects on water use." *Interims Report* IR-02–073, International Institute for Applied Systems Analysis. AIST/IIASA/UNEP workshop on lifecycle approaches to sustainable consumption in Laxenburg, Austria, November 22, 2002.

Hyde, W.F. and Amacher, G.S. (1996) "Applications of environmental accounting and the new household economics: new technical economics issues with a common theme in forestry." *Forestry Ecology and Management* 83: 137–48.

Ip, W.C., Wong, H., Jun, X., Zhu, Y., and Shao, Q. (2007) "Input-output analysis of virtual water trade volume of Zhangye." Paper submitted to the Modeling and Simulation Society of Australia and New Zealand Inc. (MSSANZ) Land, Water and Environmental Management: Integrated Systems for Sustainability Conference, December 2007, University of Canterbury, New Zealand.

Isard, W. (1968) "On the linkage of socio-economic and ecological system." *Papers of the Regional Science Association* 21: 79–99.

—— (1972) *Ecological-economic Analysis for Regional Development. Some Initial Explorations with Particular Reference to Recreational Resource Use and Environment Planning.* New York: Free Press.

Jansen, P.K. and ten Raa, T. (1990) "The choice of model in the construction of input–output coefficients matrices." *International Economic Review* 31 (1): 213–27.

Jin, D., Hoagland, P., and Dalton T.M. (2003) "Linking economic and ecological models for marine ecosystem." *Ecological Economics* 46: 367–85.

Khan, H., Seng, C.F., and Cheong, W.K. (1990) "Tourism multiplier effects on Singapore." *Annals of Tourism Research* 17: 408–18.

Khan, R.F. (1991) "The relation of home investment to unemployment." *Economic Journal* l41 (162): 173–98.

Kigyossy-Schmidt, E. (1989) "Nonmarket services in input–output analysis." *Economic Systems Research* 1 (1): 131–45.

Kim, J. (1993) "Environmental accounting in a social accounting matrix framework: the case of Mexico." Ph.D. dissertation, University of Minnesota.

King, B.B. (1985) *What Is a SAM. In Social Accounting Matrix. A Basis for Planning.* Washington D.C.: World Bank Symposium.

Klaus, J. (1994) "Computable general equilibrium models in environmental and resource economics." No 601, IVS discussion paper series from Institut für Volkswirtschaft und Statistik (IVS), University of Mannheim.

Klemperer, W.D. (1996) *Forest Resource Economics and Finance.* New York: McGraw-Hill.

Kop Jansen, P. and ten Raa, T. (1990) "The choice of model in the construction of input output coefficients matrices." *International Economic Review* 31: 213–27.

Kriström, B. (1999a) "On the incorporation of non-market outputs of forests into national accounting systems." In C.S. Roper and A. Park (eds) *The Living Forest: Non-market Benefits of Forestry.* London: Forestry Commission, pp. 400–9.

—— (1999b) *Valuing Forests*, Stockholm: MBG Press.

Leatherman, J.C. and Marcouiller, D.W. (1994) "Estimating tourism contribution to local income." Presented at the Journal City and Psijoral Community Conference, October 20–21.

—— (1996) "Income distribution characteristics of rural economic sectors: implications for local development policy." *Growth and Change* 27: 434–59.

—— (1999a) "Study area specification in forestry economic impact analysis: modifying county-level secondary data." *Northern Journal of Applied Forestry* 16 (3): 129–36.

—— (1999b) "Moving beyond the modeling of regional economic growth: a study of how income is distributed to rural households." *Economic Development Quarterly* 13 (1): 38–45.

Lee, K.-S. (1982) "A generalized input–output model of an economy with environmental protection." *The Review of Economics and Statistics* 64 (3): 466–73.

Leontief, W. (1936) "Quantitative input–output relations in the economic system of the United States." *Review of Economic and Statistics* 18 (3): 105–25.

—— (1966) *Input-output Economics.* New York: Oxford University Press.

—— (1970) "Environmental repercussions and the economic structure: an input–output approach." *The Review of Economics and Statistics* 52 (3): 262–71.

Leontief, W. and Ford, D. (1972) "Air pollution and the economic structure: empirical results of input–output computations." In A.P. Carter and A. Brody (eds) *Applications of Input-Output Analysis.* Amsterdam: North Holland Publishing, pp. 9–30.

Leung, M., Haimes, Y.Y., and Santos, J.R. (2007) "Supply- and output-side extensions to the inoperability input–output model for interdependent infrastructures." *Journal of Infrastructure Systems* 13 (4): 299–310.

Lofgren, H., Harris, R.L., and Robinson, S. (2002) *A Standard Computable General Equilibrium (CGE) Model in GAMS.* Washington, D.C.: International Food Policy Research Institute.

Lofting, E.M. and Mcgauhey, P.H. (1968) "Economic valuation of water. An input–output analysis of California water requirements." Contribution no. 116. Water Resources Center, University of California, Berkeley.

Loomis, J.B. (1995) "Four models for determining environmental quality effects on recreation demand and regional economics." *Ecological Economics* 12 (1): 55–66.

Lovelock, J.E. (1979) *GAIA: A New Look at Life on Earth*. Oxford: Oxford University Press.

Lowe, P.D. (1979) "Pricing problems in an input–output approach to environmental protection." *The Review of Economics and Statistics* 61 (1): 110–17.

Luptáčik, M. and Böhm, B. (1994) "An environmental input–output model with multiple criteria." *Annals of Operations Research* 54: 119–27.

—— (1999) "A consistent formulation of the Leontief pollution model." *Economic Systems Research* 11 (3): 263–75.

McDonald, G.W. and Patterson, M.G. (2004) "Ecological footprints and interdependencies of New Zealand regions." *Ecological Economics* 50 (1–2): 49–67.

Mapete, M. and Hassan. R. (2006) "Integrated ecological economics accounting approach to evaluation of intra-basin water transfers: an application to the Lesotho Highlands Water Project." *Ecological Economics* 60 (1): 246–59.

Marcouiller, D.W. (1998) "Environmental resources as latent primary factors of production in tourism: the case of forest-based commercial recreation." *Tourism Economics* 4 (2): 131–45.

Marcouiller, D.W. and Deller, S.C. (1996) "Natural resource stocks, flows, and regional economic change: seeing the forest and the trees." *Journal of Regional Analysis and Policy* 26 (2): 95–116.

—— (1997) "Modeling market and non-market interaction in rural resource dependent regions." Paper prepared for the presentation at the annual meeting of the Mid Continent Region Science Association, Indianapolis, June 5–7.

Marcouiller, D.W., Schreiner, D.F., and Lewis, D.K. (1995) "The distributive economic impacts of intensive timber production." *Forest Science* 41 (1): 122–39.

Martínez-Alier, J., Munda, G., and O'Neill, J. (2001) "Theories and methods in ecological economics: a tentative classification." In C. Cleveland, D. Stern, and R. Costanza (eds) *The Economics of Nature and the Nature of Economics*. Cheltenham (UK) and Northampton, MA (US): Edward Elgar, pp. 34–56.

Martínez-Anguita, P. (1999) "Introduction of environmental accounts into a social accounting matrix." Unpublished master's thesis, State University of New York College of Environmental Sciences and Forestry, Syracuse, NY.

Masui, T. (2005) "CGE model development based on U&V matrix." National Institute for Environmental Studies (NIES) AIM Training Workshop, November 7–11.

Matete, M. and Hassan, R. (2006) Integrated ecological economics accounting approach to evaluation of inter-basin water transfers: an application to the Lesotho Highlands Water Project, *Ecological Economics* 60: 246–59.

Merlo, M. and Boschetti, A. (2001) Environmental accounting in agriculture and forestry: a stepwise approach. In *Sistemas y Recursos Forestales*. (special issue on New Forestlands Economic Accounting: Theories and Applications) 10 (1): 69–90.

Merlo, M. and Briales, E.R. (2000) "Public goods and externalities linked to Mediterranean forests: economic nature and policy." *Land Use Policy* 17: 197–208.

Merlo, M. and Jöbstl, H. (1999) "Incorporating non-market values into the accounting systems of publicly and privately-owned forest enterprises: an operative stepwise approach." In C.S. Roper and A. Park (eds) *The Living Forest: Non-market Benefits of Forestry*. London: Forestry Commission, pp. 341–72.

Miller, R.E. (1998) "Regional and interregional input–output analysis." In W. Isard, K.J. Azis, M.P. Drennan, R.E. Miller, S. Saltzman, and E. Thorbecke (eds) *Methods of Interregional and Regional Analysis*, Adershot: Ashgate Publishing Limited.

Miller, R.E. and Blair, P.D. (1985) *Input-Output Analysis: Foundations and Extensions*. Englewood Cliffs, NJ: Prentice Hall.

—— (2009) *Input-output Analysis: Foundations and Extension* (second edition). Cambridge: Cambridge University Press.

Munda, G. (1997) "Environmental economics, ecological economics and the concept of sustainable development." *Environmental Values* 6 (2): 213–33.

Naess, A. (1984) "Intuition, intrinsic value and deep ecology." *The Ecologist* 14: 5–6.

NAICS (North American Industry Classification System) (2007) *Office of Management and Budget, Executive Office of the President of the United States of America*. Washington D.C.: US Census Bureau.

Nordhaus, W.D. and Tobin, J. (1973) "Is growth obsolete?" In M. Moss (ed.) *The Measurement of Economic and Social Performance*. New York: Columbia University Press for NBER, pp. 1–80.

Nordhaus, W.D. and Kokkelenberg, E.C. (eds) (1999) *Nature's Numbers: Expanding the National Economic Accounts to Include the Environment*. Washington D.C.: National Academic Press.

Odum, E.P. (1989) *Ecology and Our Endangered Life Support Systems*. Sunderland, MA: Sinauer Associates.

Office of Management and Budget (OMB) (1987) *Standard Industrial Classification Manual*. Executive Office of the President.Washington, D.C.: OMB.

Oosterhaven, J. (1989) "The supply-driven input–output model: a new interpretation but still implausible." *Journal of Regional Science* 29 (3): 459–65

Park, J.Y. (2007) *The Supply-driven Input-output Model: A Reinterpretation and Extension*. Los Angeles: School of Policy, Planning, and Development, University of Southern California.

Pearce, D.W. (ed.) (1992) *The MIT Dictionary of Modern Economics* (fourth edition). Cambridge, MA: The MIT Press.

—— (1993) *Economics Values and the Natural World*, London: Earthscan.

Pearce, D.W. and Atkinson, G. (1995) "Measuring sustainable development." In D.W. Bromley (ed.) *The Handbook of Environmental Economics* Oxford: Blackwell, pp. 166–81.

Pearce, D.W. and Turner, R.K. (1990) *Economics of Natural Resource and the Environment*. Baltimore: Johns Hopkins Press.

Percoco, M. (2006) "A note on the inoperability input–output model." *Risk Analysis* 26 (3): 589–94.

Peyron, J.L. (1998) *Élaboration d'un sytème de comptes économiques articulés de la forêt au niveau national*. Nancy: ENGREF.

Piggot, J. and Whaley, J. (1991) "Public good provision rules and income distribution: some general equilibrium calculations." *Empirical Economics* 16: 25–33.

Polo, C., Roland-Holst, D.W., and Sancho, F. (1991a) "Descomposición de Multiplicadores en un modelo multisectorial: una aplicación al caso español." *Investigaciones Económicas* 15 (1): 53–69.

—— (1991b) "Análisis de la Influencia Económica en un Modelo Multisectorial." *Investigaciones Económicas* (supplement): 125–9.

Prato, T. (1998) *Natural Resource and Environmental Economics*. Ames: IA: Iowa State University Press.

Proops, J.L.R. (1988) "Energy intensities, input–output analysis and economic development." In M. Ciaschini, (ed.) *Input-output Analysis, Current Developments*. New York: Chapman and Hall, pp. 201–15.

Proops, J.L.R., Faber, M., and Wagenhals, G. (1993) *Reducing CO$_2$ emissions. A Comparative Input-output Study for Germany and the U.K.* Berlin: Springer-Verlag.

Propst, D. (ed.) (1985) *Assessing the Economic Impacts of Recreation and Tourism*. Asheville, NC: USDA Forest Service, Southeastern Forest Experiment Station.

Pyatt, G. and Round, J.I. (1979) "Accounting and Fixed price multipliers in a social accounting matrix framework." *The Economic Journal* 89 (356): 850–73.

—— (1985) Accounting and fixed-price multipliers in a social accounting matrix framework. In G. Pyatt, and J.I. Round (eds) *Social Accounting Matrixes: A Basis for Planning*. Washington, D.C.: The World Bank.

—— (eds) (1985) *Social Accounting Matrixes: A Basis for Planning*. Washington, D.C.: The World Bank.

Randall, A. and Stoll, J.R. (1983) "Existence value in a total valuation framework." In Robert D. Rowe and Lauraine G. Chestnut (eds) *Managing Air Quality and Scenic Resources at National Parks and Wilderness Areas*. Boulder, CO: Westview Press.

Rescher, N. (1968) *Introduction to Value Theory*. Englewood Cliffs, NJ: Prentice-Hall.

Resosudarmo, B.P. (2003) "River water pollution in Indonesia: an input–output analysis." *International Journal of Environment and Sustainable Development* 2 (1): 62–77.

Resosudarmo, B.P. and Thorbecke, E. (1996) "The impact of environmental policies on household incomes for different socio-economic classes: the case of air pollutants in Indonesia." *Ecological Economics* 17 (2): 83–94.

Rhee, J.J. and Miranowski, J.A. (1984) "Determination of income, production, and employment under pollution control: an input–output approach." *The Review of Economics and Statistics* 66 (1): 146–50.

Rideout, D.B. and Hesseln, H. (1995) *Principles of Forest and Environmental Economics*. Resource and Environmental Management, LLC, Colorado.

Robinson, M.H. (1986) "Spatial and nonspatial approaches to economic impact assessment: the case of rural lumber production." Ph.D. dissertation, University of Utah.

Robinson, S. and Roland-Holst, D. (1988) "Macroeconomic structure and computable general equilibrium models." *Journal of Policy Modeling* 10 (3): 353–75.

Rodríguez-Morilla, C. and Llanes Diaz-Salazar, G. (2005a) "Estimación anual de matrices de contabilidad social usando el métdo de minimizacón de la entropía cruzada: aplicación a la economía española del año 2000." *Estudios de Economía Aplicada* 23 (1): 279–302.

—— (2005b) "Multiplicadores domésticos SAMEA en un modelo multisectorial económico y ambiental de España." Studies on the Spanish economy 184. Seville: Fundación de Estudios de Economía Aplicada (FEDEA), pp. 1–31.

—— (2007) "Matriz de contabilidad social y medioambiental: aplicación a las emisiones de gases efecto invernadero de la economía española del año 2000." Studies on the Spanish economy 175, Fundación de Estudios de Economía Aplicada (FEDEA).

Rodríguez-Morilla, C., Llanes Diaz-Salazar, G., and Cardenete, A. (2007) "Economic and environmental efficiency using a social accounting matrix." *Ecological Economics* 60 (4): 774–86.

Rokeach, M. (1973) *The Nature of Human Values*. New York: The Free Press.

Roland-Holst, D.W. (1989) "Bias and stability of multiplier estimate." *Review of Economics and Statistics* 71: 718–21.

Rose, A., Steven, B., and Davis, G. (1988) *Natural Resource Policy and Income Distribution*. Baltimore: Johns Hopkins Press.

—— (1989) "Assessing who gains and who losses from natural resource policy." *Resource Policy* 15 (4): 282–91.

Rueda-Cantuche, J.M. (2005) "Estimating interregional trade flows in Andalusia (Spain)." ERSA conference paper ERSA05, p. 245, European Regional Science Association.

—— (2006) "Análisis input–output de descomposición estructural aplicado a los casos de Andalucía y Madrid." *Revista de Métodos Cuantitativos para la Economía y la Empresa* 1: 38–57.

Rueda-Cantuche, J.M. and ten Raa, T. (2005) "Análisis de las Producciones

Secundarias en la Economía Andaluza." *Revista de Estudios Regionales* 73 (2): 43–78.

Sánchez Chóliz, J. and Duarte, R. (2003a) "Analyzing pollution by way of vertically integrated coefficients, with an application to the water sector in Aragon." *Cambridge Journal of Economics* 27: 433–48.

—— (2003b) "Production chains and linkage indicators." *Economic Systems Research* 15 (4): 481–94.

—— (2004) "CO_2 emissions embodied in international trade: evidence for Spain." *Energy Policy* 32: 1999–2005.

—— (2005) "Water pollution in the Spanish economy: analysis of sensitivity to production and environmental constraints." *Ecological Economics*, 53 (3): 325–38.

—— (2007) "Environmental impact of household activity in Spain." *Ecological Economic* 62 (2): 308–18.

Santos, J.R. and Haimes, Y.Y. (2004) "Modeling the demand reduction input–output (I–O) inoperability due to terrorism of interconnected infrastructures." *Risk Analysis* 24 (6): 1437–51.

Scandizzo, S. (2003) "Connectivity and the measurement of operational risk: an input–output approach." *Soft Computing* 7: 516–25.

Skanberg, K. and Kriström, B. (2001) "Monetary forestry accounting including environmental goods and services." In *Sistemas y Recursos Forestales*. (special issue on New Forestlands Economic Accounting: Theories and Applications) 10 (1): 5–6.

Spash, C.L. (2000) "Ecosystems, contingent valuation and ethics: the case of wetland re-creation." *Ecological Economics* 34: 195–215.

Stone, R. (1985) "The disaggregation of the household sector in the national accounts." In G. Pyatt and J. Round (eds) *Social Accounting Matrices: A Basis for Planning*. Washington D.C.: The World Bank Press, pp. 145–85.

Subramanian, A. and Qaim, M. (2009) "Village-wide effects of agricultural biotechnology: the case of Bt cotton in India." *World Development* 37 (1): 256–67.

Subramanian, S. (1988) "Production and distribution in a dry-land village economy in the West Indian Deccan." Ph.D. dissertation, University of California.

Sullivan, J. and Gilles, J.K. (1989) "Cumulative employment effects on Northern California's wood products industries from national forest timber harvests." *Forest Science* 35 (3): 856–61.

—— (1990) "Hybrid econometric/input-output modeling of the cumulative economic impact of national forest harvest levels." *Forest Science* 36 (4): 863–77.

Taniguchi, K. (2004) "Village level social accounting matrices: data requirements." In J. Dixon, K. Taniguchi, and H. Wattenbach (eds) *Approaches to Assessing the Impact of globalization on African Smallholders: Household and Village Economy Modeling*, Proceedings of Working Session, Globalization and the African Smallholder Study. Rome: World Bank and FAO (AGS and ESA).

184   *Bibliography*

Taylor, J.E. and Adelman, I. (1996) *Village Economies: The Design, Estimation, and Use of Villagewide Economic Models*. Cambridge: Cambridge University Press.

ten Raa, T. (1986) "Dynamic input–output analysis with distributed activities." *The Review of Economics and Statistics* 68 (2): 300–10.

ten Raa, T. and Kop Jansen, P. (1998) "Bias and Sensitivity of Multipliers." *Economic Systems Research* 10: 275–83.

ten Raa, T. and Rueda-Cantuche, J.M. (2003) "The construction of input–output coefficients matrices in an axiomatic context: some further considerations." *Economic Systems Research* 15 (4): 439–55.

—— (2005) "Output and employment input–output multipliers on the basis of use and make matrix." Presented at 45th Congress of the European Regional Science Association, Amsterdam, August 23–27.

—— (2007) "Stochastic analysis of input–output multipliers on the basis of use and make matrices." *Review of Income and Wealth* 53 (2): 318–34.

Thomas, M. and Bautista, R.M. (1999) "A 1991 social accounting matrix (SAM) for Zimbabwe." TMD Discussion Paper No. 36, Trade and Macroeconomics Division, International Food Policy Research Institute Washington D.C.

Thorbecke, E. (1985) "The social accounting matrix and consistency—type planning models." In G. Pyatt and J.I. Round (eds). *Social Accounting Matrices: A Basis for Planning*. A World Bank Symposium. Washington, D.C.: The World Bank.

—— (1998) "Social accounting matrices and social accounting analysis." In W. Isard, K.J. Azis, M.P. Drennan, R.E. Miller, S. Saltzman, and E. Thorbecke (eds) *Methods of Interregional and Regional Analysis*. Adershot: Ashgate Publishing Limited.

Thorbecke, E. and Jung, H.-S. (1996) "A multiplier decomposition method to analyze poverty alleviation." *Journal of Development Economics* 48: 279–300.

Toss, R. and Wiik, K. (1974) "A linear decision model for the management of water quality in the Ruhr." In J. Rothenberg and I.G. Heggie (eds) *Management of Water Quality and the Environment*. London: McMillan.

Treloar, G.J. (1997) "Extracting embodied energy paths from input–output tables: towards an input–output-based hybrid energy analysis method." *Economic Systems Research* 9 (4): 375–91.

Treloar, G.J., Love, P., and Holt, G. (2001) "Using national input–output data for embodied energy analysis of individual residential buildings." *Construction Management and Economics* 19 (1): 49–61.

Turner, R.K., Pearce, D., and Bateman, I. (1993) *Environmental Economics: An Elementary Introduction*. Baltimore: Johns Hopkins University Press.

United Nations (1993) *Integrated Environmental and Economic Accounting. Handbook of National Accounting*. Studies in Methods 61. Sales No. E.93.XVII.12.

—— (2000) *Integrated Environmental and Economic Accounting. An Operational Manual*. Studies on Methods 78. Sales No. E.00.XVII.17.

Uriel, E., Beneito, P., Ferri, J., and Moltó, M.L. (1998) *Matriz de Contabilidad Social de España 1990*. Madrid: Instituto Nacional de Estadística.

USDA Forest Service (1992) *User Manual for Interactive Computer Access to Midsouth Forest Resource Data*. Starkville, MS: Southern Experiment Station.

Van Dieren, W. (ed.) (1995) *Taking Nature into Account: A Report to the Club of Rome*. New York: Springer-Verlag.

Vanoli, A. (1998) "Modeling and accounting work in national and environmental accounts." In K. Uno and P. Bartelmus (eds) *Environmental Accounting in Theory and in Practice*. Boston: Kluwer Academic Publishers, pp. 355–73.

Velázquez, E. (2001) "El consumo de agua y la contaminación hídrica en Andalucía." Ph.D. dissertation, Universidad Pablo de Olavide, Sevilla.

—— (2003) "Modelo input–output del agua: análisis de las relaciones intersectoriales del agua en Andalucía." Working Paper. Seville: CentrA Foundation.

—— (2006) "An input–output model of water consumption: Analyzing intersectoral water relationships in Andalucia." *Ecological Economics* 56 (2): 226–40.

Victor, P.A. (1972) *Pollution: Economy and Environment*. London: Allen and Unwin.

Vincent, J.R. (1999) "A framework for forest accounting." *Forest Science* 45 (4): 552–61.

Vincent, J.R. and Hartwick, J.M. (1997) *Accounting for the Benefits of Forest Resources: Concepts and Experience*. Rome: FAO Forestry Department.

Vitousek, P., Ehrlich, P., Ehrlich, A., and Matson, P. (1986) "Human appropriation of the products of photosynthesis." *Bioscience* 34 (6): 368–73.

Wackernagel, M. and Rees, W. (1996) *Our Ecological Footprint: Reducing Human Impact on the Earth*. Gabriola Island, BC: New Society.

Wagner, J.E. (1996) "Developing a social accounting matrix to examine tourism in the area of proteção ambiental de Guaraqueçabá, Brazil." Working Paper 58. Triangle Park, NC: Southeastern Center for Forest Economic Research, FPEI.

—— (1997) "Estimating the economic impacts of tourism." *Annals of Tourism Research* 24 (3): 592–608.

Wagner, J.E., Deller, Steven C., and Alward, G. (1992) "Estimating economic impacts using industry and household expenditures." *Journal of the Community Development Society* 23 (2): 79–102.

Wang, F.C., Odum, H.T., and Costanza, R. (1980) "Energy Criteria for Water Use." *Journal of the Water Resources Planning and Management Division* 106 (1): 185–203.

Water, C., Holland. D.W., and Weber, B.A. (1994) "Interregional effects of reduced timber harvests: the impact of the northern spotted owl listing in rural and urban Oregon." *Journal of Agricultural Economics* 19 (1): 140–60.

Wear, D.N. and Hyde, W.F. (1992) "Distributive issues in forest policy." In P.N. Nemetz (ed.) *Emerging Issues in Forest Policy*. Vancouver: University of British Columbia Press, pp. 301–14.

Wiedmann, T., Minx, J., Barret, J., and Wackernagel, M. (2006) "Allocating ecological footprints to final consumption categories with input–output analysis." *Ecological Economics* 56 (1): 28–48.

Xie, J. (2000) "An environmentally extended social accounting matrix." *Environmental and Resource Economics* 16: 391–406.

Xikang, C. (2000) "Shanxi water resource input-occupancy-output table and its application in Shanxi province of China." Thirteenth International Conference on Input-output Techniques. August 21–25, Macerata, Italy.

Xu, P., Tsanis, I.K., Anderson, W.P., and Kanaroglou, P. (1994) "An economic input–output analysis for urban storm water quality planning." *Water Resource Management* 8: 1–14.

Yúnez Naude, A. and Taylor, J.E. (1999) "Manual para la elaboración de Matrices de Contabilidad Social con base en encuestas socioeconómicas aplicadas a pequeñas poblaciones rurales." Working Paper No. XIV–1999. Centro de estudios económicos, El colegio de México.

Index

188   *Index*

*For Product Safety Concerns and Information please contact
our EU representative GPSR@taylorandfrancis.com Taylor & Francis
Verlag GmbH, Kaufingerstraße 24, 80331 München, Germany*

T - #0084 - 230425 - C0 - 216/138/11 - PB - 9780415539838 - Gloss Lamination